Maya Jaber

Integral Design Thinking for Sustainability Management

Maya Jaber

Integral Design Thinking for Sustainability Management

A Framework for Organizational Culture Change and Innovation

DE GRUYTER

ISBN 978-3-11-170502-6
e-ISBN (PDF) 978-3-11-170528-6
e-ISBN (EPUB) 978-3-11-170539-2

Library of Congress Control Number: 2025948532

Bibliographic information published by the Deutsche Nationalbibliothek
The Deutsche Nationalbibliothek lists this publication in the Deutsche Nationalbibliografie;
detailed bibliographic data are available on the internet at http://dnb.dnb.de.

www.degruyterbrill.com
Questions about General Product Safety Regulation:
productsafety@degruyterbrill.com

———

This book is dedicated to my mother and father whose guidance, love, and support helped guide my passions that paved my path, your loss is felt every day. To my three amazing boys for their unwavering love and encouragement "Never give up on your dreams." To my village, all of those whose support, advice, love, and positivity kept me moving forward through all the challenges of life, you know who you are! And to my big brothers, your love makes my heart sing.

Preface

Welcome. I'm so glad you're here.

This book is for the leaders, the change agents, the curious minds, and the everyday professionals who sense deep down that things could be better, more aligned, more meaningful. Whether you're navigating organizational transformation, designing new strategies, embedding sustainability practices, or simply trying to create lasting, positive change in your corner of the world this book was written with you in mind.

We are living through a time of accelerating complexity. Markets shift overnight. Social and environmental challenges grow more urgent. Technologies evolve faster than most organizations can adapt. And in the midst of it all, we are still human working, leading, learning, and trying to make sense of what change really requires.

What I've learned over two decades of working with leaders, building strategies, and researching sustainability transformation is this: ***change is not hard because people resist it, change is hard because we don't always understand how to align the system around it.*** We focus on policies without addressing culture. We push initiatives without engaging people. We act without truly seeing.

This book offers a new way to see. A new way to think. And most importantly, a new way to **design** the change you want to lead.

At the heart of it is the **Integral Design Thinking (IDT) Holistic Strategy Framework**, a field-tested, human-centered, and systems-aware tool for navigating organizational transformation. But this book is not just about the framework. It's about building your capacity as a leader to observe clearly, think critically, and act courageously.

You'll find research here, yes. But you'll also find reflection. Tools, yes. But also, perspective. This is a book that invites you to think deeply and work practically bridging insight with action, and vision with execution.

So take your time. Mark up the margins. Have conversations. Try things out. Come back to sections as your work evolves. My hope is that this book becomes not just a one-time read, but a trusted reference and companion on your leadership journey.

Let's begin.

https://doi.org/10.1515/9783111705286-202

Contents

Part II: **Frameworks, Tools & Applications**

Leadership mindset

Who was the most inspiring person you've ever worked with or worked for?

It's a question I often pose to students and professionals at the start of our conversations about leadership. Take a moment to reflect: who shaped you? A teacher, a coach, a manager, a mentor? What did they do that stayed with you? How did they make you feel?

When people answer, they rarely talk about titles or technical brilliance. They talk about being seen, supported, or challenged with kindness. The best leaders, it turns out, are remembered not just for what they accomplished but for how they made others feel in the process. **Leadership, at its core, is a deeply human act**.

This book and the Integral Design Thinking (IDT) Strategy Framework within it is ultimately about that kind of leadership. The kind that leads with vision and heart. That creates conditions for people to grow, systems to evolve, and organizations to thrive.

But before we can transform systems, we must first reflect on the mindset we bring into them. This section is your starting point: an invitation to develop what I call an **Integrated Leadership Mindset** a fusion of two essential leadership approaches that, together, prepare you to lead meaningful, sustainable change in any organization.

Two Foundations: Transformational and Servant Leadership

To drive change in today's fast-moving and complex world, two leadership styles rise to the surface as essential:

- **Transformational Leadership**, introduced by James MacGregor Burns (1978),[1] is about inspiring others with bold vision, purpose, and the courage to challenge the status quo. These leaders fuel innovation, ignite intrinsic motivation, and shape culture through influence, not force.

Transformational leader is somebody who inspires and motivates others to achieve outcomes by transforming their attitudes, beliefs, and goals to align with a shared vision. This leadership style goes beyond managing day-to-day operations; it's about fundamentally shifting an organization's cultural direction and purpose. Scott & Bruce's[2] research findings reveal that Transformational leaders tend to change the followers' motivational level and state of mind toward enhanced innovative tendencies by establishing

---

1 Burns, James MacGregor, 1978. Leadership. 1st ed. New York: Harper & Row.
2 Scott, Susanne G. and Reginald A. Bruce, 1994. "Determinants of innovative behavior: a path model of individual innovation in the workplace", Academy of Management Journal(3), 37:580–607. https://doi.org/10.5465/256701

https://doi.org/10.1515/9783111705286-204

an organizational culture that values creativity and innovation. Some foundational traits of transformational leaders are that they articulate a clear, compelling vision of the future, they use storytelling, enthusiasm, and a strong sense of purpose to energize others, they encourage creativity and critical thinking to challenge the status quo and promote innovation, they mentor and support people individually recognizing their unique needs and potential, and they lead with integrity and demonstrate values that others want to emulate.

– **Servant Leadership**, coined by **Robert K. Greenleaf** (1983),[3] focuses on leading through empathy, humility, and service to others. Servant leaders prioritize the well-being and growth of their teams, their communities, and the broader systems they touch. They don't lead from above; they lead from within.

A servant leader is someone who leads by putting the needs of others first, especially their team members, the organization, and the community in which they touch. These individuals do not focus on power or authority but prioritize service, empathy, the growth and well-being of people, and the systems they are part of. Servant leadership attributes create a collaborative culture that results in a significant positive effect on organizational performance; this mindset fosters a culture of collaboration by breaking barriers to teamwork and promoting cross-functional partnerships between employees and leadership.[4]

The main trait of servant leadership is emotional intelligence, which is achieved by genuinely understanding and sharing the feelings of others. They are actively listening, seeking input, and feedback to create a space where others can be heard; this drives them to create an environment that repairs and supports others' emotional well-being while demonstrating self and situational awareness. These individuals also influence through dialogue and trust, not coercion; they anticipate change and plan for it, so they lead with a long-term view. They function as caretakers of the organization and its people in values while they invest in the personal and professional development of others. Through all of this, servant leaders foster a sense of belonging and connectedness to the organization and the communities it resides in.

Transformation Leadership and Servant Leadership are similar and are connected in the behaviours of this leadership mindset and action. Leading with both transformational and servant leadership mindsets is to blend vision with humility and strategy with empathy. The Transformational leader drives bold change by inspiring others with a compelling vision, while servant leadership ensures that every step of the journey centres on people, relationships, and a shared purpose. Together, they create a leadership style that is both future-focused and deeply human.

---

3 Greenleaf, Robert K., 1970. The Servant as Leader. Indianapolis: Robert K. Greenleaf Center.

4 Nauman, Shazia, Sabeen Hussain Bhatti, Hassan Imam, and Mohammad Saud Khan, 2021. "How servant leadership drives project team performance through collaborative culture and knowledge sharing", Project Management Journal (1), 53:17–32. https://doi.org/10.1177/87569728211037777

A combination of both of these leadership styles is an **INTEGRATED LEADER-SHIP MINDSET**. This integrated mindset empowers leaders to challenge the status quo while nurturing trust, inclusion, and growth. It's about shaping systems and cultures through fearless innovation and doing so with listening, care, and collaboration at the core. In today's complex world, leaders who embody both approaches are the ones most capable of fostering lasting, meaningful change.

Each of these styles on its own is powerful. But when integrated, they create something truly transformative: **a leadership mindset that is both visionary and grounded, strategic and human, bold and deeply collaborative**.

What Does an Integrated Leadership Mindset Look Like?

An Integrated Leader is both an architect and a gardener. They design strategy and structure, while also nurturing trust, collaboration, and emotional well-being across the organization. They lead with purpose and clarity, while also listening deeply and adapting with humility.

In sustainability work especially where change must be cultural, not just operational this INTEGRATED MINDSET is essential. Leaders with this mindset, design strategic visions while cultivating the conditions for people to thrive. This dual approach is vital in sustainability leadership, where success depends not just on bold ideas but on the collective energy, wisdom, and resilience of those who bring them to life. The most effective leaders today are those who can navigate complexity with clarity and compassion, shaping organizations that are agile, equitable, and aligned with a higher purpose.

The Integrated Mindset is the mindset you will want to build on as you adopt the Integral Design Thinking strategic framework into your organization. As stated, an Integrated Mindset has the alignment of Transformational and Servant leadership. The following Table 1 highlights how these leadership styles converge into a unified leadership approach:

Table 1: Alignment of Transformational and Servant Leadership to an Integrated Mindset.

Leadership Dimension	Transformational Leadership	Servant Leadership	Integrated Mindset
Purpose & Vision	Articulates a compelling vision to drive change and inspire growth	Grounds leadership in service to others and the common good	**Lead with a bold vision rooted in shared values and collective wellbeing**
Motivation & Influence	Motivates through charisma, inspiration, and intellectual stimulation	Motivates through trust, empathy, and meaningful relationships	**Inspire others while building trust and encouraging co-creation**

Table 1 (continued)

Leadership Dimension	Transformational Leadership	Servant Leadership	Integrated Mindset
Focus on People	Focuses on developing followers into leaders and change agents	Focuses on supporting individuals' personal and professional growth	**Develop people through empowerment, mentorship, and emotional connection**
Decision-Making	Often visionary and future-oriented, makes strategic decisions for large-scale impact	Seeks consensus and input from others; emphasizes shared decision-making	**Blend vision-driven action with inclusive decision processes**
Communication Style	Charismatic, persuasive, and often top-down for mobilization	Deep listening, reflective, and bottom-up	**Communicate to energize *and* empathize**
Power & Authority	Uses positional influence to shape change and inspire transformation	Leads from behind, sharing power and decentralizing authority	**Use authority responsibly while creating space for others to lead**
Organizational Culture	Seeks to transform systems, mindsets, and behaviors	Builds culture through care, community, and servant-first values	**Create cultures of care *and* innovation**
Change & Innovation	Champions disruptive change, rethinking the status quo	Encourages change through trust-building and commitment to people	**Drive innovation while preserving psychological safety and dignity**
Ethical Foundation	Rooted in values and moral responsibility to the collective	Rooted in ethics of service, humility, and compassion	**Anchor change in both moral clarity and care for human dignity**
Legacy	Aims to leave a transformational impact on systems and people	Aims to leave others stronger, more capable, and more whole	**Leave a legacy of both systemic change *and* personal empowerment**

Why This Matters for Sustainability and Change

The combination of these two leadership styles to an Integrated Mindset align perfectly with the focus of this book. The IDT framework is about human-centric, holistic, and empathetic dimensions that drive culture change rooted in values, not just metrics. Overcoming resistance to sustainability initiatives by modelling trusted empowerment. Creating agile and adaptive organizations where leadership is distributed, not just top-down. Also, the IDT framework looks to lead in complex and evolving environments. It aids in driving cultural shifts by aligning people with a higher purpose, supporting a systematic change by fostering commitment rather than compliance, and empowering sustainability leaders to navigate uncertainties and lead ethically with vision and courage.

Assess Yourself: Are You Leading with an Integrated Mindset?

To begin building or strengthening your own Integrated Mindset, start with self-reflection. Use the following questionnaire to assess where your leadership style currently aligns and where there's room to grow.

Integrated Leadership Self-Assessment Questionnaire

Evaluate Your Leadership Style Across Transformational and Servant Dimensions
 Instructions: For each statement, rate how true it is for you on a scale of 1 to 5.1 = Never (0 points), 2 = Rarely (2 points), 3 = Sometimes (4 points), 4 = Often (8 points), 5 = Always (10 points)Use the space provided to total your score and reflect on areas of strength and growth.

Purpose & Vision

I articulate a clear and compelling vision for the future. [1] [2] [3] [4] [5]
My vision reflects shared values and serves a greater good. [1] [2] [3] [4] [5]

Motivation & Influence

I inspire others through vision, passion, or ideas. [1] [2] [3] [4] [5]
I build trust and connection through empathy and consistency. [1] [2] [3] [4] [5]

Focus on People

I actively support the development of those I lead. [1] [2] [3] [4] [5]
I foster both personal and professional growth in my team. [1] [2] [3] [4] [5]

Decision-Making

I make strategic decisions with long-term impact in mind. [1] [2] [3] [4] [5]
I seek input from others and value shared decision-making. [1] [2] [3] [4] [5]

Communication Style

I communicate in ways that energize and mobilize others. [1] [2] [3] [4] [5]
I listen deeply and create space for others to be heard. [1] [2] [3] [4] [5]

Power & Authority

I use my position to enable and uplift others. [1] [2] [3] [4] [5]
I create opportunities for shared leadership and empowerment. [1] [2] [3] [4] [5]

(continued)

Organizational Culture

I model and cultivate a culture of care and community. [1] [2] [3] [4] [5]
I encourage innovation and agility within the organization. [1] [2] [3] [4] [5]

Change & Innovation

I challenge outdated systems to spark meaningful change. [1] [2] [3] [4] [5]
I create a safe space where people feel supported during change. [1] [2] [3] [4] 5]

Ethical Foundation

I lead with a strong sense of ethics and integrity. [1] [2] [3] [4] [5]
Compassion and humility guide my leadership decisions. [1] [2] [3] [4] [5]

Legacy

I think about the long-term impact of my leadership. [1] [2] [3] [4] [5]
I aim to leave others more empowered and capable than before. [1] [2] [3] [4] [5]
Total Score: _____ / 100

Use this assessment to spark honest reflection. Reflect on your lowest and highest scoring areas. What patterns do you notice? Where are your strengths? What small shifts could you make to grow?

This book supplies a few versions of this reflection from Word and Excel form documents to help you build on this mindset and continuously assess yourself as you look to help others in the transformation process. These documents can also be used to help other leaders in your organization adopt this mindset. Use QR to download the documents available for this book.

Remember, the first step to leading others is knowing ourselves, our values, and leading with authenticity.

Part I: **Building Foundational Understanding**

Foundations may be invisible,
but they hold up everything that matters and everything that shines.

1 A New World Economy & Leadership For the 21st Century

We cannot solve 21st-century problems with 20th-century thinking. Sustainability leadership demands a new mindset, one rooted in empathy, systems awareness, and creative problem-solving.

It's good to be here with you. Thank you for taking this journey with me. For us to understand where we need to go and what tools will help us get there, we need to start by understanding what is happening in a global business setting. As we look at the world around us, we can see a new economic movement beginning as the world transitions, and we saw this transition at the beginning of the 21st century. This brought the paradigm of a movement where environmental, social, and individual health pushed for an industrial revolution – we can see it in the world around us as it keeps changing, and nothing is like it was traditionally. Organizations are beginning to understand the need to transition and transform into more environmentally and socially focused entities. This shift is driven by growing pressures across climate, economic, cultural, and innovation-related domains. Embracing this transformation not only improves a company's image, but also strengthens employee and customer loyalty. At the same time, it supports the development of risk strategies that enhance internal processes and reduce operational costs.

Not only are organizations realizing the need for change, but so are our consumers. Consumers have realized their purchasing power, and the power they have when they unify as a group or community can affect a business's behavior or success. This realization by organizations has also pushed some to be more focused on their environmental, social, and governance footprints, as they acknowledge that transforming to a more environmentally and socially focused company improves the firm's image, leads to higher sales, lowers operational costs, and improves risk management. Organizations are now attempting to tackle the issue through sustainability management as they are acknowledging the responsibility for their actions.

As our global systems continue to evolve, the expectations placed on businesses are expanding. It's no longer enough to focus solely on financial returns, today's organizations are being asked to actively contribute to the health and well-being of individuals, communities, and the ecosystems they operate within. Leaders in sustainability are being challenged to navigate the complex intersections of economic performance, social responsibility, and environmental stewardship. And in response, many companies are beginning to embed resilience not just into their operations, but into the very cultural DNA of their organizations.

Meanwhile, digital transformation and new technologies are dismantling old barriers to communication and information. We're witnessing the emergence of a new economic order, one that demands agility, innovation, and deep adaptability. Organizations that want to attract and retain top talent, inspire investors, and earn con-

https://doi.org/10.1515/9783111705286-001

sumer trust must evolve. The era of the first Industrial Revolution, with its single-minded pursuit of growth and profits, often at the expense of people and planet, is no longer a viable model.

Today's employees and consumers are far more informed, connected, and values-driven. They expect safe workplaces, healthy environments for their families, equity and inclusion, and transparent, ethical practices. They are using their voices, their choices, and their wallets to demand change. Burns (2012)[5] concludes that the message is clear: the status quo is unsustainable.

To survive and thrive organizations must now rethink how they operate. They need to build transparent systems, foster evidence-based cultures, and develop new capabilities that allow them to pivot quickly in response to shifting conditions. As Ferdig and Ludema (2005)[6] remind us, change itself is a generative force. The discomfort it brings can be a spark fueling new ideas, innovations, and pathways forward. But this only happens when leaders are willing to lean into the uncertainty rather than shy away from it.

What's becoming increasingly obvious is this: transformation in today's context can't be managed with yesterday's tools. Many leaders understand that change is needed, but they lack a guiding framework to build the kind of holistic strategies that truly move the needle. Sustainability isn't a silo, it's a systems-level challenge. It touches everything: governance, operations, stakeholder engagement, values, and even the design of our daily processes.

And change isn't coming only from the top. Around the globe, we're witnessing powerful movements rising from the ground up. From climate strikes led by millions of students to city governments aligning with global agreements like the Paris Accord, it's clear: **transformation is being demanded from every direction**. Corporations that wish to stay relevant in this new reality must commit to deep, structural shifts, not just in policy, but in purpose.

This is where leadership becomes pivotal. Not just the kind of leadership that holds titles and sits in boardrooms but human-centered, adaptive, and ethical leadership. The kind that recognizes the unpredictable nature of our current era and embraces it as an opportunity. As Gitsham (2019)[7] argues, future-ready leaders are those who can craft strategies that are not only flexible but regenerative capable of evolving in sync with the markets and communities they serve.

5 Burns, T. (2012). The sustainability revolution: A societal paradigm shift. *Sustainability, 4*, 1118–1134; doi:10.3390/su4061118, www.mdpi.com/journal/sustainability.

6 Ferdig, M. A., and Ludema, J. D. (2005). Transformative interactions: Qualities of conversation that heighten the vitality of self-organising change. In Pasmore, W. and Woodman, R. (Eds.). *Research in Organisational Change and Development*, (p. 15). Emerald Publishing Limited ISBN 978-1-78052-807-6, DOI 10.1108/S0897-3016(2012)20

7 Gitsham, M. (2019). The changing role of business leaders, and implications for talent management and executive education. In G. G. Lenssen and N. C. Smith (Eds.), *Managing sustainable business* (pp. 671–682). Springer Netherlands. https://doi.org/10.1007/978-94-024-1144-7_31

Ferdig (2007)[8] describes these leaders as "informed, aware, realistic, courageous, and personally hopeful" and perhaps most importantly, able to attract others to the shared work of co-creating the future. They build cultures of inquiry and learning, take smart risks, and openly share their lessons learned. They don't pretend to have all the answers, but they know how to ask the right questions.

In an interconnected, globalized economy, relying on old playbooks just won't work. Leaders must be fluent in complexity. They must be able to integrate strategy, communication, systems thinking, and culture-building into one cohesive approach. Trompenaars and Hampden-Turner (2002)[9] offer a view of modern leadership that is both strategic and deeply human balancing analysis with empathy, delegation with decisiveness, and inspiration with clear execution.

This isn't easy work. But it is essential. The leaders who will shape the 21st century will be those who can hold these tensions, who can think across silos, inspire across disciplines, and act with both courage and care. The future is not something we wait for. It's something we design together.

1.1 Design Thinking, Change Processes, and Bottom-Up Creative Innovation

Sustainability management isn't linear. It's layered, messy, and deeply contextual requiring organizations to think not just strategically but systemically. It asks leaders to move beyond surface-level fixes and instead reimagine how their organizations learn, adapt, and evolve. This is where design thinking becomes essential not as a trendy buzzword, but as a powerful strategic mindset.

At its best, design thinking helps leaders do three critical things: see the big picture, empathize with stakeholders, and experiment boldly. When applied with intention, it becomes a compass that guides teams through complexity anchoring strategy in purpose, creativity in practicality, and change in human experience. And in the realm of sustainability, that's exactly what's needed.

For more than a decade now, design thinking has been explored and adopted within strategic management circles. It's proven itself useful in unlocking innovation, surfacing unspoken needs, and building alignment across silos.[10,11] Yet, even as its in-

8 Ferdig, M. (2007). Sustainability leadership: Co-creating a sustainable future. *Journal of Change Management*, 7(1), 25–35, DOI: 10.1080/14697010701233809 (p. 33)

9 Trompenaars, F., and Hampden-Turner, C. (2002). *21 leaders for the 21st century.* McGraw-Hill.

10 Elsbach, K. and Stigliani, S. (2018). Design thinking and organisational culture: A review and framework for future research. *Journal of Management*, 1–33.

11 Johansson-Sköldberg, U., Woodilla, J., and Çetinkaya, M. (2013). Design Thinking: Past, present, and possible futures. *Creativity and Innovation Management, 22*, 121–146.

fluence has grown, there's still a critical gap: many sustainability leaders are struggling to implement change in a way that's integrated, lasting, and culturally embedded.

What's holding them back isn't a lack of tools, it's a lack of clarity around where and how to intervene. There's often no roadmap for understanding the real levers of culture, or for designing change that people actually embrace. As both a design researcher and a practitioner, I've seen this firsthand: ambitious sustainability goals falter not because the ideas are flawed, but because they aren't grounded in a process that honors the human systems they hope to transform.

The problem is rarely motivation. It's knowing how to move from intention to execution, how to translate a vision into daily behaviors, mindsets, and systems that stick.

That's where embedding design thinking directly into the culture of an organization makes a difference. It offers not just a method for generating ideas, but a language for navigating change especially the kind of change that requires both top-down direction and bottom-up ownership. In fact, the most sustainable transformations I've observed are the ones that include voices across the hierarchy, where employees co-design the very systems they're asked to live within.

Scholars and practitioners alike have explored this from many angles: the role of innovation in transformation,[12,13] the evolution of strategic design as a competitive advantage[14], and the ways cultural repositioning can unlock deeper impact.[15,16] What's emerging is a growing consensus: to change culture, you must engage it, meaningfully, inclusively, and persistently.

Top-down leadership can set direction. But it's the bottom-up creativity the agency of people within the system that truly accelerates change. When staff are invited into the design process, they're not just implementing a strategy. They're owning it. And that makes all the difference.

To build sustainable organizations in the truest sense, we must get better at designing not only for outcomes, but for the experience of change itself. We need to ask: How do people feel while going through transformation? Are they empowered, or alienated? Inspired, or burned out?

---

12 Dunne, D., and Martin, R. (2006). Design thinking and how it will change management education. *Academy of Management Learning and Education, 5,* 512–23.

13 Liedtka, J., and Kaplan, S. (2019). How Design Thinking opens new frontiers for strategy development. *Strategy and Leadership,* 47(2), 3–10.

14 Martin, R. (2009). *The design of business: why design thinking is the next competitive advantage.* Harvard Business School Press.

15 Greenwood, R., and Hinings, C.R. (1996). Understanding radical organizational change: Bringing together the old and the new institutionalism. *The Academy of Management Review,* 21(4), 1022–1054.

16 Romanelli, E. and Tushman, M.L. (1994). Organisational transformation as punctuated equilibrium: an empirical test. *The Academy of Management Journal,* 37(5), 1141–1166.

The answers to these questions are where cultural shifts succeed or stall. And design thinking, when applied as an ongoing practice, not just a workshop, can provide the structure, empathy, and creativity to guide the way forward.

1.2 Books Aims and Objective

This book is written for the changemakers, the people who walk into an organization and ask, "What's working here, and what's quietly getting in the way?" Whether you're a sustainability manager, a CEO, a change consultant, or someone simply tasked with leading a transition be it technological, cultural, structural, or environmental this book is designed to be your companion and your compass.

At its heart, **Integral Design Thinking (IDT)** is about helping you see clearly. It's a framework for critical thinking, yes, but more than that, it's a lens for observing the inner workings of an organization in motion. Because real, lasting change doesn't happen in isolated silos. It happens when the right systems, relationships, values, and behaviors are working in unison.

The goal of this book is simple but powerful: To help you understand what needs to be aligned functionally and culturally for any form of change to not just occur but take root and grow.

Too often, change initiatives fail not because the ideas were wrong but because the conditions weren't right. Teams weren't aligned. Systems weren't connected. People weren't engaged. And so, the energy behind the change dissipates. This book gives you the tools to recognize those invisible misalignments and to do something about them.

The **IDT Strategy Framework** helps build a shared cultural mindset across your organization. It provides a structure for analyzing the moving parts, a language for engaging others, and a guide for aligning the tangible with the intangible strategy with culture, operations with values, and leadership with everyday behavior.

You don't have to be leading a large-scale transformation to use this framework. Even if you're focused on a single initiative, a new tool, a redesigned process, or a better way of working the IDT approach ensures that your efforts are not isolated or temporary, but integrated and sustainable.

In other words, this book is here to help you answer the essential questions:
- What *has* to be working together before any change can succeed?
- Where are the pressure points, the gaps, the strengths?
- How can I help this organization become more adaptive, resilient, and human-centered?

This isn't just a strategy book. It's a mindset book. It's a guide for building organizations that can change not once, but continuously because they've built the capacity to do so from within.

1.3 Research, Philosophy & Methodology

This book is grounded in years of hands-on research, real-world application, and a simple but urgent question: **How can organizations transform faster and with less friction in today's constantly evolving economy?**

The research behind this work didn't begin in a lab. It began in the field with conversations, collaborations, and case studies involving real people trying to implement real change. What I discovered is that many organizations want to become more sustainable, more adaptive, and more human-centered, but they often lack a cohesive framework to help them navigate that transformation. This is the gap that Integral Design Thinking (IDT) seeks to fill.

To develop the IDT Holistic Strategy Framework, I designed a research approach rooted in both **rigor and relevance**. The methodology blends **design science**, **action research**, and **holistic design thinking**, three approaches that not only study problems but actively engage with them in real time, helping create solutions through cycles of learning, testing, reflection, and iteration.

The Approach in Practice

This research was both cross-national and cross-sector. It included:
- **Interviews** with sustainability leaders and policy actors across the UK and the US.
- **Three in-depth case studies** across public and private sectors: a sustainable vineyard, a city Department of Education office, and a global real estate firm.
- **Analysis of policy environments**, internal cultural factors, and organizational change efforts at multiple levels.

Each case study followed the same five-phase cycle:
1. Identify the problem
2. Co-create an intervention
3. Design the solution (the "artefact")
4. Implement (when possible)
5. Reflect and refine

This design–test–learn loop allowed me to adapt the research in real-time, and it ensured that the framework being built was not just theoretical but practical, applicable, and grounded in the realities of organizational life.

Why This Methodology Matters

Too often, change is framed as slow, painful, and hard. But what if that's only true because we keep using tools designed for yesterday's problems? Through this research, I found that when you bring people into the process, clarify the systems at play, and co-design change with empathy and insight, transformation accelerates.

Design science helped me ensure the framework was functional and results-oriented. Action research kept the focus on context, collaboration, and real-time learning. And holistic design thinking brought it all together integrating systems thinking, culture, and human behavior into one strategic lens.

This wasn't just research for knowledge's sake, it was research for action.

The result is the **Integral Design Thinking Holistic Strategy Framework**: a field-tested, deeply human approach to change that equips leaders with the clarity, structure, and insight to transform their organizations not just once, but continuously.

1.4 Book Structure

This book is your roadmap for navigating organizational change especially the kind that is complex, cultural, and sustainability-driven. Whether you're a leader stepping into a new organization, a consultant helping to guide transformation, or a professional trying to make change that lasts, this book is designed to meet you where you are and move with you.

The structure is deliberate. I begin with the **why** and the **what**, the foundations you'll need to understand the evolving world of change and sustainability management. Chapters 1 through 6 provide essential knowledge, insights, and lenses that will help you assess and understand your own organization, your role within it, and the systems that shape it.

Then, in Chapters 7 through 10, we move into the **how**. This is where you'll be introduced to the **Integral Design Thinking (IDT) Holistic Strategy Framework**, a tool designed to help you think, design, and act differently. You'll learn how to apply it, how to adapt it to your unique context, and how to use its tools to accelerate alignment, embed sustainability into culture, and build an organization that is agile, human-centered, and future-ready.

Here's how the book unfolds:

Introduction A welcome into the mindset required for leading change in today's dynamic world.

Leadership Mindset What it takes to lead transformation today with courage, empathy, and systems awareness.

Integrated Leadership Self-Assessment A reflection tool to help you understand where you are and where you may need to grow.

Part I – Building Foundational Understanding

(Chapters 1–6)

1. **A New World Economy & Leadership for the 21st Century**
    Understand the shifting landscape economic, cultural, and social and what it means for leadership and organizations today.
2. **Design Thinking, Change Processes, and Bottom-Up Creative Innovation**
    Explore how design thinking can become your strategic superpower for navigating complexity and igniting change from within.
3. **Book Aims and Objectives**
    A deeper look at what this book offers you and how to use it as both a reference and a guide in your work.
4. **Research, Philosophy & Methodology**
    An accessible look at the research behind this book spanning interviews, case studies, and field-based application.
5. **Designs for Life: Sustainability Business, Sustainable Organizations**
    Unpack how sustainability is defined and practiced within organizations and why it matters now more than ever.
6. **Evolution of Perception and Theoretical Frameworks**
    Trace how our understanding of sustainability, systems, and strategy has evolved and where your work fits within that legacy.

Part II – Frameworks, Tools & Application

(Chapters 7–10)

7. **Discussion and Framework Introduction**
    Synthesizing research insights and introducing the Integral Design Thinking Strategy Framework.
8. **The IDT Strategy Framework**
    A deep dive into the framework itself how it works, what it includes, and how to begin using it in your organization.
9. **Creative-Thinking Tools for Strategy and Action**
    Practical tools based on design science to help you apply the framework, spark dialogue, and support decision-making.

10. **Leading Organizations Toward a Sustainable Future**
    Guidance for implementation, team development, and embedding these princi-
    ples into long-term culture with space for reflection, celebration, and forward
    planning.

This structure is designed to be both **practical and reflective**. You'll be challenged to
think critically, observe more deeply, and act more intentionally. Because transformation doesn't start with a checklist, it starts with clarity. And that's exactly what this
book aims to give you.

2 Designs for Life: Sustainability Business, Sustainable Organizations

To build a better future, we must first redefine what success looks like,
for business, for society, and the planet.

The idea of "sustainability" is everywhere from government policies and corporate reports to product labels and brand missions. But what does it *actually* mean within a business context? And more importantly, how does it become more than a buzzword?

In this chapter, we define sustainability in ways that are relevant and actionable for organizations. We'll look at what's driving the shift from rising consumer expectations to new regulations and how businesses are responding (or failing to respond). Whether you're in the public or private sector, understanding the forces reshaping this landscape is critical if you're trying to lead change that lasts.

This isn't just about being green. It's about aligning business strategy with long-term well-being for people, communities, and the environment. And doing so in a way that drives innovation, resilience, and future readiness.

We are at a tipping point in how we understand the role of business in society. Across the globe, conversations about sustainability are moving from the margins to the mainstream. No longer confined to environmental science departments or sustainability offices, the language of sustainability has entered boardrooms, government chambers, factory floors, and digital platforms. But the term itself still carries a certain ambiguity. What does sustainability really mean in practice, and more importantly, what does it *demand* of today's leaders, professionals, and change agents?

This chapter begins with an exploration of how sustainability is defined within a business context not just conceptually, but practically. The goal here is not only to understand the definitions but to explore how these definitions inform real-world decision-making, market shifts, and organizational behavior. Sustainability in business is not simply about environmental concern; it encompasses broader considerations, including social equity, economic resilience, and ethical governance. Together, these dimensions shape what is commonly referred to as the Environmental, Social, and Governance (ESG) framework.

Understanding sustainability from this integrated perspective is essential because it touches everything: from supply chains and stakeholder relationships to hiring practices, branding, and financial performance. For today's organizations, sustainability is no longer a niche concern; it is a strategic imperative. Businesses that fail to adapt are increasingly being left behind, not only by regulators and investors but by the very consumers and communities they aim to serve.

https://doi.org/10.1515/9783111705286-002

This chapter also looks at the dual forces shaping this transformation: bottom-up pressure from consumers and top-down pressure from regulatory bodies. We will explore how people's values and expectations have shifted, especially among younger generations who are not just working in organizations but actively choosing where they shop, invest, and engage based on ethical and environmental criteria. Simultaneously, local and state governments are stepping into leadership roles, creating policies and regulations that are fundamentally reshaping market dynamics.

The central premise of this chapter is that sustainability is no longer about isolated initiatives or public relations campaigns. It is about embedding a new way of thinking into the core of how businesses operate. Sustainability must be seen not as a constraint but as a lens for innovation, resilience, and long-term success. This chapter sets the stage for that deeper understanding by providing the foundational knowledge needed to engage meaningfully with sustainability in business.

In doing so, I also begin to challenge the prevailing mindset that "change is hard." Change, especially toward sustainability, becomes significantly more possible when organizations are equipped with the right frameworks, leadership, and culture. The Integral Design Thinking (IDT) Strategy Framework introduced later in this book is built on this very idea: that sustainability and strategic change can be human-centered, systemic, and actionable.

As we move forward, keep this in mind: sustainability is not about perfection. It is about progress, alignment, and commitment. It is about understanding the complex web of relationships and systems in which businesses exist and learning how to design change that is both responsible and regenerative. This chapter will give you the context you need to begin seeing sustainability not as a separate issue, but as central to the future of every organization. My long-time motto has been that "Sustainability needs to be second nature to our business practices and intent."

Let us begin with defining what sustainability truly means in the context of business and why that matters more than ever before.

2.1 Sustainability Defined in a Business Context

Sustainability has become one of the defining challenges of our time. But in the realm of business, it's often misunderstood, misused, or limited to surface-level activities. True sustainability in a business context goes beyond corporate social responsibility (CSR) statements or green marketing campaigns. It means fundamentally rethinking how a business operates, what it values, and how it contributes to or detracts from the broader ecological and social systems in which it exists. Scientists, civic leaders, and experts on the subject have been trying to educate the public, industry, and policymakers on the need to change behaviors in sustainable business;[17,18] the key competitive advantage is environmental management.[19]

In this section, we explore the evolution of sustainability as it applies to business, diving into its foundational concepts and the ways it is being operationalized through Environmental, Social, and Governance (ESG) frameworks. This section will also consider how sustainability is interpreted differently across industries and sectors and how these interpretations impact both internal organizational cultures and external stakeholder expectations.

Sustainability in business is not a fixed set of actions or practices; it is a mindset and a continuous process of alignment. It challenges organizations to examine the long-term consequences of their decisions, and to reimagine success in a way that includes the well-being of people and the planet. It asks businesses to operate within ecological limits, respect social boundaries, and practice good governance.

The concept of a triple bottom line, people, planet, and profit, captures this expanded understanding of value. Rather than focusing solely on short-term financial performance, businesses are being asked to take a more integrated view. This includes:

- **Environmental Sustainability:** Managing natural resources responsibly, reducing carbon footprints, minimizing waste, and supporting regenerative practices.
- **Social Sustainability:** Fostering equitable, inclusive workplaces; ensuring human rights and fair labor practices; engaging with local communities.
- **Governance:** Practicing transparency, ethical decision-making, and accountability in leadership and organizational structures.

When organizations commit to sustainability in this holistic way, it opens the door to innovation and resilience. Companies that integrate sustainability into their core strategy are not only better equipped to anticipate risks they are also better positioned to seize emerging opportunities. This includes access to new markets, increased investor confidence, stronger employee engagement, and deeper brand loyalty.

In reality, however, many organizations struggle to embed sustainability into their culture and decision-making processes.[20] They have reviewed and analyzed

17 Camou, M., and Green, L. (2016). Modeling sustainability futures: Cultural shift strategies for sustainability leaders case study New York City's Department of Education's Office of Sustainability. *The International Academic Forum (IAFOR) ECSS/ECSEE/ECSEE/ECPEL/EBMC Conference*, 53–69.

18 Goodall, C (2012). *Sustainability: All that matters*. McGraw-Hill Education.

19 Singh, S. K. (2019). Sustainable business and environment management. *Management of Environmental Quality: An International Journal*, *30*(1), 2–4.

20 Martinez, F., Peattie, K., and Vazquez-Brust, D. (2019). Beyond win–win: A syncretic theory on corporate stakeholder engagement in sustainable development. *Business Strategy and the Environment*, *28*(5), 896–908. https://doi.org/10.1002/bse.2292

both strategic and influential levels internally and externally of an organization to try to understand the micro environmental analysis, which could include resources, internal stakeholders, and overall behavior. This is often due to a lack of clarity on what sustainability entails, conflicting priorities, or internal resistance to change. That's why developing a clear, accessible definition of sustainability one that resonates across departments and levels of leadership is a vital first step.

The next sections will explore the drivers behind the growing demand for sustainability, starting with the role of the modern consumer and continuing with the regulatory landscape that is accelerating change. Together, these forces are reshaping what it means to be a successful business in the 21st century.

2.1.1 Sustainability Defined

At its most basic, sustainability refers to the capacity to endure to continue to function and thrive over time without exhausting resources or causing harm to the systems that support life. In a business context, this definition expands beyond ecological impact to include how an organization sustains its value, relevance, and positive impact within an interconnected world.

Historically, sustainability efforts were often limited to environmental compliance or philanthropic side projects. Today, that view is no longer sufficient. The evolving landscape of sustainability demands a systemic, integrated approach that acknowledges the interconnected nature of economic, environmental, and social systems.

A sustainable business considers:

- **Its inputs:** What resources are being used, how they are sourced, and their environmental and social impact.
- **Its processes:** How those resources are transformed, and whether practices are efficient, ethical, and inclusive.
- **Its outputs:** What products or services are delivered, how they are used, and what legacy they leave behind.

This broader lens also means acknowledging the influence of global supply chains, employee wellbeing, customer relationships, investor expectations, and community engagement. These are not separate silos; they are interdependent elements of a thriving, sustainable enterprise.

Sustainability in business is not just about reducing harm, it is about adding value in a way that is regenerative. That means designing systems and strategies that contribute positively to the environment, society, and the economy. For example, rather than simply reducing emissions, a company might invest in circular economy models or clean energy innovation. Rather than just hiring diversely, an organization might actively reshape workplace culture to center equity and belonging.

From an operational perspective, defining sustainability also includes setting measurable goals and frameworks. Common tools include but are not limited to:

- **The United Nations Sustainable Development Goals (SDGs):** A global blueprint for achieving a better and more sustainable future by 2030.
- **Global Reporting Initiative (GRI):** Guidelines for transparent sustainability reporting.
- **B Corporation Certification:** Verification of a company's social and environmental performance, accountability, and transparency.

These tools help organizations move from intention to action. There are so many different reporting tools that can help a company define its metrics and help develop guidelines on how to move forward. They allow companies to track progress, benchmark against peers, and communicate efforts credibly to stakeholders. The initial steps are to understand what your organization's values are and how this ties to the mission and vision, as well as how this can bring value and purpose to these foundations. The UN SDGs are a great starting point to help with that analysis, as they all can be broken down into Environmental, Social, and Governance areas for review. The following Table 2 shows the breakdown:

Table 2: UN SDG's Aligned to ESG Foundations.

UN SDG's Aligned to ESG Foundations		
Environmental (E)	**Social (S)**	**Governance (G)**
SDG 6 Clean Water and Sanitation	**SDG 4** Quality Education	**SDG 1** No Poverty
SDG 7 Affordable and Clean Energy	**SDG 5** Gender Equality	**SDG 2** Zero Hunger
SDG 12 Responsible Consumption and Production	**SDG 10** Reduced Inequalities	**SDG 3** Good Health and Well-being
SDG 13 Climate Action	**SDG 11** Sustainable Cities and Communities	**SDG 8** Decent Work and Economic Growth
SDG 14 Life Below Water	**SDG 16** Peace, Justice, and Strong Institutions	**SDG 9** Industry, Innovation and Infrastructure
SDG 15 Life on Land	**SDG 17** Partnerships for the Goals	**United Nations 17 Sustainable Development Goals**

Ultimately, defining sustainability in business is about shifting from a mindset of extraction and exploitation to one of stewardship and systems thinking. It means understanding the business as part of a larger ecosystem where long-term success depends on the health of that entire system. This definition lays the foundation for everything else this book will explore: strategy, innovation, change management, and cultural transformation toward a more just, resilient, and sustainable future. Just remember, each organization is its own living entity, just like every person; we have foundational medical care, but each of us needs different medications, vitamins, and nourishment, just as organizations do, so foundational understanding is necessary to understand how to proceed.

2.1.2 Consumer Demand and Organizational Response

Consumer behavior is a powerful driver of change in today's economy. Over the past decade, consumers have become increasingly aware of their purchasing power, and they are using it to demand more ethical, sustainable, and transparent business practices. This shift is not just anecdotal; it is backed by data across multiple markets and sectors. From food and fashion to finance and real estate, buyers are asking hard questions: Where did this come from? Who made it? How was it made? What impact does it have on people and the planet?

The rise of the conscious consumer has ushered in a new era of accountability for businesses. A 2021 global study by IBM and the National Retail Federation found that 62% of consumers are willing to change their shopping habits to reduce environmental impact, and more than 70% of purpose-driven consumers say they pay an added premium for brands aligned with their values. In addition, Gen Z and Millennials, two of the largest and most influential consumer groups, expect companies to take clear stands on environmental and social issues.[21] Not only are these groups the largest consumers, but they are also the predominant members of the workforce as of 2026.[22]

These expectations have created a landscape where sustainability is now a market differentiator. Brands that lead with transparency, integrity, and action are not only attracting customers, but also building long-term loyalty and advocacy. This is a stark contrast to earlier decades when companies could rely on glossy marketing to cover unsustainable practices. Today's consumers are savvy, skeptical, and well-informed, thanks to digital platforms and global connectivity, they can quickly research a company's supply chain, labor practices, and carbon footprint.

Organizations have responded in varying ways. Some have made bold, systemic changes to align their operations with sustainability goals. These are companies that

---

21 IBM, 2021. Comsumers want it all: Hybrid shopping, sustainability, and purpose-driven brands, downloaded from IBM.COM, 2025. https://www.ibm.com/downloads/documents/us-en/10c31775c8540243
22 World Economic forum, 2025. The Future of Jobs Report 2025, downloaded 2025. https://reports.we forum.org/docs/WEF_Future_of_Jobs_Report_2025.pdf

embed sustainability into their business model rethinking everything from product design and logistics to energy use and supplier relationships. Others, however, have taken a more superficial approach, implementing isolated green initiatives or issuing CSR reports without real operational changes. This latter strategy, often referred to as "greenwashing," is increasingly risky as watchdogs, activists, and consumers alike demand proof, not promises.

In addition to product and service transparency, consumers are also influencing how organizations engage socially and politically. Silence or inaction on critical issues such as climate change, racial justice, or workers' rights can result in backlash and reputational damage. As a result, brands are now navigating a more complex landscape where business strategy must integrate ethical leadership and active social engagement.

We are also seeing the rise of **co-creation models**, where companies involve consumers directly in product development, sustainability initiatives, and advocacy efforts. For example, some fashion brands invite consumers to vote on sustainable collections or contribute ideas for recycling programs. This participatory approach not only builds trust but also reinforces the idea that sustainability is a shared responsibility. Some examples of companies doing this is highlighted in Table 3 below.[23]

Table 3: Industry Co-Creation Models.

Industry Co-Creation Models				
Company	Industry	Platform/ Initiative	Co-Creation Approach	Impact/Outcome
Unilever	Consumer Goods	Open Innovation Platform	External collaboration, customer-sourced ideas	Over 1,000 proposals; 60% of research projects involve external partners
IKEA	Furniture/ Retail	Co-Create IKEA	Customer input, bootcamps, university collaborations	Thousands of suggestions, rewards for selected ideas, prototyping resources
Sodexo	Facilities & Food Management	Innov'Hub via Braineet	Employee and client idea platform	Global engagement, internal talent development, +60 NPS
DeWalt	Power Tools	Insight Community	Engaging professional and home users for product development	Saved $6M in research costs; 12,000+ users

---

23 Braineet.com, Customer Co-Creation Examples: 12 Companies Doing It Right, Open Innovation, referenced 2025. https://www.braineet.com/blog/co-creation-examples

Table 3 (continued)

Industry Co-Creation Models

Company	Industry	Platform/ Initiative	Co-Creation Approach	Impact/Outcome
LEGO	Toys	LEGO Ideas	Fan-submitted product ideas	Over 1M contributors; 23 products launched; revenue growth
Heineken	Beverages	Open Design Explorations	Designers + customer collaboration for club concepts	Media attention, low-cost creative marketing
DHL	Logistics	Innovation Centers	Workshops with customers and employees	6,000+ co-creation sessions; innovations like drone delivery
Anheuser-Busch	Beverages	Crowdsourced Product & Commercial Dev	Consumer tastings, brewer competitions, crowdsourced media	Created Black Crown; commercials with 35,000+ contributors
BMW	Automotive	Co-Creation Lab	Innovation contests for design and features	300+ ideas; global judging; continued contests
Accor	Hospitality	Innovation Funnel	Customer co-creation tied to strategy across regions	Cross-regional idea management, strategy-aligned innovation
General Mills	Food Products	Worldwide Innovation Network	Startup + customer collaboration platform	Product/packaging updates via open proposals
Coca-Cola	Beverages	Local Co-Creation Strategy	Customer R&D engagement in Southeast Asia	Positive local product testing and strategy alignment

Internally, organizations are learning that responding to consumer demand requires cultural alignment. Employees, especially younger workers, want to work for companies that reflect their values. This means that sustainability is not just a marketing strategy, but a talent acquisition and retention tool. Businesses that are responsive to both internal and external stakeholder values are seeing stronger performance across multiple dimensions.

In summary, consumer demand is not merely reactive it is shaping the future of business. Companies that listen, adapt, and act with authenticity are emerging as leaders in a new economic paradigm. The next section will explore how regulations and public policy are also playing a pivotal role in guiding this transformation, complementing and amplifying the signals coming from the consumer base.

2.1.3 City and State Regulations Push Organizational Sustainability and Market Transformation

While consumer demand has created a bottom-up momentum for change, public policy is increasingly applying top-down pressure that is accelerating the shift toward sustainable business practices. In particular, regulations at the city and state levels have emerged as powerful levers of transformation. These regulatory bodies are often closer to the ground, more agile, and more responsive than national governments. As a result, they are playing a leading role in shaping the standards, incentives, and expectations for corporate sustainability.

Cities, for example, are on the frontlines of climate change. Urban areas consume over two-thirds of the world's energy and are responsible for more than 70% of global CO_2 emissions.[24] This reality has driven many cities to adopt ambitious sustainability goals some even more progressive than those of their national counterparts. Initiatives like the C40 Cities Climate Leadership Group, a network of nearly 100 global cities committed to taking climate action, have resulted in local ordinances that require businesses to meet stringent energy efficiency benchmarks, transition to renewable power, and invest in greener infrastructure.[25]

In the United States, cities such as New York, San Francisco, and Seattle have implemented comprehensive sustainability mandates that touch everything from waste management and building codes to transportation and labor practices. These local policies are often binding, enforceable, and backed by financial penalties or incentives. For example, New York City's Local Law 97 mandates that large buildings reduce their greenhouse gas emissions significantly over the coming decades, directly impacting how real estate firms, landlords, and developers plan their future investments, with a target of Net Zero greenhouse gas emissions from buildings by 2050.[26]

State-level legislation is also driving market transformation. In California, for instance, progressive environmental laws have had ripple effects across industries. The state's Cap-and-Trade Program, Clean Energy and Pollution Reduction Act, and the California Consumer Privacy Act (CCPA) all reflect a broader commitment to sustainability not just environmental, but also social and ethical. These laws often serve as models that other states, and sometimes entire industries, later adopt.

What's particularly powerful about city and state regulations is their ability to create change through both mandates and market incentives. On one hand, they establish minimum compliance standards that all organizations must meet. On the

---

24 United Nations, 2020. Urban Climate Action Is Crucial to Bend the Emissions Curve 5 October 2020, Article referenced 2025. https://unfccc.int/news/urban-climate-action-is-crucial-to-bend-the-emissions-curve

25 C40 Cities 2025. Website referenced 2025, https://www.c40.org/

26 NYC Gov, 2025. Website accessed 2025, https://www.nyc.gov/site/buildings/codes/ll97-greenhouse-gas-emissions-reductions.page

other, they reward innovation, investment in green technologies, and responsible governance. These dual pressures encourage businesses not just to follow the rules but to lead in sustainability.

Moreover, many cities and states now require companies to disclose ESG (Environmental, Social, and Governance) performance metrics. An example of this is California's SB-253 & 261, passed in September of 2022, the purpose of which is to increase transparency regarding corporate greenhouse gas emissions and to promote accountability in addressing climate change. So, companies that work nationally and internationally have to transform their organizational culture to be able to be competitive in multiple markets. For instance, the European Parliament adopted the **Corporate Sustainability Reporting Directive (CSRD)** in November 2021, which came into effect in January 2024. It is a legislative framework aimed at improving and standardizing sustainability reporting by companies across the EU. The objective is to enhance transparency and accountability in corporate sustainability practices and emphasize the importance of sustainability in long-term business strategies. Any organization that wants to work in any EU country will have to have the capabilities to report to these mandates. Why is this important? Transparency requirements help standardize sustainability reporting and level the playing field. They also make it easier for investors, consumers, and communities to evaluate which companies are truly committed to sustainable development and which are merely checking boxes.

It is important to note that regulatory leadership at the subnational level often fosters a culture of collaboration between government, business, and civil society. Programs such as public-private partnerships, urban innovation labs, and sustainability incubators are enabling new solutions to emerge and scale. In many cases, these partnerships have led to job creation, improved community wellbeing, and increased business resilience.[27]

In summary, city and state regulations are not merely bureaucratic hurdles, they are catalysts for change. By setting clear expectations and creating supportive ecosystems for innovation, these policies help guide businesses toward practices that are both ethically responsible and economically advantageous. As we'll explore in the next section, when this regulatory momentum is combined with shifting consumer expectations and internal cultural transformation, it creates a powerful foundation for redefining the role of business in society.

---

27 Hallin, J., Fredriksson, E., Altman, R., and Zhou, S. (2016). Developing a Human Centred Business Index – Leading with Purpose, Empathy, Systems-Approach and Resilience in 'Business Beyond Sustainability'. *European Public and Social Innovation Review, 1*(1). https://doi.org/10.31637/epsir.16-1.3.

2.1.4 Section Synthesis: Sustainability Defined in a Business

As we bring together the insights from this section, a clear picture emerges: sustainability in business today is not an isolated initiative or a side department it is a transformative force shaping how organizations think, operate, and evolve. It is a strategic, systemic, and values-driven orientation that responds to the demands of an interconnected world. Sustainability, in this integrated sense, is not only about environmental stewardship; it is about how organizations design for resilience, lead with ethics, and co-create value with their stakeholders.

I began with defining sustainability in a business context, establishing that it goes far beyond the occasional green campaign or compliance requirement. It is about integrating environmental, social, and governance (ESG) considerations into the DNA of business decision-making. Whether it's product development, operations, or leadership structures, sustainability must be designed to serve both long-term viability and immediate impact.

Next, we examined how consumer demand is radically transforming the marketplace. Today's customers are not passive buyers; they are active participants in shaping the identities and practices of the brands they support. Businesses that respond authentically to these demands by building transparency, trust, and value alignment into their operations are better positioned to thrive in this evolving environment. Importantly, consumers are also employees, investors, and community members, which amplifies the reach and influence of their expectations.

On the policy side, city and state regulations are proving to be critical accelerators of sustainable transformation. Local governments, often acting more swiftly and boldly than national bodies, are setting the bar higher through mandates and incentives that nudge or push businesses toward more responsible behavior. These actions not only level the playing field but also cultivate innovation ecosystems that support sustainable development as a shared mission across sectors.

Taken together, these forces, bottom-up demand and top-down regulation are converging to create a powerful momentum for organizational change. Businesses are no longer being asked whether they should engage in sustainability; the question is *how well* they are doing it and *how deeply* it is embedded in their culture and strategy. In this sense, sustainability is becoming a competitive necessity and a moral imperative.

However, to truly meet this moment, organizations must move beyond fragmented or performative responses. Sustainability must be treated as a design challenge one that calls for critical thinking, cross-functional collaboration, and cultural alignment. This is where the Integral Design Thinking (IDT) Strategy Framework comes into play. As we progress through this book, the IDT framework will offer a path to operationalize sustainability through systems thinking, human-centered leadership, and creative strategy.

Ultimately, the organizations that succeed in today's changing economy will be those that can see the big picture without losing sight of the details. They will be the ones who understand that sustainability is not about choosing between people, planet, and profit, but about finding synergy among them. This synthesis sets the stage for the next chapters, where we explore the historical, strategic, and design-based perspectives that inform how sustainable transformation can be led from within.

We now turn our attention to Chapter 3: Evolution of Perception and Theoretical Frameworks a journey through how sustainability has been understood, defined, and modeled by leading thinkers and organizations across the globe.

3 Evolution of Perception and Theoretical Frameworks

Sustainability is not just about saving the planet,
it's about changing how we think, relate, and lead.

To lead change in sustainability, we must understand how the very idea of sustainability has evolved over time, how it has shifted in meaning, in urgency, and in strategy. This chapter invites you into that evolution, tracing how our collective understanding has grown from a narrow focus on environmental preservation to a more integrated vision that considers systems, culture, psychology, and ethics.

In the early days, sustainability was often seen as a technical issue, something to be solved with the right regulations, metrics, or innovations. But as the consequences of unsustainable practices grew more visible, so too did the realization that the roots of these problems are social, philosophical, and psychological. Sustainability is not just about carbon footprints and recycling bins, it's about how we see the world, what we value, and how we choose to relate to one another and to the planet.

This chapter explores that deeper terrain. I begin by examining the historical arc of sustainability awareness, from its emergence on the global stage to its expansion into business, governance, and civil society. I then turn to the contributions of key thinkers, Ken Wilber, Otto Scharmer, Bob Doppelt, and Chris Laszlo, whose theoretical frameworks help us understand the kind of leadership, mindset, and systems thinking required for sustainable transformation.

These frameworks are not academic abstractions; they are practical lenses for action. They show us that transformation requires not just a shift in policy or technology, but a shift in consciousness. They remind us that empathy, collaboration, and integrated vision are not "soft skills", they are core strategies for resilience and innovation.

Together, the thinkers and models introduced in this chapter form the intellectual and philosophical foundation for the Integral Design Thinking (IDT) Strategy Framework presented later in this book. They equip you with the perspective needed to see the interconnectedness of the challenges you face and to design solutions that are as integrated and adaptive as the systems you seek to change.

Now, let's begin with the evolution of the perception of sustainability, and how it has shaped today's call to lead with purpose, empathy, and systems wisdom.

3.1 Evolution of the Perception of Sustainability

The idea of sustainability has come a long way since it was formally introduced into the global discourse. What began as a scientific and environmental concern has trans-

https://doi.org/10.1515/9783111705286-003

formed into a broad-based organizational and societal imperative, evolving with shifts in political will, economic necessity, and human consciousness. In this section, I trace the historical arc of how sustainability has been perceived, from its earliest definitions to its current incarnation as an integrated value system that touches nearly every aspect of organizational life.

The modern sustainability movement took a decisive turn with the release of the Brundtland Report in 1987 by the World Commission on Environment and Development. This foundational document defined sustainable development as "development that meets the needs of the present without compromising the ability of future generations to meet their own needs.[28]" Crucially, the report recognized that true sustainability involves more than ecological responsibility; it requires social equity and economic reform as well. This holistic framing laid the groundwork for everything that followed.

But the Brundtland Report also made it clear: achieving sustainability in the real world would require deep, systemic change. It challenged prevailing social and political structures, calling for policy frameworks that account for unequal access to resources and the disproportionate distribution of both benefits and harms. From this emerged the now-critical concept of **intergenerational equity**, justice not only within a generation but between generations.

Fast forward to the early 2000s and beyond, sustainability conversations became more urgent. The notion of "overshoot and collapse," described by Brown (2006),[29] captured a grim possibility: humanity's consumption had already outpaced what Earth's ecosystems could sustainably regenerate. The reality of climate change, environmental degradation, and social inequality began to shift sustainability from an abstract goal to a matter of survival. Policymakers and business leaders alike began to recognize that business-as-usual was not just untenable—it was actively dangerous.

By 2012, at the United Nations Conference on Sustainable Development in Rio de Janeiro, global sustainability had matured into a formal, actionable agenda. The conference led to the production of the Sustainable Development Goals (SDGs),[30] a set of 17 interconnected objectives ranging from eradicating poverty to ensuring clean energy and justice. These SDGs signaled a new era, one in which sustainability was framed not just as a government responsibility but as a collaborative challenge requiring action from businesses, civil society, and individuals alike.

The corporate world, particularly in the U.S., began to respond in 2019 with a major pivot from shareholder to stakeholder capitalism. Over 200 of the world's largest corporations signed the Business Roundtable Statement on the Purpose of a Corpo-

---

28 United Nations, 1987. Report of the World Commission on Environment and Development, p. 54, retrieved 2025. https://digitallibrary.un.org/record/139811?v=pdf
29 Brown, L. (2006). *Plan B 2.0: Rescuing a planet under stress and a civilization in trouble.* Norton and Company, Inc.
30 United Nations, 2015. SDG History, retrieved from website 2025. https://sdgs.un.org/goals

ration, which declared that businesses exist to serve all stakeholders, such as customers, employees, suppliers, communities, and shareholders. This shift, often referred to as a move from the "triple bottom line" (people, planet, profit) to the "quadruple bottom line" (adding purpose), reflected an evolution in both perception and accountability.

As these paradigms evolved, so too did the awareness that sustainability cannot be tackled in silos. Systems thinking, cross-sector collaboration, and a deep understanding of interdependencies became essential. Scholars and thought leaders such as Dryzek[31], Capra[32], and Senge[33] emphasized the interconnectedness of global challenges and the need for solutions that reflect this complexity. Their work emphasized that no single initiative, regulation, or business model would suffice. What was needed was a new way of seeing and a new way of leading.

This leads us into the need for interdisciplinary integration. In this age of volatility and uncertainty, effective sustainability strategies are those that synthesize environmental science, economics, sociology, ethics, and innovation management. The goal is no longer to optimize for one variable but to harmonize across many, to seek not just growth, but regenerative impact.

In short, the perception of sustainability has evolved from niche concern to moral and strategic imperative. The sustainability leader of today must be fluent not only in environmental data but in systems thinking, organizational psychology, and cultural dynamics. They must be able to build coalitions, challenge assumptions, and lead organizations through ambiguity with empathy and purpose. As we continue this chapter, we'll explore how this broadening perception has given rise to new global frameworks and theoretical tools that guide this transformation.

Next, we'll take a look at the global perspective of sustainability, understanding how nations, institutions, and local movements have responded to this challenge through policies, partnerships, and practice.

3.2 Global Perspective of Sustainability

Twenty years into the 21st century, the world is navigating heightened levels of volatility across environmental, economic, and social domains. While the phrase "global sustainability" is often used in policy or corporate reports, its real implications cut much deeper. A truly global perspective acknowledges that sustainability cannot be compartmentalized within regions or industries. Instead, it recognizes the deeply in-

---

31 Dryzek, J., Norgaard, B., and Schlosberg, D. (2012). *The Oxford handbook of climate change and society*. doi: 10.1093/oxfordhb/9780199566600.003.0001
32 Capra, F. (2002). *The hidden connections: A science for sustainable living*. Anchor Books.
33 Senge, P., Smith, B., Kruschwitz, N., Laur, J., and Schley, S. (2008). *The necessary revolution: how individuals and organisations are working together to create a sustainable world*. Doubleday.

terconnected nature of ecological systems, economic structures, and human communities. This understanding demands a collaborative, planetary mindset, one that honors both local ingenuity and global solidarity.

Despite decades of well-intentioned action, including from the international community, scientists and scholars warn that humanity may be reaching a critical threshold, where the accumulated damage from industrialization and unsustainable consumption might become irreversible.[34,35] We are living in an era shaped by the consequences of the first Industrial Revolution and the linear economic model it introduced, one of extraction, production, consumption, and waste. The result: rising temperatures, shrinking biodiversity, widening inequalities, and mounting global health and humanitarian crises.

But where there are challenges, there is also opportunity, especially for innovation, leadership, and local action. Researchers Seelos and Mair (2005)[36] proposed that locally generated, community-based solutions hold powerful potential for addressing sustainability challenges. They advocate for integrating the unique strengths of local cultures and institutions into broader sustainability efforts. This insight remains vital today, especially as businesses and governments recognize that context matters and that no single sustainability model can apply universally.

For decades, global frameworks have attempted to guide this evolving understanding. These include milestone initiatives like the Universal Declaration of Human Rights (1948), the Convention on the Rights of the Child (1989), and Agenda 21 from the 1992 Earth Summit. More recently, the Millennium Development Goals (2000–2015) and the Sustainable Development Goals (2015–2030) have further institutionalized global efforts to link environmental, social, and economic concerns into an actionable roadmap. The 2015 Paris Agreement on climate change, with its unprecedented international collaboration, has become one of the most potent symbols of collective responsibility and shared action.

However, treaties and policies only go so far without active translation into local-level initiatives. As McKnight (1993)[37] argued, sustainable transformation often begins in communities, where people have the most at stake and the greatest capacity to co-create solutions. One example is the socially focused B Corporation 4Ocean, which was founded in 2017 to address ocean plastic pollution. By linking their business model to a tangible ecological outcome, removing over 40 million pounds of plastic

---

34 Brown, L. (2006). *Plan B 2.0: Rescuing a planet under stress and a civilization in trouble.* Norton and Company, Inc.

35 Sachs, J. (2005). *The end of poverty: Economic possibilities for our time.* Penguin Books.

36 Seelos, C., and Mair, J. (2005b). Sustainable Development: How social entrepreneurs make it happen. [Working Paper]. IESE Business School, University of Navarra.

37 McKnight, J. (1993). *Building communities from the inside out: A path toward finding and mobilizing a community's asset.* ACTA Publications.

from the ocean[38], 4Ocean illustrates how purpose-driven companies can bridge global concerns with localized, measurable impact.

Moreover, as supply chains have become increasingly globalized, the web of environmental and social consequences has expanded in complexity. A product might be designed in one country, assembled in another, and shipped halfway around the world to be consumed and eventually discarded. Consumers, once unaware of these pathways, are now asking harder questions about ethics, transparency, and sustainability. This growing awareness is pushing companies to go beyond compliance and begin rethinking their business models.

Leading thinkers like Laszlo (2005)[39] emphasize the need for a new kind of business ethos, one that shifts from a shareholder focus to stakeholder management. This involves honoring the needs and perspectives of employees, communities, ecosystems, and future generations, not just financial investors. In this model, sustainability is no longer an add-on. It becomes embedded into the purpose, governance, operations, and innovation practices of the organization.

The call for global sustainability is, in essence, a call for new consciousness, one that honors interconnectedness as a foundational reality. Capra (2002)[40] and Senge et al. (2008)[41] urge leaders to recognize the systems within which they operate, not only as economic players but as ethical stewards. Organizations that can align their purpose with this broader, integrated vision are the ones best poised to lead transformative change, not just for profit, but for people and planet alike.

This global view prepares us to dive deeper into the integral theories and models that inform sustainable leadership in the next sections, beginning with Wilber's Integral Vision.

3.3 Wilber's Integral Vision

As the complexity of sustainability challenges has become more evident, there has been a growing recognition that we need a more holistic way to make sense of the

---

38 Blue Podcast Network. 2024. How to Protect the Ocean. 4Ocean: 40 Million Pounds and Counting – The Impact of 4ocean on Ocean Cleanup Efforts. Retrieved 2025, https://www.speakupforblue.com/show/speak-up-for-the-ocean-blue/4ocean-40-million-pounds-and-counting-the-impact-of-4ocean-on-ocean-cleanup-efforts/

39 Laszlo, C. (2003). *The sustainable company: How to create lasting value through social and environmental performance.* Island Press.

40 Capra, F. (2002). *The hidden connections: A science for sustainable living.* Anchor Books.

41 Senge, P., Smith, B., Kruschwitz, N., Laur, J., and Schley, S. (2008). *The necessary revolution: how individuals and organisations are working together to create a sustainable world.* Doubleday.

systems we operate within. This is where Ken Wilber's "Integral Vision"[42,43] becomes especially relevant. Wilber proposes that no single perspective be it scientific, cultural, psychological, or spiritual, can fully capture the dynamics of the human experience. Instead, he offers a model called AQAL (All Quadrants, All Levels) that invites leaders to understand sustainability through a multidimensional lens that can be seen in Figure 1.

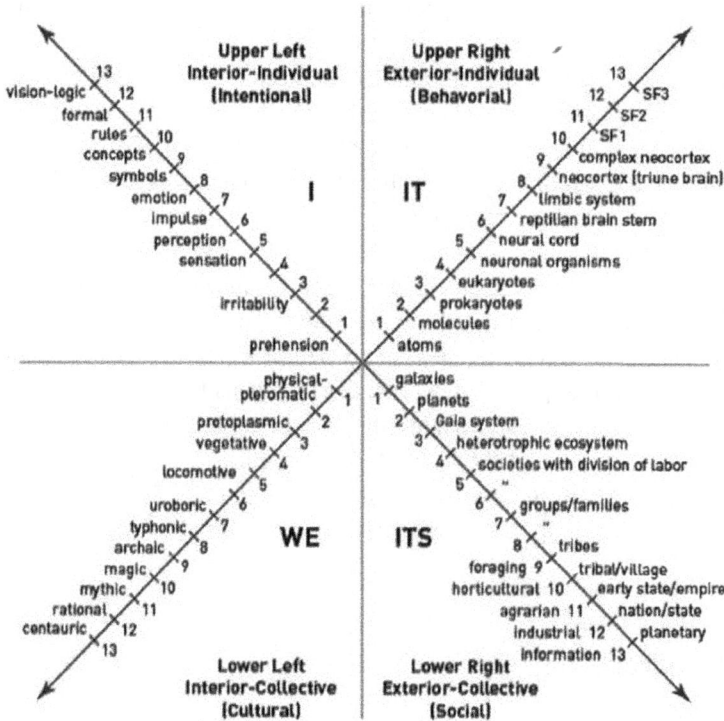

Figure 1: Integral Vision Represented by All Quadrants, All Levels (AQAL) (Source: Wilber's, 2001).[44]

Wilber's framework divides experience into four quadrants: the internal individual ("I"), the internal collective ("We"), the external individual ("It"), and the external collective ("Its"). These quadrants represent different ways of knowing the world subjective, intersubjective, objective, and interobjective. By accounting for all four, Wilber insists we can better comprehend and influence the systems around us.

---

42 Wilber, K. (2001). *A theory of everything: an integral vision for business, politics, science and spirituality.* Shambhala Publication, Inc.

43 Wilber, K. (2007). *The integral vision.* Shambhala Publications, Inc.

44 Image retrieved from Jaber, M., 2021. Integral Design Thinking: A Novel Cross-national Framework for Sustainability Management, PhD Thesis, pg. 24.

Why does this matter for sustainability? Because sustainability is inherently multidimensional. It is not only a technical challenge of emissions and resources (external), but also a challenge of mindset, behavior, and values (internal). A business that focuses solely on carbon audits and reporting metrics without addressing employee values, company culture, or community relationships will likely fall short of genuine sustainability.

In a practical sense, Wilber's AQAL framework provides a kind of "organizational x-ray." It helps leaders diagnose challenges and design interventions that are comprehensive, not just cosmetic. For instance, if a company wants to shift toward regenerative practices, it cannot simply revise its supply chain logistics (external individual). It must also engage employees in meaningful dialogue about purpose and impact (internal collective), revise its strategic vision (internal individual), and collaborate across sectors and stakeholders (external collective).

Critics have argued that Wilber's framework is too abstract or philosophically dense for practical use. But proponents like **Young** (2002)[45] highlight its interdisciplinary value, noting how it bridges science, philosophy, and practice. Importantly, it empowers sustainability leaders to see both the forest and the trees, to zoom in on operational challenges while keeping the whole system in view.

This integrative approach resonates with today's most urgent sustainability demands. As Pavez et al. (2020)[46] suggest, we are entering an era where sustainability leadership is defined not just by innovation, but by a deep shift in worldview. Businesses are increasingly being asked to operate from a perspective of interconnectedness, where the health of the planet, people, and profit are woven together not treated as separate goals.

Wilber's Integral Vision doesn't provide a checklist. Instead, it provides a map—a way to think and act more systemically, empathetically, and strategically. It aligns well with the Integral Design Thinking (IDT) framework explored later in this book. Just as IDT seeks to align design, systems thinking, and cultural change, Wilber's model helps leaders become aware of the deeper patterns that shape individual and collective behavior.

In today's volatile, interdependent world, the leaders who thrive will be those who see across quadrants, think across disciplines, and act across boundaries. Wilber's Integral Vision provides the philosophical scaffolding for that kind of leadership and it's time we bring it into the heart of our sustainability conversations.

---

45 Young, J. E. (2002). A spectrum of consciousness for CEOs: A business application of Ken Wilber's spectrum of consciousness. *International Journal of Organisational Analysis, 10*(1), 30–54.

46 Pavez, I., Kendall, L., and Lazlo, C. (2020). Positive-impact companies: Toward a new paradigm of value creation. *Organ Dyn*, https://doi.org/10.1016/j.orgdyn.2020.100806

3.4 Empathy and Sustainability

As sustainability becomes a driving force in modern organizations, one critical yet often underexplored element is emerging as essential: empathy. While most discussions around sustainability focus on emissions targets, resource efficiency, or governance frameworks, empathy plays a foundational role in shaping how we relate to each other, the natural world, and the systems we inhabit. Without empathy, sustainability becomes transactional; with it, sustainability becomes transformational.

Empathy allows us to recognize that sustainability is not simply an external goal, it's a relational one. It challenges us to step outside of self-interest and consider the broader impacts of our actions on people, communities, ecosystems, and future generations. This emotional and cognitive bridge is especially necessary in a world where the consequences of climate change, social inequity, and economic instability are deeply interconnected.

In business, the rise of stakeholder capitalism has created space for a more human-centered approach to leadership. Researchers like Hallin et al. (2016)[47] have argued that for organizations to operate effectively in today's volatile and interconnected world, they must embrace four core leadership principles: purpose, empathy, systems thinking, and resilience. Empathy is not a feel-good accessory to these principles, it is their emotional engine. It powers an organization's ability to see, feel, and act beyond its narrow interests.

Sustainability leaders must therefore be skilled not just in strategy but in emotional intelligence. They must develop the capacity to understand different perspectives, listen deeply, and manage the discomfort that comes with change. This is especially important when leading transformation efforts, where fear, cynicism, and resistance often surface. Empathy becomes the key to unlocking trust and cooperation, which are vital for any long-term change initiative.

Empirical studies affirm this view. Scholars like Schultz (2000)[48] and Czap et al. (2012)[49] have consistently shown that empathy correlates with pro-environmental behavior. People are more likely to act sustainably when they feel emotionally connected to the issue, whether that's the plight of future generations, the suffering of marginalized communities, or the degradation of natural ecosystems. Empathy helps us build those emotional connections.

---

47 Hallin, J., Fredriksson, E., Altman, R., and Zhou, S. (2016). Developing a Human Centred Business Index – Leading with Purpose, Empathy, Systems-Approach and Resilience in 'Business Beyond Sustainability.' *European Public and Social Innovation Review, 1*(1). https://doi.org/10.31637/epsir.16-1.3.
48 Schultz, P.W., (2000). Empathizing with nature: The effects of perspective taking on concern for environmental issues. *J. Soc. Issues, 56*, 391–406.
49 Czap, N.V., Czap, H.J., Khachaturyan, M., Lynne, G.D., and Burbach, M.E., (2012). Walking in the shoes of others: Experimental testing of dual-interest and empathy in environmental choice. *J. Socio. 41*, 642–653.

Design thinking methodology has played a major role in institutionalizing empathy within organizations. As Elsbach and Stigliani (2018)[50] explain, design thinking encourages iterative learning, cross-functional collaboration, and above all, a deep understanding of user needs. This "empathize-first" mindset is not only a design principle, it's a leadership principle. It enables organizations to better understand the human impact of their actions and to innovate in ways that are inclusive, ethical, and future-focused.

Otto Scharmer's Theory U[51] further deepens this perspective. In his model, seen in Figure 2, empathy is more than a trait, it is a practice. Scharmer argues that leaders must cultivate "presencing," a state of deep awareness where individuals can connect with their highest future potential. This requires a shift from ego to eco, moving from a self-centered mindset to one that prioritizes the whole. Scharmer's U-shaped model is a roadmap for this journey, guiding leaders through a process of letting go, listening, co-sensing, and co-creating.

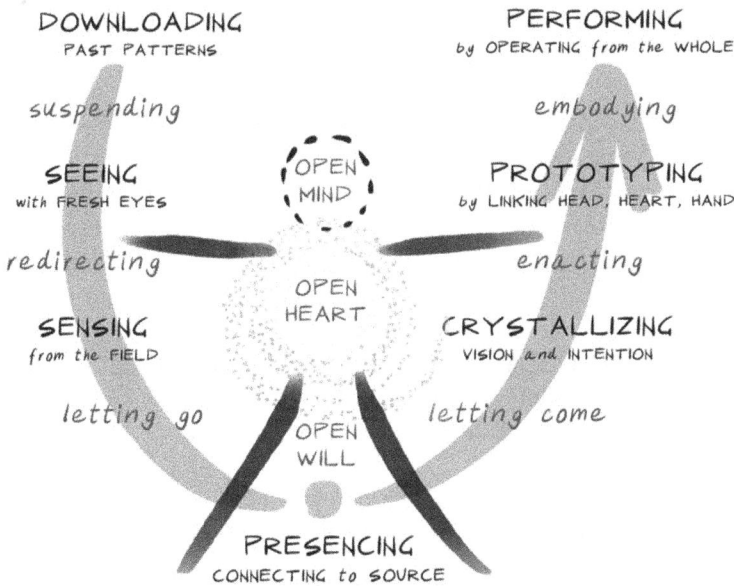

Figure 2: Theory U: Seven Ways of Attending and Co-Shaping (Source: Scharmer, 2018).[52]

---

50 Elsbach, K. and Stigliani, S. (2018). Design thinking and organisational culture: A review and framework for future research. *Journal of Management*, 1–33.

51 Scharmer, O. (2007). *Theory U: Leading from the future as it emerges*. The Society for Organisational Learning, Inc.

52 Image retrieved from Jaber, M., 2021. Integral Design Thinking: A Novel Cross-national Framework for Sustainability Management, PhD Thesis, pg. 26.

This isn't easy. As Schein (1992)[53] notes, organizations are often locked into "basic underlying assumptions" that make new behaviors feel inconceivable. Empathy helps break through these cognitive walls. It allows leaders and teams to see with fresh eyes, engage with humility, and reimagine possibilities together.

Empathy also plays a strategic role in decision-making. When organizations incorporate empathy into their culture, they are better able to anticipate stakeholder needs, navigate conflict, and build stronger partnerships. This creates a competitive advantage, not just in terms of brand loyalty or employee retention, but in resilience. Empathetic organizations adapt more quickly because they are attuned to subtle shifts in stakeholder expectations and social dynamics.

Perhaps most importantly, empathy shifts our measurement of success. It moves us from short-term profit to long-term flourishing. It encourages businesses to ask not only, "What do we gain?" but also, "Who might be left behind?" and "How do we repair harm?" These are moral questions, but they are also practical ones. In an age of rising transparency and accountability, empathy is a business imperative.

As the UN Global Compact-Accenture CEO Study (2023)[54] shows, 98% of CEOs see sustainability as critical to future success and core to their role. Yet many still struggle to move from compliance to transformation. The missing link is often mindset. Empathy offers a pathway to deepen that mindset, fostering cultures where listening, learning, and collaboration become standard practice.

In sum, empathy is not a soft skill, it is a systems skill. It connects people to purpose, drives inclusive innovation, and supports the deep cultural change that sustainability requires. It also aligns seamlessly with the Integral Design Thinking framework of this book, which places empathy, co-creation, and shared value at the heart of sustainable strategy.

In the next section, we will explore how Bob Doppelt's seven interventions offer practical tools to institutionalize these mindsets and how they help organizations embed empathy into the very fabric of their systems and structures.

3.5 Doppelt's Seven Interventions for Sustainability

As sustainability initiatives continue to evolve, many organizations find themselves stuck, not because of a lack of intention, but due to systemic inertia, outdated mental models, and fragmented strategies. Bob Doppelt's[55] work offers a way forward. Through years of research and consulting across the private and public sectors, Dop-

53 Schein, E. (1992). *Organisational culture and leadership*. Jossey Bass.

54 UN Global Compact, 2023. The 12th United Nations Global Compact–Accenture CEO Study. Accessed 2025. https://www.globalcompactusa.org/news/the-12th-united-nations-global-compact-accenture-ceo-study

55 Doppelt, B. (2003). Overcoming the seven blunders of sustainability. *The systems thinker, 14*(5), 2–7.

pelt identified seven common "blunders" that impede sustainability efforts, and more importantly, seven strategic interventions to overcome them.

Doppelt's core argument is that sustainability isn't just about greening operations or drafting better policies, it's about **transforming organizational culture**. This requires deep shifts in how power is distributed, how decisions are made, and how learning happens. His framework helps leaders recognize that sustainable transformation must be both systemic and participatory. It is not something "done" by a department, it is a shared and evolving commitment.

The Case for Cultural Change

One of Doppelt's[56] central insights is that sustainability often fails not because of external barriers, but because organizations do not challenge their internal assumptions. Many leaders mistakenly believe that compliance with environmental regulations or launching a few CSR initiatives is sufficient. But these actions rarely address the root causes of unsustainable behavior, such as hierarchical governance, siloed departments, or a lack of psychological safety for employees to speak up. To help address this, he developed the Seven Blunders[57] for review, visualized in Figure 3.

Doppelt urges organizations to confront these foundational issues by rethinking how they design their systems. His research, which included sustainability leaders from companies like IKEA, Starbucks, and Interface, revealed that the most successful organizations shared two critical traits: (1) distributed governance, and (2) visionary, emotionally intelligent leadership. Together, these create the enabling conditions for change.

The Seven Blunders: Why Sustainability Gets Stuck

Before transformation can take root, we have to be honest about what's holding us back. And not just at the surface level. Real change means interrogating the *habits, assumptions, and structures* that quietly run the show in most organizations.

Doppelt outlines seven blunders, recurring pitfalls that stall or sabotage sustainability efforts before they can take off. These aren't just organizational oversights; they're cultural blind spots. Let's walk through each one and unpack why it matters.

---

56 Doppelt, B. (2014). Leading change toward Sustainability: A change-management guide for business, government and civil society. *International Journal of Sustainability in Higher Education.* Volume 5 Issue 2https://doi.org/10.1108/ijshe.2004.24905bae.005.

57 Doppelt, B. (2003). Overcoming the seven blunders of sustainability. *The systems thinker, 14*(5), 2–7.

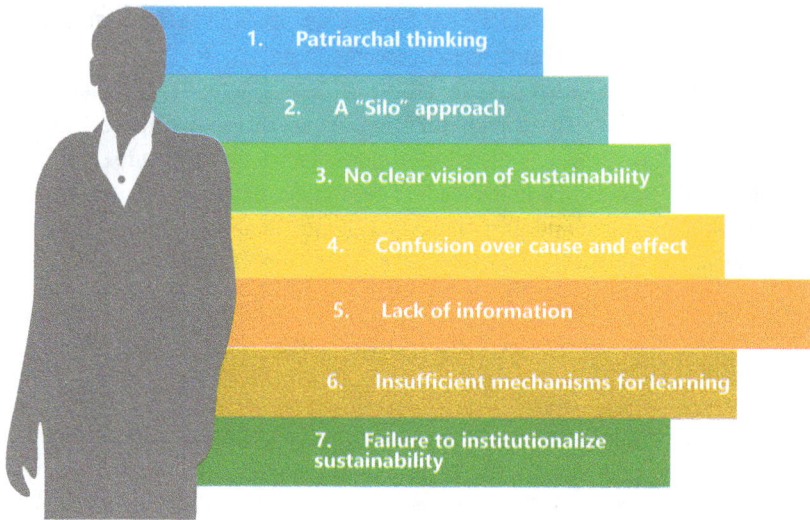

Figure 3: The Seven Blunders for Sustainability (Source: adapted from Doppelt, 2003).[58]

1. **Patriarchal Thinking**
   This is the classic top-down, command-and-control leadership model. While it may offer clarity, it breeds dependency, stifles creativity, and sends a clear (even if unspoken) message: innovation is not your job unless you're at the top. But sustainability thrives on collaboration and distributed leadership, not hierarchy.

2. **Siloed Approaches**
   Ever heard "that's not my department"? That's the voice of fragmentation. When teams and departments operate in isolation, there's no shared vision, just competing priorities and duplicated efforts. Sustainability is systemic. It doesn't live neatly inside a single function.

3. **Lack of a Clear Vision**
   If people can't articulate *why* sustainability matters or *what success looks like*, they'll default to business as usual. Without a compelling and shared vision, initiatives are scattered, reactive, and let's be real, often forgotten by the next quarter.

4. **Misdiagnosing Root Causes**
   It's tempting to chase symptoms: rising energy costs, employee disengagement, low ESG scores. But without digging into the structural and behavioral roots, why these issues are happening, organizations waste time treating the surface while the deeper issues grow.

---

58 Image retrieved from Jaber, M., 2021. Integral Design Thinking: A Novel Cross-national Framework for Sustainability Management, PhD Thesis, pg. 28.

5.   **Poor Information Flow**
     In many organizations, information travels one way: from the top down. But meaningful change requires *dialogue*. When feedback loops are broken or non-existent, learning stalls. Transparency and cross-level communication aren't luxuries; they're necessities.
6.   **Inadequate Learning Mechanisms**
     Change is messy. You have to try, fail, reflect, and improve. But if there's no space (or grace) to do that, people play it safe. Organizations that don't build systems for ongoing learning become brittle, unable to adapt when conditions shift, as they inevitably do.
7.   **Failure to Institutionalize**
     Sustainability isn't a one-off campaign or the job of one department. If it's not embedded into hiring, onboarding, performance evaluations, and core strategy, it stays on the margins. Institutionalization is what turns good intentions into new norms.

> Let's take a moment and reflect on this section. Are these showing up where you work? Think back to an organization you've worked in or the one you're in now.
>   Which of these blunders feel uncomfortably familiar?
> –   Was there a compelling, shared vision that made people feel connected to something bigger than themselves?
> –   Were decisions made by a select few, while others just waited for direction?
> –   Did departments collaborate across silos, or protect their turf?
> –   Was learning encouraged, or punished?
>
> These questions aren't about blame, they're about clarity. Because if we can't name what's broken, we can't begin to build something better.
>
>   So take a moment.
>   Write down one blunder you've seen in action.
>   Then ask: *What would it look like to do the opposite?*
>   That's the beginning of change.

The Seven Interventions: A Systems Wake-Up Call

If you've been with me since the beginning of this book, you'll know we started with the idea that real change starts with the self with a shift in personal mindset. That same principle holds true for organizations. In fact, it might be even more critical there. Because if an individual can keep themselves stuck with outdated thinking, an organization can institutionalize it.

That's why I find Doppelt's Seven Interventions so powerful, visualized in Figure 4. They're not just a checklist, they're a systemic diagnosis of what's holding organizations back and how to rewire them for a sustainable future; they create a roadmap for embedding sustainability into an organization's core DNA. Let's walk through each one, not just to understand what they are but to pause and reflect on what they demand from us.

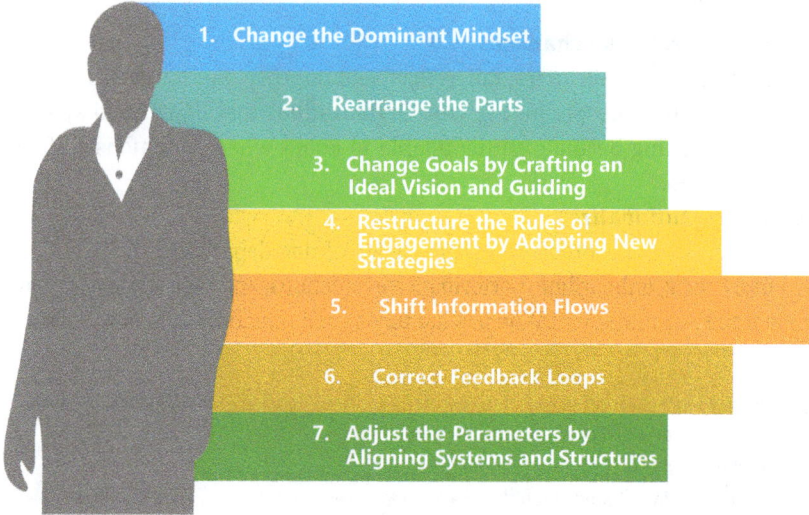

Figure 4: The Seven Interventions for Sustainability (Source: adapted from Doppelt, 2003).[59]

1. **Shift the Dominant Mindset**
    Change starts with belief. Organizations need to challenge deeply embedded assumptions, those invisible scripts that tell people "this is just how we do things." Instead, sustainability must be framed not as a side project or compliance task, but as a moral obligation and a strategic opportunity. If leadership doesn't believe that, no one else will.
2. **Rearrange the Organizational Structure**
    Silos kill innovation. Doppelt suggests creating cross-functional teams to lead transition efforts, not just for optics, but to build collective ownership. These teams aren't just task forces; they're experimental hubs where knowledge can cross-pollinate and new solutions can take root.
3. **Establish a Guiding Vision and Principles**
    You can't lead transformation with vague intentions. Leaders and teams must co-create a vision of what sustainability *looks like* in their context. These guiding principles become a cultural compass, used not only for big strategic moves but also in everyday decisions.

---

59 Image retrieved from Jaber, M., 2021. Integral Design Thinking: A Novel Cross-national Framework for Sustainability Management, PhD Thesis, pg. 29.

4. **Redesign Rules and Procedures**

   Culture eats strategy for breakfast, but rules reinforce culture. You need to adjust the "rules of the game" to support new behaviors: things like performance metrics, incentives, budgeting models, and communication flows. Otherwise, old structures will quietly strangle new intentions.

5. **Improve Information Flows**

   Feedback is a lifeline. For organizations to learn and adapt, communication must move *across*, *down*, and *up* the hierarchy. Leaders must listen as much as they talk. When information flows freely, it builds trust, accelerates learning, and strengthens shared ownership.

6. **Correct Feedback Loops**

   Learning means nothing without iteration. You need systems in place to capture lessons, measure progress, celebrate wins, and course-correct failures. Think of this as the organization's nervous system, constantly sensing, responding, and evolving.

7. **Institutionalize Sustainability Thinking**

   Ultimately, sustainability should live in the DNA of the organization. That means it's embedded in hiring practices, onboarding, training, branding, and stakeholder engagement. When it becomes second nature, how we work, not an extra task, that's when real transformation sticks.

Let's be honest. These interventions sound straight forward, but living them is anything but. What Doppelt is really asking us to do is to design *systems that learn*, *cultures that care*, and *structures that evolve*. And that takes courage.

It takes:

- **A shift in mindset** not just once, but repeatedly.
- **Open, cross-functional collaboration** that's not about control, but co-creation.
- **Transparent communication** where people feel safe speaking the hard truths.
- **Decision-making at all levels**, not just the C-suite.
- **Prototyping and testing**, not waiting for perfect answers.
- And a commitment to **continuous learning**, not one-and-done solutions.

These are the same things we ask of individuals when they commit to growth. The difference is: when an organization does it, the ripple effect is massive.

So here's my question to you, whether you're a leader, a team member, or a change agent from the outside:

Where is your organization clinging to an old mindset, and what's one conversation you can start this week to help shift it?

Why This Matters

Doppelt's interventions are powerful because they acknowledge that culture eats strategy for breakfast.[60] You can craft the most elegant sustainability plan in the world, but if it clashes with how people actually think, decide, and behave day to day, it won't stick. Without cultural alignment, even the best-laid plans will fail. These interventions offer more than just a diagnosis, they offer a pathway for healing. They help organizations move from fragmented, short-term sustainability projects to deep, structural, culture-wide transformation.

And here's the real shift: leadership isn't about control anymore. It's about designing the conditions for transformation to emerge. That means modeling the values you want to see, empowering others to lead, and building in the humility to listen, learn, and evolve. These principles speak directly to the *Integrated Mindset* we explored earlier, a mindset that's adaptive, inclusive, and grounded in purpose.

In sustainability work, the ground is always shifting. Regulations evolve. Technologies emerge. Public expectations rise. Organizations that cling to rigid systems will be left behind. But those that internalize Doppelt's principles, making them part of how they think, hire, train, budget, and measure success, will be positioned not just to survive, but to lead.

They'll be resilient. They'll be human-centered. And they'll be aligned with the future that's already unfolding.

Next, we'll explore the work of Chris Laszlo, who takes us deeper into how businesses can evolve from isolated ESG efforts into systems that create lasting, purpose-driven value.

3.6 Laszlo's Eight Disciplines of Value Creation

As the sustainability conversation matures, so does our collective expectation: it's no longer enough for organizations to simply reduce harm. Today, they're called to actively create value, value that is ethical, regenerative, and aligned with the needs of all stakeholders. Chris Laszlo's[61] work stands at the forefront of this shift. Through his *Integrated Bottom Line* model and the *Eight Disciplines of Sustainable Value Creation*, Laszlo offers a clear, actionable pathway for organizations to move beyond risk management and into the realm of purposeful impact.

Where Doppelt helps us look inward, focusing on culture, mindset, and systems that support transformation from within, Laszlo challenges us to look outward and

---

60 Peter Drucker, 1950's to 2000's, a renowned management consultant, educator, and author who wrote extensively about management and organizational culture, this phrase came from his writing.
61 Laszlo, C. (2005). *The sustainable company: How to create lasting value through social and environmental performance.* Island Press.

forward. His core message? Sustainability is not a side initiative. It's not branding. It's not a checkbox. It's a business model. A mindset. A way of working that drives innovation, resilience, and long-term success.

From Shareholder to Stakeholder Thinking

Laszlo's framework begins with a deep shift: moving from the traditional shareholder model, where success is measured in quarterly gains, to a stakeholder approach, where value is defined more broadly and more meaningfully. Laszlo's work emerges from a recognition that the traditional shareholder model of business, focused narrowly on quarterly profits, is ill-equipped to deal with today's ecological, social, and systemic risks.

Why does this matter now? Because the world is changing fast.

Global supply chains are being disrupted. Climate threats are escalating. Social unrest and institutional distrust are rising. In this context, the narrow pursuit of profit no longer protects companies, it exposes them. What once worked is no longer enough.

This isn't just a moral imperative. It's a strategic one.

Consumers, employees, and investors are demanding transparency, authenticity, and action. They're watching closely. The companies that meet this moment with courage and creativity, those that embed purpose into how they create value, are the ones that will innovate, adapt, and thrive.

The CEO's Journey to the Integrated Bottom Line

Laszlo illustrates this transformation through the lens of a CEO navigating change. At first, the focus is on traditional, efficiency, risk avoidance, and shareholder returns. But as the journey unfolds, a deeper opportunity emerges: to align profit with purpose.

Along this journey, the organization shifts:
- From **compliance** to **innovation**
- From **linear metrics** to **systems thinking**
- From **internal optimization** to **external collaboration**
- From **risk minimization** to **opportunity creation**

This journey culminates in what Laszlo calls the *Integrated Bottom Line*, a framework that unites financial, social, and environmental performance. In this model, business success is not separate from human and ecological flourishing. It's interdependent.

The Eight Disciplines of Value Creation

To operationalize this transformation, Laszlo introduces eight disciplines that serve as building blocks for embedding sustainability into the core strategy of the business. These disciplines aren't one-and-done actions. They're part of a living, breathing strategy cycle. They fall into three categories: **Discovering Value**, **Creating Value**, and **Enabling Value**. Figure 5 shows his thought process of the flow of these eight disciplines, and as we can see, it is a constant flow for improvements and innovation.

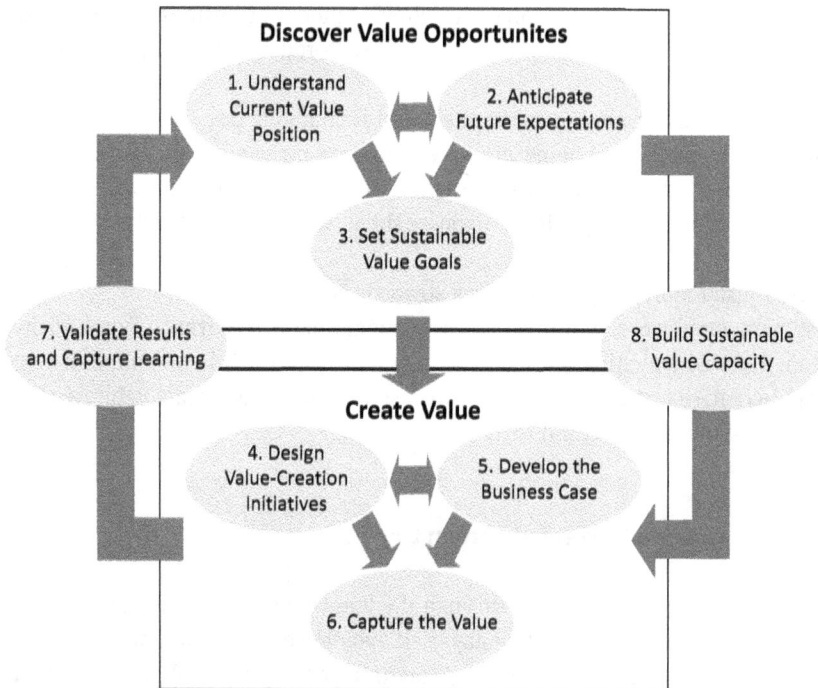

Figure 5: The eight disciplines of value creation (Source: Laszlo, 2003, p. 123).[62]

1. **Understanding Current Value Proposition, Getting Real** Start with honesty. Take a hard look at your sustainability performance, stakeholder perceptions, risks, and opportunities. Without clarity, there's no credible path forward.
2. **Anticipate Future Experiences, Defining the Opportunity Space** Identify where unmet social or environmental needs overlap with your organization's

---

62 Image retrieved from Jaber, M., 2021. Integral Design Thinking: A Novel Cross-national Framework for Sustainability Management, PhD Thesis, pg. 32.

unique capabilities. These intersections are where impact and growth can thrive together.

3. **Set Sustainable Value Goals** Go beyond compliance. Set bold, measurable goals that reflect long-term value for all stakeholders, not just shareholders. Establish goals that move beyond compliance, goals that are aspirational, measurable, and rooted in long-term stakeholder value.

4. **Design Value-Creation Initiative** Map out what needs to change: processes, products, partnerships, and practices. This step includes co-creating with internal and external stakeholders.

5. **Make the Business Case** Show the value. Link sustainability initiatives to tangible outcomes, brand equity, customer loyalty, innovation, employee engagement, or cost savings. Demonstrate how sustainability initiatives create tangible business value.

6. **Capture Value** Execute the strategy. Build the systems to monitor progress, learn from feedback, and adapt in real time. Success depends on agility and cross-functional commitment.

7. **Validate Results and Capture Learning** Reflect and refine. Question assumptions, measure impact, and stay attuned to a changing environment. This stage focuses on learning from implementation, challenging assumptions, and staying responsive to change. The goal is not perfection, but evolution.

8. **Build Sustainable Value Capacity** Make it last. Develop leaders, invest in infrastructure, and weave sustainability into the organization's DNA through training, incentives, and long-term planning. Examples of this are leadership development, talent pipelines, infrastructure investment, and long-term planning.

These disciplines aren't a straight line, they're a cycle. A rhythm. A way of working that keeps organizations responsive and relevant in a complex world. By continuously discovering, creating, and enabling sustainable value, organizations remain relevant and responsive in a rapidly changing world. When sustainability becomes part of how value is discovered, created, and enabled, strategy comes alive.

And more importantly, it becomes future-fit.

Implications for Strategic Leadership

What makes Laszlo's model so compelling is its accessibility, clarity, and practicality. It bridges the gap between purpose and process, vision and metrics, leadership and value creation. It reminds us that doing good and doing well aren't trade-offs; they're interdependent forces that strengthen one another. In this model, sustainability isn't a cost center. It becomes a **strategic advantage**. Organizations that embrace this mindset don't just reduce risk, they unlock innovation, attract top talent, earn deeper customer trust, and build more resilient partnerships across their supply chains. They also become more resilient in the face of economic, social, or environmental shocks.

But to lead this kind of transformation, something deeper must shift.

The *eight disciplines* aren't just operational; they're personal. They call for leaders who think in systems, lead with empathy, and act with humility. Leaders who are willing to move from command-and-control to inquiry and co-creation. Leaders who see themselves not just as decision-makers but as **facilitators of learning**, **architects of culture**, and **stewards of long-term value**.

This is the leadership that the future demands and the kind that builds organizations ready to meet it.

Building the Bridge to Integral Design Thinking

Laszlo's work aligns naturally with the *Integral Design Thinking (IDT)* framework we'll explore in the next chapters. Both approaches emphasize **holistic value creation**, **cross-functional collaboration**, **systems thinking**, and **design for transformation**. And both recognize a deeper truth: sustainability isn't a fixed endpoint, it's a living journey. One that demands vision, courage, and a willingness to evolve.

As you consider how to lead sustainability, whether in your organization, your community, or your own sphere of influence, Laszlo's model offers more than inspiration. It's both **a compass and a toolkit**. It gives you the language, structure, and momentum to move from intention to impact, to translate ideals into innovation, and strategy into lasting systems of change.

Next, we'll weave together the ideas presented in this chapter and reflect on how the evolution of perception and theory has laid a powerful foundation for integrated, human-centered sustainability leadership.

3.7 Section Synthesis: Evolution of Perception and Theoretical Frameworks

In this chapter, we've traced a rich and evolving landscape of ideas, frameworks, and perspectives, each offering a lens into the shifting meaning and mandate of sustainability. From early environmental concerns to complex systems thinking, and from stakeholder engagement to inner transformation, the sustainability conversation has matured into something far deeper and more urgent. What began as a call to protect the environment has grown into a far-reaching conversation about how we live, lead, and organize for a flourishing future.

Sustainability today is no longer just a technical challenge, it is a **transformational endeavor.** It asks us to think in systems, act with integrity, and lead with empathy. Yes, it requires new tools, but more importantly, it requires new ways of seeing.

We began with the evolution of sustainability perception, from the Brundtland Report's foundational call for intergenerational equity to today's integrated ESG frameworks. What was once focused narrowly on environmental preservation now embraces a fuller spectrum: equity, purpose, well-being, and justice. The move from a triple to a **quadruple bottom line** marks a paradigm shift, one that expands organizational accountability beyond shareholders to a broader ecosystem of stakeholders and future generations.

This evolution is mirrored on the global stage. From sweeping international declarations to grassroots movements like 4Ocean, the mandate for sustainability is now universal, spanning institutions, communities, and supply chains. But while its scope is global, its power lies in the local. The term *"glocal"*[63] captures this: the ability to align global responsibility with local relevance.

To meet this challenge, we explored several **theoretical frameworks** that stretch and deepen our understanding:

- **Ken Wilber's Integral Vision** offers a map for navigating complexity through multiple lenses: internal and external, individual and collective. It reminds us that systems don't operate in silos, they are shaped by culture, consciousness, and context.
- **Empathy as a strategic capability,** through the work of Brown, Scharmer, and others, reveals that meaningful change requires emotional intelligence. Empathy fuels innovation, deepens trust, and enables collaboration across boundaries as it connects people to purpose. It is not a "soft" skill; it's a strategic and necessary one.
- **Doppelt's seven interventions** provide a roadmap for dismantling the cultural and structural barriers to sustainability. His work reinforces that without a shift in mindset and governance, even the most well-intended initiatives can falter.
- **Laszlo's eight disciplines** offer a practical blueprint for embedding sustainability into business strategy. His model reframes sustainability not as a constraint, but as a multiplier, a driver of innovation, resilience, and stakeholder loyalty.

Taken together, these perspectives converge on a powerful insight:

Sustainability is a journey of **integration**.

It calls us to align our inner worlds, our beliefs, values, and intentions, with our outer systems, structures, and behaviors. It's about creating coherence between what we *say* and what we *do*, between our purpose and our performance.

---

63 Robertson, Roland (1995). "Glocalization: Time-Space and Homogeneity-Heterogeneity," in *Global Modernities*, edited by Mike Featherstone, Scott Lash, and Roland Robertson. Sage Publications.

For leaders, this demands more than new strategies. It calls for a **new conscious-ness.** One that holds complexity without paralysis. One that sees the organization not as a machine to be optimized, but as a living system to be nurtured. One that recognizes sustainability not just as *what we do,* but as *how we are.*

This is the foundation of the **Integral Design Thinking (IDT) Strategy Framework**, which you will encounter in the next chapters. IDT builds directly on the philosophical and practical foundations we've explored here. It offers a way to translate systems thinking, empathy, creativity, and purpose into a living strategy for real organizational transformation.

As you reflect on this chapter, ask yourself:

- What worldview is guiding your decisions?
- What assumptions are shaping your leadership?
- Where is there a gap between your values and your actions?
- And what might change if sustainability became the lens for everything your organization does, not a project, but a principle?

The answers to these questions will shape not only the future of your organization,but the world we are all designing together.

4 Strategy and Strategic Thinking

Strategy is not just a plan, it's a mindset that helps us navigate complexity,
unlock purpose, and create meaningful change.

In a world defined by rapid change, uncertainty, and complexity, strategy can no longer be seen as a static plan on paper. For today's sustainability leaders, strategy must evolve into something more dynamic: a mindset, a compass, and a daily leadership practice.

This chapter redefines what it means to think and act strategically in the context of sustainability. Traditional definitions focused narrowly on market share, efficiency, or short-term gains; they simply don't hold up in a world where long-term resilience, ethical alignment, and adaptive capacity are essential to survival and success.

Instead, strategy must be **holistic**. It must account for shifting environmental, social, and economic forces while remaining rooted in organizational purpose. As Freedman (2013)[64] notes, strategy is not merely about targets and tasks, it's about aligning goals, activities, and resources in a way that remains flexible enough to adapt over time. In this sense, strategy becomes a living system, evolving as conditions change and new insights emerge. This chapter will cover:

– **Strategic Positioning: Finding Your Place in an Ever-Changing Landscape**
I will begin by unpacking the concept of ***strategic positioning***, the process by which organizations define their role and relevance within an ever-shifting landscape. Strategic positioning isn't just about market competition. It's about clarifying where and how a company can deliver **unique, sustainable value** that aligns internal capabilities with external opportunities. As Michael Porter (1986)[65] argued, true strategy is "about being different." It requires organizations to choose deliberately, selecting a distinct set of activities to deliver a unique mix of value to stakeholders. For sustainability leaders, this means carving out a position that integrates environmental and social goals with business objectives, rather than treating them as parallel tracks.

Strategic positioning also requires internal alignment. Andrews (1980)[66] emphasized that strategy must reflect a pattern of decisions that guide not only what an organization aims to achieve but also how it intends to show up in the world. This includes decisions about social impact, workforce development, and philanthropic commitments, all of which are increasingly central to sustainability leadership. In sustainability contexts, positioning is also adaptive. Mintzberg (1994)[67] reminds us that strategies are not just plans; they're patterns that emerge over time as intentions

---

64 Freedman, L. (2013). *Strategy.* Oxford University Press.
65 Porter, M. (1986). *Competitive strategy.* Harvard Business School Press.
66 Andrews, K. (1980). *The concept of corporate strategy,* (2nd ed.). Dow-Jones Irwin.
67 Mintzberg, H. (1994). *The rise and fall of strategic planning.* Prentice-Hall

https://doi.org/10.1515/9783111705286-004

meet reality. This is especially true in fast-moving markets where regulatory shifts, climate risks, and stakeholder expectations require organizations to stay responsive and flexible.

– Strategic Thinking: A Way of Seeing, Not Just Planning

If strategic positioning is about defining where you stand, *strategic thinking* is about developing the vision to see what's coming and the agility to respond.

Strategic thinking is not about predicting the future perfectly. It's about preparing for it wisely. As Mintzberg and Quinn (1996)[68] noted, it combines pattern recognition, scenario planning, and the courage to make decisions under uncertainty. Strategic thinking requires leaders to zoom out and see the big picture while also zooming in to act with clarity and intention.

For sustainability leaders, this mindset is essential. Climate change, shifting regulations, and evolving consumer expectations are not challenges with fixed solutions. They are complex, adaptive problems that demand ongoing reflection, innovation, and learning. Engert et al. (2016)[69] emphasize that sustainability strategy must integrate both external analysis and internal awareness. Leaders must be attuned to broader forces, economic shifts, ecological constraints, and societal demands while also understanding their organization's culture, capabilities, and constraints.

This is why strategic thinking for sustainability requires more than linear planning. It requires **systems thinking**, **empathy**, and a deep understanding of interconnectedness. It asks leaders to engage with the complexity of the world, not to tame it, but to work with it.

– From Tactical Action to Purpose-Driven Alignment

One of the key distinctions in strategic leadership is the difference between tactical action and strategic alignment. Tactical actions might feel productive in the short term, but without a clear strategic foundation, they often fail to create lasting impact. As Steiner (1979)[70] pointed out, strategy must be grounded in organizational purpose and mission. It must guide actions, answer questions, and provide direction through uncertainty. This is particularly true in sustainability management, where isolated initiatives without strategic integration often lose momentum or fail to scale.

When strategy is treated as a living framework, as a complex web of thoughts, insights, goals, experiences, and expectations, leaders can align people, processes, and systems with a higher purpose. That's what transforms action into impact.

---

68 Mintzberg, H., and Quinn, J.B. (1996). *The strategy process: concepts, contexts, cases.* Prentice Hall.
69 Engert S., Rauter R., and Baumgartner R.J. (2016). Exploring the integration of corporate sustainability into strategic management: A literature review. *J. Clean. Prod.,* 2833–2850.
70 Steiner, G. (1979). Strategic Planning. Free Press.

4.1 Strategic Positioning

In the evolving landscape of sustainability management, success depends not only on what an organization does but also on how it defines its place in the world. Strategic positioning, in this context, is not a fixed label or competitive stance. It's a dynamic process of **aligning purpose, capability, and context** repeatedly as conditions change. This work begins with awareness of both the internal ecosystem (culture, people, resources) and the external environment. Frameworks like PESTEL (Political, Economic, Social, Technological, Ecological, and Legal) provide a useful lens for mapping the broader forces that shape risks and opportunities. But analysis alone is not enough. Strategic positioning requires *interpretation*, and the courage to act on that insight in ways that are bold, differentiated, and deeply values-driven.

As Michael Porter (2009)[71] asserted, strategic positioning means deliberately choosing a distinct set of activities that deliver a unique mix of value. It's not about being everything to everyone. It's about clarity, understanding what you stand for, whom you serve, and how your work creates meaning in a shifting world. In sustainability, this clarity is vital. How an organization positions its products, services, and social impact directly shapes its **relevance**, **resilience**, and **license to operate**.

This is where design thinking breathes new life into strategy. As Liedtka and Kaplan (2019)[72] argue, design principles, empathy, iteration, and possibility help organizations uncover unmet needs and co-create solutions that are not only innovative but also inclusive. This approach is especially powerful when applied to stakeholder ecosystems, which are rarely linear or static. Employees, regulators, communities, suppliers, and customers each hold a piece of the puzzle, and each must be engaged with care.

Tools like Wilber's Integral Vision and stakeholder mapping models help make sense of this complexity. They offer multidimensional views of power, influence, and alignment, guiding leaders as they navigate competing interests and overlapping priorities. When used well, they illuminate not only who matters, but how to foster relationships built on trust, transparency, and mutual value.

But strategy doesn't live in diagrams, it lives in **culture**. Culture is where strategy either takes root or quietly dissolves. It is made up of stories, rituals, power dynamics, unspoken assumptions, the informal rules that shape how things really work. Johnson et al. (2017)[73] describe this as the "cultural web," a constellation of seven interconnected elements that collectively define an organization's identity in action. For sus-

---

71 Porter, T. (2009). Three views of systems theories and their implications for sustainability education. *Journal of Management Education*, 33(3), 323–347.

72 Liedtka, J., and Kaplan, S. (2019). How Design Thinking opens new frontiers for strategy development. *Strategy and Leadership*, 47(2), 3–10.

73 Johnson, G., Whittington, R., Scholes, K., Angwin, D., and Regner, P. (2017). *Exploring strategy: Text and cases*, (11th ed.). Pearson.

tainability strategy to succeed, it must move through this web with intention, aligning purpose not only with processes, but with people's lived experiences of work.

This is especially important when dealing with **subcultures**, regional branches, departments, or teams that may operate with different norms or values. These subcultures can be sources of innovation or resistance, depending on whether they feel seen, heard, and included in the change process. Cultural alignment, then, becomes a **strategic imperative**, not just an HR concern. At the heart of all of this is **organizational identity**. Clear, consistent, and authentic identity acts as the emotional anchor for employees and the reputational signal for stakeholders. In a sustainability context, identity must not be performative. It must reflect a genuine commitment, where sustainability is not an initiative, but an expression of who the organization is and what it exists to do.

Ultimately, strategic positioning is not just about market advantage. It is about embedding sustainability into the very **DNA of the organization**, its strategy, culture, relationships, and sense of self. It is an ongoing act of leadership, one that invites the whole system to move in the direction of purpose, coherence, and transformation. Table 4 is a summarized list of the framework and tools discussed for review and reflection:

Table 4: Summary: Strategic Positioning Frameworks & Tools.

Framework / Tool	Description	How It Supports Sustainability Strategy
PESTEL Analysis	Analyzes macro-environmental factors: Political, Economic, Social, Technological, Ecological, Legal	Helps organizations identify external forces shaping risks, opportunities, and market dynamics
Michael Porter's Positioning Theory (2009)	Emphasizes deliberate choices to deliver a unique mix of value through distinct activities	Encourages clarity, differentiation, and purpose-driven strategic direction
Design Thinking (Liedtka & Kaplan, 2019)	Uses empathy, iteration, and possibility to uncover needs and co-create solutions	Encourages innovation, inclusivity, and stakeholder-centered design in strategy development
Stakeholder Mapping (Freeman, 2010; Mendelow, 1991)	Identifies stakeholders based on power, influence, and interest	Facilitates thoughtful engagement and alignment across complex internal and external ecosystems
Integral Vision (Wilber, 2001)	A multidimensional lens integrating individual/collective and internal/external perspectives	Encourages holistic analysis and integration across values, behavior, systems, and structures
Cultural Web (Johnson et al., 2017)	A model mapping seven elements of organizational culture (paradigms, rituals, stories, etc.)	Reveals hidden dynamics that can support or resist sustainability transitions
Organizational Identity	The authentic narrative of who an organization is and what it stands for	Serves as a foundation for internal engagement and external credibility

4.2 Strategic Thinking

Strategic thinking is the **cognitive backbone** of effective leadership. It's more than planning, it's a way of perceiving, questioning, and navigating the world. It is about **Seeing the Whole While Acting with Intention**. In sustainability management, strategic thinking combines structured analysis with intuition, systems awareness, and creativity. It allows leaders to move beyond short-term fixes and toward decisions that are coherent, long-term, and deeply aligned with purpose.

Freedman describes strategy as a process of setting targets, determining priorities, and mobilizing resources. In this light, strategic thinking isn't just a leadership competency, it becomes a **cultural and organizational imperative**. It shapes how decisions are made, how opportunities are framed, and how meaning is created across the system.

Michael Porter likened strategy to a kind of glue, something that binds disparate initiatives, functions, and priorities into a coherent whole. Mintzberg echoed this, arguing that true strategic thinking produces an *integrated perspective* of the organization—one that sees across silos, through time, and into possibility.

In the context of sustainability, this integration is critical. Strategic thinking must be **both top-down and bottom-up**. Yes, vision matters, but so does participation. The true power of strategy emerges when people at every level of the organization not only understand the direction but also feel part of shaping it. Bouhali et al. (2015)[74] emphasize the need to embed meaning and purpose throughout the organization. That doesn't happen by accident; it requires intentional communication, education, and empowerment.

This is where **design thinking** becomes a powerful ally. With its emphasis on empathy, co-creation, and iteration, design thinking brings strategy to life as a living, learning process. It invites experimentation and makes space for feedback. And it recognizes that innovation doesn't always come from the top, it often emerges from the edges, from those closest to the work and to the people served.

Scholars like Liedtka (1998),[75] Bonn (2001),[76] and Graetz (2002)[77] highlight the importance of developing adaptive, creative thinkers across all levels of an organization. In an era marked by complexity, volatility, and rapid change, this kind of distributed intelligence is not optional, it's essential. Table 5 demonstrates a flow from strategic thinking to strategic culture for reflection:

---

74 Bouhali R., Mekdadb Y., Lebsirc H., and Ferkha L (2015). Leader roles for innovation: Strategic thinking and planning. *Procedia – Social and Behavioural Sciences, 181*, 72–78.

75 Liedtka J.M. (1998). Lining strategic thinking with strategic planning. *Strategy and leadership*, 30–35.

76 Boon, I. (2001). Developing strategic thinking as a core competency. *Management Decision, 39*(1).

77 Graetz, F. (2002). Strategic thinking versus strategic planning: Towards understanding the complementarities. *Management Decision, 40*(5).

Table 5: How organizations move from mindset to system-wide impact.

Strategic Thinking and Communication		
	Ask:	**Mindset:**
1. Strategic Thinking	Where are we going? What matters most? What patterns are emerging?	Systems awareness Creativity & curiosity Intuition & analysis
↓	**Actions:**	**Outcome:**
2. Strategic Communication	Share purpose with clarity Align vision with language Create space for dialogue & feedback	Shared understanding Psychological safety Meaning-making at all levels
↓	**Behaviors:**	**Outcome:**
3. Strategic Participation	Empower across levels Collaborate cross-functionally Encourage co-ownership of outcomes	Innovation from the edges Distributed intelligence Values-driven engagement
↓	**Culture Markers:**	**Result:**
4. Strategic Culture	Decisions aligned with purpose Continuous learning loops Adaptive, resilient systems	Strategy is embedded in how we work Sustainability becomes identity, not initiative

In the chapters ahead, we'll look more closely at how Integral Design Thinking draws on these principles to build not just strategic plans, but **strategic cultures**, ones where creativity, systems thinking, and purpose-driven action are embedded into the fabric of decision-making.

4.2A Systems Thinking

Strategic thinking and systems thinking are natural allies. Where strategic thinking asks "What direction should we take?", systems thinking responds with "What patterns are we a part of?" Together, they provide the cognitive tools for leaders to navigate complexity with clarity, humility, and intention.

Systems thinking is about seeing the whole, not just the parts, but the relationships between them. It helps us understand **interdependencies, feedback loops, and emergent behaviors**, which is exactly what sustainability demands: a way of making sense of the long-term, ripple-effect consequences of our choices.

Reed (2006)[78] describes systems thinking as a way of uncovering interconnections and tracing their effects. In sustainability work, this approach is essential. Actions rarely have isolated outcomes. What we do in one part of the system often reverberates in ways we cannot immediately see. Checkland and Haynes (1994)[79] further evolved systems thinking through their development of **Soft Systems Methodology (SSM)**, a more human-centered, adaptive approach. Unlike traditional models that seek to solve problems in linear ways, SSM encourages learning through real-world engagement. It treats organizational challenges not just as problems to fix, but as opportunities to generate insight, build relationships, and reimagine possibilities. Tools like narrative modeling, stakeholder dialogue, and iterative reflection are central to this approach.

Building on this foundation, **Porter (2009)**[80] introduced the idea of **Complex Adaptive Systems (CAS)**, living networks that are constantly changing, self-organizing, and evolving. In a sustainability context, this means designing systems that can learn, adapt, and regenerate over time. Porter emphasized that not all systems are alike. There is no universal blueprint. Effective leadership in complex environments means developing the capacity to sense context, foster feedback, and **design for emergence** rather than control.

This is where systems thinking truly expands the potential of strategic thinking. It transforms strategy from a static document into a living, evolving process, one shaped by learning, feedback, and shared responsibility. It's not about predicting every outcome; it's about staying responsive to what unfolds.

In my own research, I integrated **design thinking** with the principles of **Complex Adaptive Systems** to create the *Holistic Design Thinking Methodology*. This methodology reimagines traditional systems analysis through a more creative, human-centered, and flexible lens. This method will be explored in depth in later chapters, but for now, it serves as a preview of how strategy, systems, and design can be woven together to lead change that is both sustainable and systemic.

4.3 Section Synthesis: Strategy and Strategic Thinking

At its core, **strategy is about direction, meaning, and alignment**. It's the translation of purpose into behavior through plans, priorities, processes, and, most importantly, culture. It is about embedding purpose, learning, and alignment into how we lead. In the context of sustainability, this means moving far beyond static documents or top-

---

78 Reed, G. (2006). Leadership and systems thinking. *Defence ATandL*, 10–13.

79 Checkland, P., and Haynes, M. (1994). Varieties of systems thinking: The case of soft systems methodology. *System Dynamics Review, 10*(2–3), 189–197.

80 Porter, T. (2009). Three views of systems theories and their implications for sustainability education. *Journal of Management Education,* 33(3), 323–347.

down plans. It means building a living system of **strategic and systems thinking** that is embedded into the way an organization sees, learns, and acts.

Strategic positioning gives an organization clarity about its role within larger environmental, social, and economic systems. It helps leaders assess both the macro forces (through models like PESTEL) and the micro realities of stakeholders, identity, and culture. Without this clarity, sustainability efforts risk becoming fragmented or worse, purely symbolic.

Strategic thinking, meanwhile, ensures that leadership is not reactive but **generative**, rooted in vision, shaped by learning, and capable of navigating change. When integrated with **systems thinking**, strategic thinking becomes not just more effective, but more human. It brings in complexity without paralysis. It supports adaptability without losing focus. These aren't aspirational extras—they're foundational capabilities for any leader working toward sustainability.

At the heart of this integration is **culture**. Johnson et al.'s *cultural web* reminds us that organizations don't transform through strategy alone, they transform through the stories they tell, the rituals they keep, the structures they uphold, and the symbols they reinforce. These elements can be seen as **strategic anchors**, grouped into themes of communication, brand identity, and organizational community. When aligned, they provide the continuity needed to evolve without losing coherence.

In a world that is increasingly fast, interconnected, and uncertain, sustainability leaders must become more than planners. They must become **sense-makers, storytellers, and system shapers**. They must inspire participation, mobilize diverse actors, and cultivate a culture that can adapt and learn in real time.

Strategy, in this sense, is not a fixed roadmap, it's a compass. One that orients us not only toward success, but toward **regeneration, inclusion, and long-term resilience**.

> **To reflect on this chapter, consider the following:**
> - What assumptions shape the way your organization approaches strategy?
> - Where do planning, purpose, and people feel aligned?
> - Where do they feel disconnected?
> - If strategy were treated as a living process, what would you change tomorrow?

5 Design Thinking

Reimagining Problems, Possibilities, and Purpose

Design thinking is more than a methodology—it's a way of seeing, thinking, and acting. It offers a powerful lens through which we can understand and respond to the complex challenges organizations face today. Grounded in **creativity, empathy, and iteration**, design thinking has grown far beyond its academic roots to become a vital capability for leaders navigating the demands of modern sustainability management.

This chapter explores how design thinking functions as a **human-centered, systems-aware, and solution-oriented approach** to change. We'll begin by tracing its conceptual roots in *designerly thinking* and follow its evolution into a practical methodology now embraced across industries and sectors worldwide.

Drawing on decades of theory, research, and application, we'll examine how design thinking provides both a **philosophical foundation** and a **tactical framework** for addressing today's most urgent challenges—from climate change and resource scarcity to social equity and innovation.

But more than that, we'll explore how design thinking helps organizations **bridge the gap between aspiration and action**. It's not only about designing better products or services—it's about **rethinking how we work, how we engage with others, and how we align values with strategy**. For sustainability managers, change agents, and leaders across all sectors, design thinking offers a critical toolkit for shaping futures that are not only viable, but just and regenerative.

In the sections ahead, we'll explore:
- The origins of designerly thinking
- The foundational principles of design thinking
- Its strategic relevance in sustainability leadership
- Its influence on culture, systems, and decision-making

Each concept is grounded in real-world application—making the case that design thinking is not a trend, but an **indispensable mindset** for leading transformative, long-term change.

Let's begin by exploring the origins: how designerly thinking laid the groundwork for what design thinking would become.

5.1 Designerly Thinking

Before "design thinking" became a staple in boardrooms and business schools, there was **designerly thinking**, a foundational concept born within the design disciplines themselves. It framed designers not merely as problem-solvers, but as practitioners

https://doi.org/10.1515/9783111705286-005

with a unique way of engaging the world, blending logic and intuition, creativity and structure, ingenuity and iteration. It was a way of seeing and shaping that invited both rigor and imagination.

The formal beginnings of this thinking can be traced to Herbert A. Simon, whose seminal book *The Sciences of the Artificial* (1969)[81] laid out a clear, structured vision for design as a process of purposeful change (Visualized in Figure 6). Simon introduced a **seven-stage model**: define, research, ideate, prototype, choose, implement, and learn, offering a rational and methodical approach to designing human-made systems. Importantly, he viewed design not just as functional planning, but as a **discipline of transformation**, focused on shaping what *ought* to be, rather than accepting what *is*. For example, he emphasized the role of design in engineering and planning, viewing it as a discipline of transformation, a way of directing change through intentional, human-made constructs.

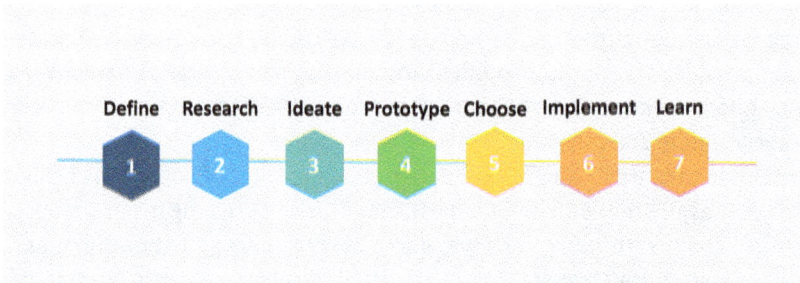

Define   Research   Ideate   Prototype   Choose   Implement   Learn

1   2   3   4   5   6   7

Figure 6: Seven stages of the Design Process (Source: Adapted from Simon 1969).[82]

Yet design, as practiced, is rarely linear. As the field evolved, scholars like Donald Schön challenged Simon's technical framing. In *The Reflective Practitioner* (1983),[83] Schön introduced the concept of **reflection-in-action**, emphasizing that real-world design involves improvisation, intuition, and dynamic sense-making. For Schön, design wasn't about executing a perfect plan, it was about "dancing with complexity."

Later scholars like Krippendorff (2006)[84] further deepened this lineage, defining design as *"making sense of things."* This view emphasized **meaning-making**, relationship, and the symbolic dimensions of design. It also opened the door for design to be recognized not just as a tool for innovation, but as a language of culture, ethics, and purpose. This shift opened up the field to richer, more nuanced perspectives. Nigel

---

81 Simon, H.A (1969). *The sciences of the artificial.* MIT Press.

82 Retrieved from Jaber, M. (2021). *Integral Design Thinking: A Novel Cross-national Framework for Sustainability Management.* PhD Thesis, Birmingham City University, retrieved pg. 43.

83 Schon, D. (1983). *The reflective practitioner: How professionals think in action,* (pp. 102–104). Basic Books.

84 Krippendorff, K. (2006). *The semantic turn: A new foundation for design.* Taylor and Francis.

Cross (2011)[85] described design as a **third culture of thinking**, distinct from the sciences or humanities, characterized by synthesis, tacit knowledge, and creative exploration. Bryan Lawson (2006)[86] highlighted the interplay between **problem framing and problem solving**, noting that designers often redefine the problem as they explore it. This recursive, reframing mindset is a signature of designerly thinking. In fact, recursion is not a flaw, it's a **feature**. Unlike technical planning that moves in a straight line, designerly thinking loops back again and again, revisiting assumptions, reimagining constraints, and refining understanding. It invites **ambiguity as a resource**, rather than something to be minimized. And it values multiple forms of knowing: **analytical, emotional, experiential, and social**. It enables deeper understanding and more nuanced solutions. The goal is not just to fix a problem, but to explore its full dimensions and potential through iterative engagement. Table 6 highlights scholarly work in the area of Designerly Thinking.

Table 6: Designerly Thinking in Action.

Element	Description
Define → Learn	Simon's 7-stage model of rational design thinking
Reflect-in-action	Schön's dynamic, intuitive engagement with complexity
Tacit knowledge	Cross's recognition of design as a third way of knowing
Reframing the problem	Lawson's insight into the fluidity of problem definition
Making sense	Krippendorff's etymological and philosophical approach to design

As these traditions moved from studio practice to strategic environments, the principles of designerly thinking were distilled into what we now call **design thinking**. But behind every post-it note and prototype lies this deeper heritage, a way of thinking that is not only practical but philosophical. For leaders working in sustainability, innovation, or systems change, understanding the roots of designerly thinking is more than academic. It helps avoid superficial applications of design thinking and reminds us that transformation requires not just ideas, but a **mindset of openness, reflection, and generative inquiry**.

Ultimately, **designerly thinking is about shaping futures**. It empowers people to imagine what could be and to act with empathy, courage, and creativity to bring that vision into being. As we move through this chapter, it is this foundation that will ground our exploration of design thinking as a strategic, cultural, and systems-based tool for sustainable leadership.

---

85 Cross, N. (2011) Design Thinking: Understanding how Designers Think and Work. Berg Publishers Ltd., Oxford.
86 Lawson, B. (2006). *How designers think: The design process demystified*, (4th ed.). Architectural Press.

5.2 Design Thinking Foundations

Design thinking is not just a set of tools, it's an evolution of **designerly thinking**, extending its core values of reflection, iteration, and empathy beyond the studio and into the heart of organizational life. If designerly thinking is the **DNA**, then design thinking is the **living organism** dynamic, adaptive, and increasingly vital for navigating the complexity of today's world.

What sets design thinking apart is its **deeply human-centered orientation**. It begins with empathy not just as a buzzword, but as a practice of immersion. Practitioners are asked to step into the shoes of others, to understand their needs, frustrations, desires, and aspirations before attempting to solve anything. This act of listening is especially powerful when applied to **"wicked problems"** those messy, systemic issues that defy simple solutions and span across stakeholders, sectors, and time horizons.

While Herbert Simon provided the early structure, it was thinkers like Richard Buchanan (1992)[87] who reframed design thinking for complexity. Buchanan argued that design is a discipline of "placement," a way of constructing meaning and locating problems within their social and systemic context. In his view, design thinking is not only about creating solutions, but it's about understanding **how problems are framed** in the first place.

This academic lineage met practical momentum through the work of Tim Brown (2006)[88] and IDEO, who helped translate design thinking into a broadly accessible framework. Brown's model: *empathize, define, ideate, prototype, test*, offered a clear, repeatable process. But beneath its simplicity lies a profound shift: design is not a linear march toward answers; it's a cyclical exploration guided by empathy, experimentation, and continuous learning. Table 7 highlights the contributions of these two leaders.

Table 7: Two Lenses on Design Thinking.

Thinker	Focus	Contribution	Implications for Leaders
Richard Buchanan (1992)	*Philosophical & Contextual*	Framed design thinking as a way to tackle "indeterminate" or "wicked" problems by constructing meaning within context. Introduced "design as placement."	Encourages leaders to explore how problems are framed and who is involved in defining them, especially relevant in sustainability and equity contexts.

87 Buchanan, R. (1992). Wicked problems in design thinking. *Design Issues, 8*, 5–21.
88 Brown, T. (2009). *Change by design*. Harper Collins.

Table 7 (continued)

Thinker	Focus	Contribution	Implications for Leaders
Tim Brown / IDEO (2009)	*Practical & Process-Oriented*	Developed a 5-phase framework: *Empathize, Define, Ideate, Prototype, Test*. Made design thinking accessible across industries.	Offers a hands-on structure for innovation, collaboration, and experimentation. Fosters creativity in everyday decision-making.

Together, Buchanan provides the *why*, Brown provides the *how*. Both are essential for sustainable leadership.

Crucially, **design thinking democratized creativity**. It opened the design process to non-designers, engineers, educators, health workers, policy-makers, and anyone willing to approach problems with curiosity and openness. The goal was not to turn everyone into designers, but to unlock the **designer's mindset**: reflective, iterative, courageous, and collaborative. Figure 7 is a visual representation of the Design Thinking Methodology process with some critical thinking concepts for each stage.

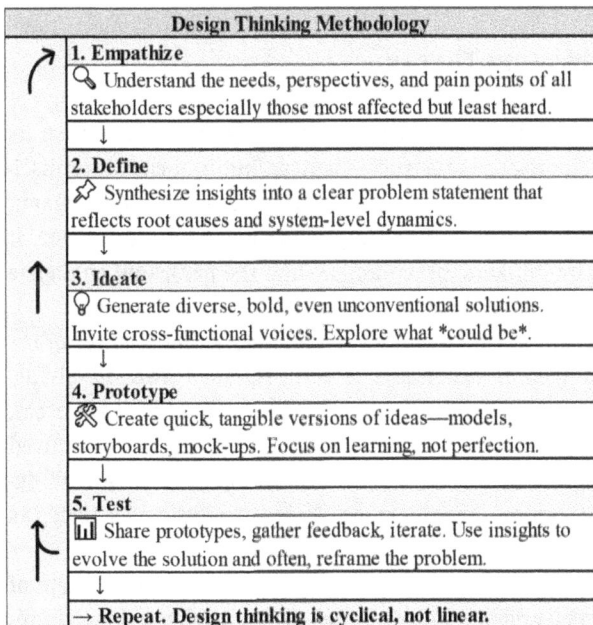

Design Thinking Methodology
1. Empathize
🔍 Understand the needs, perspectives, and pain points of all stakeholders especially those most affected but least heard.
↓
2. Define
🔖 Synthesize insights into a clear problem statement that reflects root causes and system-level dynamics.
↓
3. Ideate
💡 Generate diverse, bold, even unconventional solutions. Invite cross-functional voices. Explore what *could be*.
↓
4. Prototype
✂️ Create quick, tangible versions of ideas—models, storyboards, mock-ups. Focus on learning, not perfection.
↓
5. Test
📊 Share prototypes, gather feedback, iterate. Use insights to evolve the solution and often, reframe the problem.
↓
→ Repeat. Design thinking is cyclical, not linear.

Figure 7: Design Thinking Methodology.

A core rhythm of design thinking is the movement between **divergent and convergent thinking**. First, we expand, inviting diverse perspectives, imagining unlikely solutions, asking "What if?" Then, we focus, filtering ideas through the lenses of feasibility, viability, and desirability. This dance is what allows design thinking to stay grounded in both **possibility and practicality**. It is about dreaming big without restrictions and then analyzing the prospects of reaching those goals.

Beyond products and services, design thinking invites us to rethink **systems, experiences**, and **ways of working**. It offers structure in ambiguity and collaboration in complexity. It flattens hierarchies, encourages dialogue, and surfaces knowledge that often goes unheard. Scholars like Jeanne Liedtka, Saul Kaplan[89] and Roger Martin[90] have extended its relevance into the world of business and management. They emphasize that design thinking is not about novelty for its own sake it's about solving the **right problems** in the right ways. In sustainability leadership, this distinction is essential. The questions we ask and **who we invite into the room** to ask them can shape the future more powerfully than the answers we generate.

In essence, **design thinking is a methodology of meaning-making**. It equips leaders to hold ambiguity, listen deeply, explore boldly, and return—again and again —to the human experience at the heart of every challenge. Applied with care and intention, it becomes more than a process. It becomes a **catalyst for transformation**— personal, organizational, and systemic.

5.3 Origins of Design Thinking Theory

To understand the power and promise of design thinking, we must first trace its roots, not just to the creative studios of industrial designers, but to a rich, interdisciplinary heritage that spans psychology, engineering, architecture, and management theory. Design thinking didn't emerge from a single moment or mind; rather, it evolved over decades, shaped by thinkers, practitioners, and the persistent challenge of solving problems that defy easy categorization.

The story begins with Herbert A. Simon, whose seminal work *The Sciences of the Artificial* (1969) established the idea of design as a form of rational problem-solving. Simon framed design not as an artistic endeavor alone, but as a disciplined process: identifying what "ought to be" and developing pathways to get there. His structured approach laid the intellectual groundwork for a science of design, complete with defined stages of ideation, prototyping, and learning. This was design as logic, as method, and as measurable action.

Yet, Simon's rational model was not the only influence. Donald Schön's concept of the "reflective practitioner" (1983) added a layer of nuance, emphasizing the tacit, intuitive, and improvisational aspects of professional practice. For Schön, design was

89 Liedtka, J., and Kaplan, S. (2019). How Design Thinking opens new frontiers for strategy development. *Strategy and Leadership*, 47(2), 3–10.

90 Martin, R. (2009). *The design of business: why design thinking is the next competitive advantage*. Harvard Business School Press.

not merely about solving problems but reframing them engaging in a conversation with the materials, the context, and one's own assumptions. This interplay between structure and intuition, between method and reflection, is what gives design thinking its unique texture.

Design theorist Richard Buchanan (1992) provided a critical turning point by explicitly linking design thinking to "wicked problems", those messy, ill-defined issues that arise in social and organizational contexts. Buchanan argued that design was not confined to objects or aesthetics; it was a way of reasoning, a way of placing and connecting ideas across disciplines. His work helped shift design thinking from the studio to the boardroom and beyond, establishing it as a vital approach for navigating modern complexity.

From there, design thinking gained traction in the business world, thanks in large part to the work of practitioners like Tim Brown, Roger Martin, and David Kelley. These leaders translated the designer's mindset into actionable practices for innovation and organizational change. Tim Brown's *Change by Design* (2009) popularized a five-phase model, empathize, define, ideate, prototype, and test—that became a touchstone for teams seeking to innovate collaboratively. Roger Martin added strategic depth by suggesting that leaders must "balance the reliability of analytical thinking with the validity of intuitive thinking", in essence, to think like designers.

This convergence of theory and practice led to the institutionalization of design thinking across sectors. Business schools began to teach it. Nonprofits applied it to social innovation. Governments explored it for policy-making. And across industries, organizations began to view design not just as a function, but as a core capability.

It is also worth noting the influence of IDEO, one of the most prominent design consultancies in the world. Under Brown's leadership, IDEO demonstrated how multidisciplinary teams using design thinking could solve problems as varied as hospital workflows, urban mobility, and educational reform. Their work made the approach visible, credible, and replicable.

As design thinking entered mainstream discourse, it sparked both enthusiasm and critique. Some scholars raised concerns about oversimplification, especially when design thinking was reduced to a set of tools without its deeper philosophical underpinnings. Others cautioned against using it as a panacea for all organizational problems. Yet even these critiques underscore its impact: design thinking had arrived as a significant paradigm in how we understand and act upon the world.

Ultimately, the origins of design thinking are not linear, they are layered, evolving, and interwoven. They reflect a shift in mindset: from seeing problems as fixed to viewing them as dynamic, from acting alone to creating together, from optimizing parts to reimagining wholes. This evolution gives design thinking its staying power. It is not tied to a single industry or trend—it is rooted in how humans make meaning, solve problems, and imagine what's possible.

5.4 Importance of Design in Strategic Planning and Organizational Culture

Design is no longer confined to products or aesthetics, it's a discipline, a mindset, and increasingly, a strategic advantage. In an era defined by complexity, speed, and rising stakeholder expectations, design thinking offers more than innovation. It becomes a cornerstone of how organizations plan, adapt, and evolve.

Traditional strategic planning tends to rely on linear thinking: define goals, project outcomes, map the path. But in a volatile world, such models often fall short. Design thinking introduces a **more dynamic approach**, anchored in empathy, experimentation, and co-creation. It doesn't discard analytical rigor, but enriches it with imagination. Table 8 highlights these differences between Traditional vs. Design-Driven Strategy and Culture.

Table 8: Traditional vs. Design-Driven Strategy and Culture.

Traditional vs. Design-Driven Strategy and Culture		
Dimension	**Traditional Approach**	**Design-Driven Approach**
Starting Point	Goals, forecasts, control	Empathy, exploration, co-creation
Primary Orientation	Predictive, efficiency-focused	Adaptive, purpose-driven
Approach to Uncertainty	Minimize or avoid uncertainty	Engage with and learn from uncertainty
Decision-Making	Top-down, expert-driven	Participatory, distributed authority
Innovation Method	Linear planning and analysis	Iterative prototyping and testing
View of People	Users as end-receivers	Users as co-creators and stakeholders
Culture Norms	Risk-averse, perfectionist	Curiosity-driven, tolerant of failure
Feedback Loops	Periodic, formal reviews	Continuous, informal learning cycles
Measure of Success	KPIs, ROI, market share	Meaning, impact, system change

When applied to strategy, design thinking begins not with a spreadsheet, but with deep listening. Organizations tune into the unspoken needs of customers, employees, and communities. They challenge assumptions, ask provocative "what if" questions, and prototype possible futures before making major commitments. This iterative process turns strategy from a static roadmap into a **living, learning journey**.

But design's greatest power may lie in shaping culture.

Culture is the shared values, beliefs, and behaviors that shape how people work, and can be a formidable barrier or a transformative force. Design thinking helps organizations **reshape culture from the inside out**. It fosters curiosity over certainty, collaboration over control, and iteration over perfection. Everyone, not just senior leaders, becomes a designer of solutions. When practiced daily, design thinking creates psychological safety. Teams feel empowered to experiment, speak up, and learn from failure. This mindset is especially resonant with the emerging workforce: research shows that by 2025, over 75% of the global workforce will be Millennials and Gen Z, a generation that values purpose, co-creation, and equity[91]. Design thinking offers them not just a voice, but a method to act on it.

Design also shapes how identity is expressed through branding, communications, internal rituals, and stakeholder engagement. Every design decision signals what the organization stands for. As such, **design becomes a language of culture,** one that reinforces alignment between values and action. Scholars like Elsbach and Stigliani[92] have shown that when design thinking becomes embedded in organizational DNA, it transforms how decisions are made. It decentralizes authority, nurtures foresight, and redefines success, not just by profit margins, but by meaning, relationships, and impact.

In sustainability contexts, these cultural shifts are even more vital. Achieving long-term resilience and regenerative outcomes demands more than new strategies—it requires new stories, new behaviors, and new belief systems. Design thinking gives organizations the tools to **reimagine not just what they do, but who they are.** As we move from efficiency to resilience, from planning to participation, design emerges as a vital thread, a connective tissue between vision and execution, people and process, purpose and performance.

In short, design thinking is no longer a sideline activity. It is a **strategic and cultural imperative** for any organization serious about leading meaningful, sustainable change.

5.5 Design Influences on the Function and Sustainability of Holistic Systems

Design, at its highest potential, is not just about aesthetics or product development—it is a method of reimagining systems. When applied holistically, design becomes a powerful tool for reshaping how organizations function, connect, and evolve within the social, economic, and ecological systems they are part of. For sustainability leaders, this systems-level perspective is not a luxury, it's a necessity.

A holistic system recognizes the interdependence of its parts. Rather than optimizing individual components in isolation, it seeks coherence, balance, and integra-

91 Forbs, Timmes, M. 2022. *Millennials And Gen Z: Now Is The Time To Reshape Businesses To Harness Their Power,* Article publisher June 27,2022. Retrieved 2025, https://www.forbes.com/councils/forbescoachescouncil/2022/06/27/millennials-and-gen-z-now-is-the-time-to-reshape-businesses-to-harness-their-power/?
92 Elsbach, K. and Stigliani, S. (2018). Design thinking and organisational culture: A review and framework for future research. *Journal of Management,* 1–33.

tion across the whole. Design thinking, with its iterative and integrative mindset, provides a framework to understand and transform systems in this way. It helps leaders zoom out to identify patterns, feedback loops, and leverage points, the subtle places where small shifts create lasting impact.

This is especially crucial in sustainability contexts, where the problems we face, climate change, inequality, ecological degradation, are what Horst Rittel and Melvin Webber called "wicked problems." These issues resist linear thinking and siloed solutions. They require collaborative approaches, adaptive learning, and strategies that evolve with time. Design thinking offers both the **mindset** and the **methodology** to meet this complexity.

Across industries, leading organizations are already embracing systems-level design. They're redesigning supply chains for circularity, restructuring stakeholder relationships for shared value, and reimagining products and services through the lens of justice and regeneration. They're asking powerful questions:

– *How might we create circular economies that regenerate rather than extract?*
– *How might we embed equity into our hiring, procurement, and engagement strategies?*
– *How might we use technology not just for efficiency, but for transparency and trust?*

Design's influence also reaches into the conceptual and cultural dimensions of systems. It shapes **mental models**, the invisible assumptions that guide behavior. Through storytelling, visualization, and rapid prototyping, design helps make abstract challenges tangible. It equips people across disciplines and power structures to engage with complexity and co-create meaningful solutions.

Crucially, design supports learning. Through cycles of exploration, reflection, and iteration, organizations begin to embody what Peter Senge (1990)[93] called a **"learning organization"** one that senses change and adapts through creativity, not compliance. This adaptive capacity is foundational for sustainability. It allows systems not just to withstand disruption, but to evolve through it.

Design also challenges traditional power dynamics. It elevates marginalized voices, fosters inclusion, and brings diverse perspectives into the room. In sustainability work, this inclusivity ensures that solutions are not only effective but also just. A well-designed system does not privilege efficiency over ethics or profit over people. It seeks balance.

And perhaps most powerfully, design reconnects us with purpose. It asks:

– *What kind of world are we designing for?*
– *What kind of legacy are we leaving behind?*

---

93 Senge, P. (1990). The fifth discipline:The Art & Practice of the Learning Organization. Doubleday.

It turns strategy into moral inquiry. Sustainability becomes not a constraint, but a creative possibility, an invitation to design systems that are regenerative, inclusive, and deeply aligned with human and planetary well-being.

In practical terms, this could mean designing value chains that minimize waste and maximize reuse. It could involve cross-sector collaborations that address systemic problems. It might require building reflective spaces inside organizations where experimentation and sense-making are part of the daily rhythm. Whatever the expression, the principle is this: **sustainability cannot be retrofitted. It must be intentionally designed.**

To enable this, organizations must invest in design capabilities at every level. Train leaders in systems thinking. Empower teams to test ideas. Embed design practices into strategic planning and operations. And most importantly, adopt a core belief: change is not only possible, it can be **intentionally, inclusively, and beautifully designed.**

Design doesn't merely improve systems. It **transforms** them. And in a world that desperately needs transformation, that's not optional. It's vital.

5.6 Section Synthesis: Design Thinking

Design thinking is more than a methodology, it is a mindset, a practice, and a strategic lens through which organizations can interpret, navigate, and transform complexity. As we have explored throughout this chapter, its origins are rooted in the convergence of creativity, scientific inquiry, systems awareness, and a deep sensitivity to human needs. This makes design thinking uniquely suited to the challenges of sustainability leadership in the 21st century.

At its foundation, design thinking calls on us to reframe problems. It moves us away from asking, "What's broken?" or "What's the quickest fix?" Instead, it asks, "What kind of future do we want to create?" And just as critically: "How might we design our systems to get there?" This shift from reactive to generative thinking is critical for sustainability management. It invites innovation not only in products or services but in values, processes, and organizational cultures.

This chapter has traced the evolution from designerly thinking, rooted in Simon's structured, rational models, to a contemporary approach that embraces ambiguity, intuition, and collaboration. It has shown how scholars like Buchanan and practitioners like Brown extended the boundaries of design into strategic planning, organizational development, and systemic transformation. In this expansion, design thinking became accessible to non-designers and applicable across sectors, from healthcare to education, from urban planning to corporate strategy.

We have seen that design thinking is most powerful when it is participatory and human-centered. It requires empathy as a core competency, an ability to step into the shoes of users, stakeholders, or communities and understand their needs, values, and constraints. It turns solutions into co-creations. And shifts authority, not just downward, but across and throughout the system. For example, a municipality using design thinking to improve urban mobility might bring together city planners, cyclists, elderly residents, and rideshare drivers to co-create solutions that meet diverse accessibility needs. This kind of inclusive process surfaces blind spots, fosters trust, and leads to innovations that are more widely embraced and sustained over time.

It is also an approach deeply tied to action. Design thinking does not rely solely on analysis or abstraction; it thrives on prototyping, feedback, and learning through doing. This makes it well-suited to fast-changing, uncertain contexts where fixed plans often become obsolete. In this way, design thinking aligns with the demands of the sustainability era, where responsiveness, resilience, and reinvention are necessary for survival.

Culturally, when design thinking becomes embedded in an organization's DNA, it shifts the entire ecosystem. It encourages experimentation over perfection, cross-functional collaboration over silos, and meaning-making over mere efficiency. It reorients success metrics toward impact, well-being, and long-term value creation, not just quarterly returns. In short, design thinking humanizes strategy. It brings context. And it makes strategic processes more inclusive, more adaptive, and more alive.

For holistic sustainability to take root, we must stop seeing systems as static machines to optimize and start seeing them as living ecosystems to cultivate. Design thinking supports this shift. It helps sustainability leaders not only recognize the interdependencies within and between systems but also design interventions that honor those relationships. It builds bridges between vision and execution, between ambition and pragmatism.

Importantly, design thinking is not a one-size-fits-all solution. It is a mindset that must be continuously adapted, localized, and evolved. It thrives in cultures that value curiosity, diversity, transparency, and integrity. It requires time, trust, and a willingness to fail forward.

This synthesis makes clear that design thinking is indispensable for any organization serious about embedding sustainability into its core. It offers the tools, the language, and the philosophy to move from fragmented initiatives to integrated, regenerative strategies. It is how we can design not only better products or services but better futures.

As we move forward into subsequent chapters, I will deepen our understanding of how design thinking interconnects with systems change, leadership, and the Integral Design Thinking for Sustainability Management (IDT-SM) framework. But here, I establish the imperative: **sustainability is not an endpoint, it is a continuous design challenge. And it is one we must embrace with creativity, courage, and care.**

6 Organizational Change Management

Lasting change doesn't happen at the edges, It starts at the core, where culture, leadership, and learning meet.

In an era marked by volatility, uncertainty, complexity, and ambiguity, change is no longer the exception it is the environment in which organizations exist. It affects every dimension of organizational life: structure, processes, culture, people, and purpose. Change is no longer a momentary disruption to be managed; it is an ongoing condition to be embraced.

This chapter explores the evolving dynamics of organizational change, anchoring both classic models and contemporary insights in the context of sustainability leadership. Here, change is not just operational it is existential. It calls for reimagining not only what organizations do, but how they think, how they relate, and how they build the capacity to evolve continuously and ethically.

Effective change management is not a side initiative it is a strategic imperative. For sustainability leaders, this means going beyond implementing green policies or launching social initiatives. It involves transforming the organizational mindset, shifting governance structures, and embedding new cultural norms that support long-term resilience.

I will begin with the foundations: a review of early change theories that provide structure, process, and insight into how change has traditionally been approached. These models offer valuable tools, but they are only part of the picture. As complexity has increased, so too has the need for adaptive approaches that recognize the interdependence of systems, people, and values.

From there, we explore systems thinking particularly as framed by Peter Senge and others which, reframes organizations as living, interdependent networks rather than static hierarchies. This lens reveals how meaningful change often requires shifting not only practices but paradigms, not only strategies but stories.

Culture and leadership, two powerful forces in the change equation, receive focused attention. Culture is not simply the backdrop for transformation; it is the texture of everyday behavior. It determines how change is perceived, resisted, or embraced. Leadership, in turn, must be less about control and more about cultivation of vision, trust, and shared agency.

Finally, we conclude the chapter with a synthesis of key insights and practical applications. What does holistic, systems-aware change management look like in the real world? How can sustainability leaders move from theory to action and from intention to impact?

Together, these ideas build a foundation for the chapters ahead. If sustainability is to be more than a goal, if it is to become a way of being, then organizational change must be seen not as a disruption to endure, but as a vital force to design, lead, and steward.

https://doi.org/10.1515/9783111705286-006

6.1 Organizational Change

Organizational change is not a moment in time. It's an ongoing condition, part of the very rhythm of business life. As Peter Senge and others have emphasized, the 21st-century organizational landscape is in a constant state of flux due to factors such as globalization, technological innovation, demographic shifts, and increasing complexity in stakeholder demands. For any organization, and particularly for those committed to sustainability, learning to manage and lead through change is no longer optional; it is essential.

At its core, organizational change refers to the ongoing process of renewing an organization's direction, structure, and capabilities to meet the evolving needs of both internal and external stakeholders.[94] Whether driven by internal goals or external pressures, successful change efforts require a strategic, proactive mindset. As Cooperrider and Srivastva (1987)[95] suggested, change is inseparable from strategy itself. In fact, change *is* strategy in motion.

The accelerating pace of change has made adaptability one of the most important organizational capabilities. Scholars such as Graetz (2000),[96] Senior (2002),[97] and Kotter (1996)[98] argue that the role of leaders today is primarily to navigate this change, to guide their teams through disruption and transition with clarity, confidence, and empathy. These change agents must manage evolving goals, shifting customer expectations, competitive dynamics, and rapid innovation. Leadership today isn't just about optimizing the present, it's about preparing for what's next. It's about building the capacity to pivot, adapt, and evolve.

One important insight from the literature is that change can emerge from both inside and outside the organization. External changes, like regulatory shifts, market trends, or environmental crises, often catalyze internal reassessments. Meanwhile, internal innovations or cultural shifts can proactively drive broader transformation. This duality means that change management cannot be isolated in a single department; it must be embedded in the fabric of the entire organization, guided by a shared vision and clear values.

However, not all change is created equal. There is a difference between tactical adjustments and transformational change. Tactical change might involve improving efficiency or modifying workflows, while transformational change involves a funda-

---

94 Moran, J. W., and Brightman, B. K. (2001). Leading organisational change. *Career Development International*, 6(2), 111–118.

95 Cooperrider, D. L., and Srivastva, S. (1987). Appreciative inquiry in organisational life. In R. W. Woodman and W.A. Pasmore (Eds.), *Research in organisational change and development*, (pp. 129–169). JAI Press.

96 Graetz, F. (2000). Strategic change leadership. *Management Decision*, 38(8), 550–562.

97 Senior, B. (2002). Organisational change (2nd ed.). Prentice Hall.

98 Kotter, J. P. (1996). *Leading change.* Harvard Business Press.

mental shift in values, culture, business models, or strategic direction. Sustainability initiatives often require the latter, deep, systemic changes that touch every part of the organization and its ecosystem. This is what makes sustainability change uniquely complex, and why a thoughtful, evidence-based approach to change management is so crucial.

As Burnes (2004)[99] and others have pointed out, resistance to change is one of the most persistent challenges organizations face. This resistance may stem from fear, uncertainty, lack of trust, or simply the inertia of existing routines. To overcome it, leaders must not only design effective change strategies, they must also communicate persuasively, engage authentically, and build a culture that views change as an opportunity rather than a threat.

Effective organizational change requires alignment between vision, strategy, structure, and people. It involves translating big ideas into actionable steps and making those steps meaningful to the individuals responsible for implementing them. It requires creating feedback loops, celebrating progress, and building learning organizations that can adapt continuously.

As we move through this chapter together, we will explore early theories and evolving frameworks that help us understand the dynamics of change. We'll examine how systems thinking has reshaped our approach to transformation, and how culture and leadership play pivotal roles in the success or failure of change efforts. By deepening our understanding of these dynamics, we equip ourselves not just to manage change but to lead it. And not just any change, but the kind that endures, aligns with purpose, and reshapes the future. For instance, when Patagonia restructured its supply chain to align with regenerative agriculture principles, it didn't just tweak operations; it reshaped its entire business narrative. That's transformational change.

6.2 Early Theories and Approaches

Understanding how organizational change has been theorized and managed over time helps us appreciate the complexity and evolution of modern change strategies, especially those focused on sustainability. Early theories of organizational change largely stemmed from the belief that change was episodic, controllable, and linear. These foundational models provided essential insights but often lacked the adaptability required in today's volatile, uncertain, complex, and ambiguous (VUCA) environment.

---

99 Burnes, B. (2004). *Managing change: A strategic approach to organisational dynamics,* (4th ed.). Prentice Hall.

Kurt Lewin,[100] one of the earliest and most influential voices in change management, introduced what's now known as the 'planned approach' to change in 1947. His model, unfreeze, change (or move), and refreeze, offered a structured and sequential roadmap for transformation. First, existing behaviors and attitudes are "unfrozen," meaning old patterns must be questioned and loosened. Then, the organization moves through a transitional phase of change before "refreezing" into a new steady state. This model emphasized that for change to be successful, it must be anchored in a new culture and behavioral norm.

Lewin's work laid the foundation for many subsequent models, such as those by Judson (1991)[101] and Kotter (1995).[102] Kotter's influential eight-step model added more operational and leadership focus. It emphasized building urgency, creating coalitions, developing a clear vision, and embedding changes into the organizational DNA. These models share a common thread: they treat change as a rational, step-by-step process that leaders can manage with the right planning and communication.

However, these early approaches also assumed a level of predictability that today's business environment rarely offers. As Rieley and Clarkson (2001)[103] argued, early theories operated under the assumption that too much change would create instability and inefficiency. In contrast, modern scholars and practitioners recognize that constant change is now the norm, not the exception.

This realization gave rise to the **emergent approach** to change. Rather than treating change as a linear sequence of actions, emergent theories view it as a dynamic, adaptive process. Change emerges organically through the interactions of people, systems, and environmental conditions. Scholars like Burnes (2004)[104] and Dawson (1994)[105] highlight how the emergent model acknowledges that change is often non-linear, messy, and shaped by culture, politics, and timing. Emergent change is not about controlling every step, it's about fostering conditions in which change can flourish. It invites continuous learning, feedback, and adaptation. This approach is especially resonant in sustainability contexts, where change is both ongoing and value-driven, and where solutions must evolve with communities, ecosystems, and technologies.

---

100 Lewin, K. (1947). Frontiers in group dynamics. *Human Relations, 1,* 5–41.

101 Judson, A. (1991). *Changing behaviour in organisations: Minimizing resistance to change.* Basil Blackwell.

102 Kotter, J. P. (1995). Leading change: Why transformation efforts fail', *Harvard Business Review,* 59–67.

103 Rieley, J. B. and Clarkson, I. (2001). The impact of change on performance. *Journal of Change Management, 2*(2), 160–172.

104 Burnes, B. (2004). *Managing change: A strategic approach to organisational dynamics,* (4th ed.). Prentice Hall.

105 Dawson, P. (1994). *Organisational change: A processual approach.* Paul Chapman.

Beyond Lewin and Kotter, other models have provided rich, actionable insights. For instance, Beer et al. (1990)[106] focused on aligning organizational levers, such as structure and systems, with new strategic goals. Hiatt (2006)[107] introduced the ADKAR model, which emphasizes individual transitions across five stages: Awareness, Desire, Knowledge, Ability, and Reinforcement. Kanter et al. (1992)[108] contributed the 'Ten Commandments for Executing Change,' highlighting the importance of communication, participation, and political acumen. Galpin (1996)[109] suggested that leaders must not only communicate vision but also test and refine it collaboratively before full implementation. For example, an energy company transitioning to renewables might follow Kotter's steps to build urgency and create quick wins, but success would also hinge on the adaptive, emergent feedback loops emphasized by Burnes.

Each of these models brings something valuable to the table. However, as Stouten et al. (2018)[110] pointed out, none of them are sufficient on their own. They analyzed seven of the most recognized models and synthesized ten critical success components, including building a clear case for change, promoting shared ownership, empowering coalitions, identifying quick wins, and sustaining momentum. These can be grouped under three themes: **communication**, **branding**, and **community**, all of which are essential for modern change efforts.

Importantly, early models often assumed a top-down approach to change. But newer perspectives challenge this, advocating for participatory, bottom-up engagement that empowers employees as co-creators of change. This aligns closely with sustainability leadership, where buy-in from across the organization, especially from those on the front lines, is critical for success.

Additionally, metaphors have been used to deepen our understanding of change. Lewin likened organizations to blocks of ice that need to be unfrozen and reshaped. Later, Cameron and Green (2015)[111] expanded this metaphorical approach, encouraging change leaders to view organizations as living organisms, political arenas, or even flux-and-transformation systems. These metaphors help leaders reframe their challenges and discover creative strategies for navigating complex transformations.

---

106 Beer, M., Eisenstat, R.A., and Spector, B. (1990). *Why change programs don't produce change*. Harvard Business School Press/.

107 Hiatt, J.M. (2006). ADKAR: *A model for change in business, government, and our community: How to implement successful change in our personal lives and professional careers*. Prosci Research.

108 Kanter, R.M., Stein, B., and Jick, T.D. (1992). *The challenge of organisational change: How companies experience it and leaders guide it*. Free Press.

109 Galpin, T. (1996). *The human side of change: A practical guide to organisation redesign*. Jossey-Bass.

110 Stouten, J., Rousseau, D., and Cremer, D. (2018). Successful organisational change: Integrating the management practice an scholarly literatures. *Academy of Management Annals, 12*(2), 752–788.

111 Cameron, E., and Green, M. (2015). *Making sense of change management* (4th ed.). Great Britain, Kogan Page Limited.

In summary, while early change theories provided the foundational tools for organizational transformation, they are no longer sufficient on their own. Sustainability-focused change demands a more holistic, flexible, and systemic approach. As we move into the next sections of this chapter, we'll explore how systems thinking and organizational culture offer deeper, more resilient ways to manage meaningful and lasting change.

6.3 Organizational Systems Thinking Approach

Organizational systems thinking offers a vital lens through which sustainability change efforts can be understood and implemented. Unlike traditional change models that isolate problems and apply linear solutions, systems thinking recognizes the interdependence of parts within a whole. It asks us to explore patterns, feedback loops, structures, and mental models that sustain organizational behavior over time. In sustainability management, where problems are often "wicked" and interconnected, this approach becomes indispensable.

One of the most influential voices in this space is Peter Senge, whose 1990 book *The Fifth Discipline* introduced the concept of the "learning organization." Senge defined systems thinking as the "fifth discipline" that integrates the other four, personal mastery, mental models, shared vision, and team learning, into a coherent body of theory and practice. Without systems thinking, he argued, efforts to change organizational behavior are likely to be superficial or short-lived. Lasting change must occur at the **system level**, not merely in isolated functions or individual behaviors.

Senge and colleagues later articulated ten core capabilities essential for sustained, systemic transformation. This framework urges leaders to move beyond reactive thinking toward proactive and generative learning. For instance, one principle warns against treating symptoms rather than root causes, a common pitfall in many organizational change efforts. Another emphasizes that cause and effect are not always close in time and space, underscoring the importance of long-term, strategic thinking in sustainability work.

Building on this, Bicheno and Holweg (2009)[112] argued that traditional "unfreeze-change-refreeze" models are no longer adequate. In a world of rapid change, organizations must remain "continuously unfrozen", always adaptable, always evolving. Sustainability is not a final destination; it's an ongoing commitment to balancing environmental, social, and economic systems. Leaders need new mental models that embrace uncertainty, complexity, and interdependence.

---

112 Bicheno, J., and Holweg, M. (2009). *The lean toolbox, the essential guide to lean transformation*, (4th ed.). Production and Inventory Control, Systems and Industrial Engineering (PICSIE). Books.

Systems thinking also emphasizes the value of small, strategic wins, what Senge refers to as "micro-initiatives", that act as proof points within the organization. Rather than launching sweeping transformations all at once, which can overwhelm or desta-bilize a system, leaders can test new ideas in specific areas. These initiatives generate learning, build momentum, and reveal leverage points. As Senge noted, "Small changes can produce big results, but the areas of highest leverage are often the least obvious."

Ikujiro Nonaka (1994)[113] further deepened the field by emphasizing knowledge creation within systems. For change to be sustained, knowledge must be not only shared but also co-created. Nonaka described innovation as a process of identifying and framing problems, then generating new knowledge to address them, often through the dynamic exchange of tacit and explicit knowledge across cross-disciplinary teams. This is particularly relevant in sustainability work, where collaboration across science, policy, operations, and community is essential.

Nonaka's work reinforces the idea that systems are not fixed structures, but dynamic networks of learning and adaptation. Organizations must evolve into **learning ecosystems**, where feedback is constant, knowledge flows freely, and creative responses are encouraged. Systems thinking, in this view, becomes both a diagnostic tool and a blueprint for transformation.

Further advancing this thinking, Porter (2009)[114] outlined three paradigms for viewing systems: the functionalist (linear problem-solving), the interpretive (adjacent systems relationships), and the complex adaptive system (CAS), which best reflects the demands of today. In a CAS, networks of empowered stakeholders **self-organize around shared goals**. These systems are organic, flexible, and fueled by learning, trust, and feedback.

This complexity-aware approach aligns especially well with sustainability management. Traditional top-down change efforts often fall short because they neglect local contexts, tacit knowledge, or psychological resistance. In contrast, a systems approach cultivates bottom-up capacity. It values diversity, encourages experimentation, and adapts to emerging conditions.

Despite its promise, systems thinking is not without challenges. It demands patience, trust-building, and the courage to work within ambiguity. It also requires leaders to move beyond command-and-control mindsets and become stewards of shared purpose and learning. These leaders facilitate dialogue, hold creative tension, and help guide the organization toward alignment and coherence.

The organizational system itself must also support continuous change. Siloed departments, rigid hierarchies, and outdated metrics can stifle innovation. Agile struc-

---

113 Nonaka, I. (1994). A dynamic theory of organisational knowledge creation. *Organisation Science*, 5(1), 14–37.
114 Porter, T. (2009). Three views of systems theories and their implications for sustainability education. *Journal of Management Education*, 33(3), 323–347.

tures, interdisciplinary teams, and reflective learning cultures are essential. Success must be measured not just by outcomes, but by **feedback quality, engagement, and adaptive capacity.**

In summary, systems thinking invites us to see organizations not as machines to be fixed, but as ecosystems to be cultivated. For sustainability leaders, this shift in perspective enables deeper and more enduring change. By addressing structural and cultural roots, we design not just better interventions, we design better systems, better learning, and ultimately, better futures.

6.4 Organizational Culture Change and Leadership

Organizational culture is often described as "the way we do things around here." But beneath that simple phrase lies a rich and complex system of beliefs, values, rituals, routines, and power structures. These elements profoundly shape how change is received, resisted, or realized. In the context of sustainability management, cultural transformation is not optional; it's foundational. To create sustainable futures, organizations must cultivate cultures that embrace adaptation, collaboration, and purpose-driven leadership.

At its core, culture is a **social construct**, what Mann (2010)[115] calls a "hypothetical construct" used to explain observed behavior. It is not fixed; it evolves. And that evolution can be guided. According to Liff and Posey (2004),[116] culture can be influenced by leadership style, organizational structure, social norms, and even the physical design of the workspace. This is powerful: it means that leaders can, intentionally and strategically, shape culture to support sustainability goals.

To do this, however, they must go beyond surface-level change. True cultural transformation requires deep engagement with stakeholders across the organization. It involves listening, storytelling, modeling behavior, and creating psychological safety. As Beer et al. and Kotter argued, change must be **embedded** into daily routines, measured regularly, and reinforced through communication and action. Change cannot be a memo; it must be a movement.

Kurt Lewin's field theory laid the groundwork for understanding how culture and behavior interact. His model—unfreezing, changing, and refreezing—highlights the emotional and psychological work of letting go of old norms and internalizing new ones. Yet in today's rapidly shifting environment, many scholars suggest we no longer aim to "refreeze." Instead, **cultures must remain dynamic, continually learning and adapting.**

---

115 Mann, D. (2010). *Creating a lean culture* (2nd ed.). CRC Press, Taylor and Francis Group, Ltd.
116 Liff, S., and Posey, P. (2004). *Seeing is Believing*. American Management Association, AMACOM.

Leadership plays an essential role in this. As Senge and Nonaka have emphasized, leaders must act as **stewards of learning**. They must not just set direction, they must nurture the conditions for growth and collaboration. This involves **influencing beliefs, building trust**, and **modeling the desired future state**. Their actions carry symbolic weight: how they respond to feedback, failure, and conflict sends powerful signals about what is truly valued.

Research by Judson (1991), Edmondson (2002),[117] and Kotter (2012) further emphasizes that **championing change requires more than charisma**. It requires **infrastructure**: systems for feedback, recognition, and support. Leaders must create structures where the new culture can be rehearsed and reinforced through onboarding practices, meeting norms, performance evaluations, and communication strategies. For example, embedding sustainability stories into onboarding or celebrating "green wins" in company-wide meetings signals a cultural commitment from day one.

One of the more profound insights in cultural change literature is that **identity matters**. Organizations, like people, have identities. These are shaped by stories, who we believe we are, what we stand for, and how we engage the world. As Stouten et al. (2018) and Clark et al. (2010)[118] note, successful cultural change often involves creating a **transitional identity**, a bridge between the current culture and the desired future state. This helps stakeholders feel continuity and meaning, even as they adapt to new expectations.

Change is emotional. It can trigger fear, uncertainty, and resistance. Leaders must address this not with platitudes, but with empathy and structure. Resistance is not failure; it is a sign that something matters. The task is to **create space for dialogue**, to understand what is at stake for people, and to co-create pathways forward. As Burke and Litwin (1992) suggested, a leader's credibility rests on their ability to engage these conversations with honesty and compassion.

Trust is essential. Without it, cultural change efforts will falter. Trust is built through **transparency, consistency, and inclusion**. Leaders must involve stakeholders early and often. This is especially true in sustainability work, where values, ethics, and purpose are at the core. Inclusion means more than inviting people to meetings, it means **valuing their voice in shaping the organization's future**.

Social sustainability depends on this. When people feel seen, heard, and valued, they are more likely to engage, adapt, and innovate. Corporate Social Responsibility (CSR) efforts can reinforce this by framing sustainability as a shared responsibility, not just a leadership mandate. As Rodell and Colquitt (2009)[119] found, perceived fair-

117 Edmondson, A. C. (2002). The local and variegated nature of learning in organisations: A group-level perspective. *Organisation Science, 13*, 128–146.
118 Clark, S. M., Gioia, D. A., Ketchen, D. J. Jr., and Thomas, J. B. (2010). Transitional identity as a facilitator of organisational identity change during a merger. *Administrative Science Quarterly, 55*, 397–438.
119 Rodell, J. B. and Colquitt, J. A. (2009). Looking ahead in times of uncertainty: The role of anticipatory justice in an organisational change context. *Journal of Applied Psychology, 94*, 989–1002.

ness and shared benefit are critical for building commitment to change. This is where leadership transitions from authority to **authenticity**. Leaders must embody the values they espouse. This means walking the talk, being visible in change efforts, and holding themselves accountable. Research shows that when leaders **model new behaviors** from inclusive decision-making to sustainable practices, they give others permission and encouragement to follow.

Moreover, leaders must create **mechanisms for ownership**. Empowerment isn't a buzzword, it's a structural necessity. People need agency, clarity, and tools to make the new culture real. They need to see how their daily work connects to the larger vision. This requires ongoing communication, reinforcement of purpose, and acknowledgment of contributions.

Finally, cultural change is not a side project, it is the work. It must be integrated into strategic planning, performance management, hiring, and leadership development. It must be visible in how meetings are run, how conflicts are handled, and how success is celebrated.

To summarize: culture change is about shifting beliefs, behaviors, and systems in alignment with purpose. It requires clarity of vision, constancy of communication, and consistency of behavior. For sustainability leaders, this means cultivating a culture that values long-term thinking, equity, collaboration, and adaptability. It means becoming both a strategist and a storyteller, both an architect and a gardener.

Done well, culture becomes not just the context for change, but its engine. It becomes the soil in which sustainability can take root and thrive. And leaders are the gardeners, tending, cultivating, and protecting the conditions that allow sustainable culture to grow.

6.5 Section Synthesis: Organizational Change Management

Organizational change management (OCM) is no longer a luxury or a niche function, it is a core competency for any institution seeking to thrive in the face of complexity, sustainability challenges, and accelerating transformation. This chapter has explored how successful change efforts require the integration of strategy, systems thinking, leadership, and culture. In this synthesis, I bring these threads together to reflect on what effective, sustainable change looks like, and how it can be fostered at all levels.

At the heart of OCM is a simple but profound truth: **change is human**. It is not just about new systems, policies, or structures, it's about shifting mindsets, behaviors, and beliefs. The literature is clear: resistance to change is not only expected; it is a sign that something meaningful is at stake. This underscores the need for **empathetic leadership**, inclusive processes, and meaningful engagement with all stakeholders.

Organizational change begins with **strategic clarity**. Leaders must have a compelling vision that aligns with broader sustainability goals and articulates the "why" behind change. This vision should be consistently shared and transparently reinforced, becoming a collective narrative that anchors transformation efforts. Through **storytelling and co-creation**, people begin to locate themselves within the change and take ownership of it.

But vision alone is not enough. To move from inspiration to implementation, change must also be **systemically informed**. As Senge (1990) and Porter (2009) emphasize, organizations are complex, adaptive systems composed of interdependent layers: structures, relationships, knowledge flows, and power dynamics. Change agents must understand these dynamics and avoid one-size-fits-all solutions. Instead, they must cultivate systemic awareness, promote iterative learning, and remain flexible as feedback and conditions evolve.

A systems lens also reframes culture—not as a soft or secondary influence, but as a **strategic lever**. Culture shapes how people interpret change, how they behave under pressure, and what they believe is possible. Sustainable change requires embedding new cultural norms into daily practices, rituals, and expectations. It means recognizing informal influencers, challenging power imbalances, and building systems of reinforcement and accountability.

Change is not a single event, it is an ongoing process. While models like Lewin's three-phase process (unfreeze, change, refreeze) offered early guidance, they often fall short in today's fluid environments. Contemporary perspectives emphasize **dynamic equilibrium**, the idea that organizations must remain agile and adaptive, even after initial changes take root. In sustainability contexts, where environmental and social conditions are in constant flux, this capacity for ongoing learning is essential.

To build that capacity, organizations must become what Nonaka (1994) called **"learning organizations"** places where knowledge is continuously created, shared, and translated into innovation. These environments value curiosity, cross-functional collaboration, and open feedback loops. Failure is not feared but embraced as a source of insight. Integrating design thinking into this learning process adds empathy, agility, and creativity, turning strategy into a participatory, human-centered endeavor.

Leadership remains the critical catalyst. As this chapter has shown, leaders must go beyond managing processes, they must **model new behaviors, embody core values**, and **become champions** of the cultural and emotional dimensions of change. They must also design systems that empower others, creating a coalition of champions, distributing authority, and fostering a sense of shared purpose. Leadership in sustainability is not about command and control—it is about **inspiration, influence, and integrity**.

This leads us to the three integrated pillars emerging across the literature: **communication, branding, and community**.

- **Communication** is about clarity, consistency, and dialogue. It involves listening deeply, framing change in relatable terms, and ensuring people feel informed and heard throughout the journey.

- **Branding** refers to internal and external alignment around purpose and identity. This is not just about logos or slogans, it's about making sure the organization's actions reflect its stated values, building credibility and trust.
- **Community** is the web of relationships that sustains change. It includes coalitions, peer networks, informal influencers, and shared meaning-making. Community transforms change from a mandate into a movement.

Each of these elements must be **intentionally designed, nurtured, and maintained**. Together, they shape the terrain on which sustainable transformation becomes possible.

In conclusion, effective organizational change management is both an art and a science. It blends structure with sensitivity, systems with storytelling, and strategy with human connection. It requires leaders who can anticipate resistance, foster resilience, and build cultures rooted in learning, equity, and sustainability. **When these capabilities are in place, change doesn't just succeed—it sticks, spreads, and transforms.**

Summary and Conclusion of Part 1

The first six chapters of this book have been crafted to lay the intellectual and practical foundation for sustainability leadership and change agency in the 21st century. These chapters represent a convergence of research, lived professional experience, systems theory, and emerging innovation practices, each one addressing a critical dimension of sustainable transformation.

We began by contextualizing the urgent need for a new leadership mindset (Chapter 1), one that is attuned not just to economic performance but to ecological balance, social equity, and long-term systemic resilience. Today's leaders must navigate a world shaped by globalization, climate disruption, digital acceleration, and shifting stakeholder expectations. In this environment, the old ways of thinking are no longer sufficient. A new form of leadership, grounded in empathy, systems awareness, and integrative strategic thinking, is urgently needed.

Chapter 2 explored how sustainability is defined and operationalized in a business context. We examined how consumer demands, regulatory pressures, and shifting societal values are reshaping the expectations placed on organizations. Sustainability is no longer a peripheral CSR initiative; it is a central driver of organizational legitimacy, resilience, and competitive advantage. We identified that truly sustainable business requires reimagining how value is created, not just for shareholders, but for a broader ecosystem of stakeholders.

In Chapter 3, we investigated the philosophical and theoretical foundations underpinning change. We drew from Ken Wilber's Integral Theory, Scharmer's U Theory, Laszlo's systems thinking, and Doppelt's interventions for sustainability, we surfaced a set of guiding principles for integrative, consciousness-based approaches to transformation. These frameworks demonstrate the importance of shifting from fragmented, mechanistic views of organizations to holistic, participatory, and purpose-driven paradigms.

Chapter 4 turned our attention to strategy and strategic thinking. Here we observed that in an age of complexity and ambiguity, strategy must be adaptive, human-centered, and iterative. The literature and professional experience point to the necessity of cultivating "strategic imagination", the ability to think creatively and act boldly in service of long-term sustainability. This includes the integration of macro and micro perspectives, stakeholder engagement, and identity alignment.

In Chapter 5, we examined the origins and applications of design thinking, tracing its evolution from designerly thinking to a widely adopted strategic methodology. We highlighted its role in human-centered innovation, its capacity to navigate "wicked problems," and its value in aligning organizational culture with systems-level transformation. Design thinking provides the practical tools, such as empathy mapping, rapid prototyping, and divergent-convergent thinking—needed to turn vision into action.

https://doi.org/10.1515/9783111705286-007

Finally, Chapter 6 addressed organizational change management. We reviewed both early and contemporary change models, including Lewin's stages, Kotter's steps, and Senge's systems-based learning organization. We emphasized that effective change is not linear but dynamic, not top-down but participatory. Culture emerged as a key driver, change must be embedded into the routines, language, and shared meaning-making processes of daily organizational life. Leadership is essential in shaping this cultural fabric, and their role is as much about modeling as it is about managing.

Core Themes Emerging Across Part 1

Several consistent themes have emerged across this foundational section of the book:

- **Sustainability Demands Systems Thinking**: Isolated initiatives or one-off interventions are insufficient. Organizations must develop the capacity to see the interconnections between people, processes, culture, and the planet.
- **Leadership Must Be Transformational and Empathetic**: Traditional command-and-control models are giving way to leaders who listen deeply, build psychological safety, and inspire collective action toward shared purpose.
- **Strategy Is Now a Learning Process**: Rigid plans are being replaced by agile, feedback-driven approaches that allow organizations to respond to complexity with curiosity and adaptability.
- **Design Thinking Is the Integrative Bridge**: It offers a practical, creative, and human-centered approach to tackling the multifaceted challenges of sustainability. It encourages a culture of experimentation, collaboration, and optimism.
- **Culture Is Where Change Lives or Dies**: The best strategies will fail if they do not take root in the day-to-day beliefs and behaviors of the people inside the organization. Culture must be actively shaped, not passively endured.
- **Change Must Be Co-Created**: Whether you are a CEO, a sustainability officer, or a frontline manager, change cannot be imposed; it must be built collaboratively, with stakeholders actively involved in shaping the journey.
- **Communication, Branding, and Community** are the pillars of successful change management. These are not marketing functions; they are strategic levers to mobilize collective energy and meaning.

From Foundation to Framework

These six chapters have collectively illustrated the **why** and **what** of sustainable organizational transformation. They have shown us that we are operating in a new world economy that demands new thinking, new skills, and new kinds of leadership. They have revealed the gaps that exist, particularly in terms of strategic coherence, cultural alignment, and integrative thinking.

And now, we shift from understanding to application, from the foundation to the framework.

The next part of this book will introduce the **Integral Design Thinking (IDT) Strategy Framework**, a comprehensive, practical, and deeply human-centered approach to sustainable change. Grounded in the themes and theories explored thus far, the IDT framework offers a new kind of toolkit: one that blends design and systems thinking with change management and strategic foresight.

This framework is not a rigid model, it is a set of practices, mindsets, and tools that can be adapted to a wide range of organizational contexts. It is designed to help change agents not only implement sustainability strategies, but also cultivate the organizational culture and leadership capacity required for those strategies to succeed and endure.

As we move into the next chapters, keep in mind the key takeaway from this first section: **Sustainability is not just a set of practices, it is a way of seeing, being, and leading.** This shift begins with the individual, radiates through the culture, and ultimately transforms the system.
Let's take that next step together.

Part II: **Frameworks, Tools & Applications**

Frameworks are not fixed paths,
but living guides—meant to be shaped as much as they shape us

7 Discussion and Framework Introduction

From Insight to Strategy: Integrating the Parts to Design the Whole

By now, you've walked with me through some of the most critical foundations of sustainability leadership: the shifts in mindset, the urgency of systemic strategy, the promise of design thinking, and the complexity of managing organizational change. Along the way, you may have paused to reflect on your own context—your role, your organization, your sphere of impact. And you've likely recognized that meaningful transformation isn't linear. It's layered. And it calls for a new kind of integration.

This chapter marks a turning point in our journey—from exploration to design. From understanding what must change, to shaping how that change takes form.

Here, I introduce the **Integral Design Thinking (IDT) Strategy Framework**—a synthesis of the research, insights, and practical realities we've uncovered thus far. It's not a fixed model or prescriptive formula. Instead, it's a flexible, systems-aware approach built for leaders navigating complexity with clarity, empathy, and vision.

The IDT framework is grounded in the belief that sustainability challenges require a form of leadership that is both systems-oriented and human-centered—bold yet reflective, pragmatic yet purpose-driven. Drawing from systems thinking, change management, strategic design, and organizational culture, the framework integrates these domains into a cohesive approach leaders can actually use.

This chapter unfolds in several key sections. First, we revisit the conceptual foundations of IDT, reconnecting to the aims and motivations that shaped its development. We then explore shifts in the U.S. sustainability landscape—pressures, expectations, and emerging priorities that are redefining what effective leadership must look like.

Next, we examine the key drivers and barriers to change—internal and external forces that shape whether transformation takes root or stalls. These include lack of alignment, cultural resistance, and the absence of actionable, holistic strategy. These challenges are not theoretical; they are recurring realities that the IDT framework is designed to address.

I close the chapter with practical guidance for beginning to implement the framework—insights meant to help you translate theory into movement. Because ultimately, this framework isn't just about understanding systems. It's about designing within them. Leading from within them. And doing so in a way that aligns people, purpose, and possibility.

This is the architecture of transformation. Let's begin.

https://doi.org/10.1515/9783111705286-008

7.0 Conceptual Framework: Integral Design Thinking (IDT) Foundations

If sustainability is the goal, strategy the compass, and change management the engine—then design thinking is the bridge that connects intention to impact. Yet many existing models fall short of reflecting the real-world complexity of transformation. That's where the **Integral Design Thinking (IDT)** framework steps in—not as a replacement, but as an integration. It brings together the most effective elements from each discipline into something coherent, usable, and deeply responsive to context.

The IDT framework didn't emerge from a single theory or toolkit. It was shaped through pattern recognition—across literature, practice, interviews, and firsthand experience. It began with one core question: *What would it take to make change not only possible, but sustainable—and even inspiring?*

At its core, IDT weaves together design thinking, systems thinking, strategy, and organizational culture. But it doesn't treat these as isolated silos. It recognizes that sustainability leadership operates on multiple levels—strategic, relational, emotional, and systemic. It engages both the data and the dynamics, the measurable and the meaningful.

A Preview of the Framework

The **IDT strategy framework** consists of six core imperatives. At the center are three key focus areas—**communication, branding**, and **community** —— each serving as a strategic anchor for sustainable transformation. These are supported by two enabling disciplines: **empathy and shared language**, and **design thinking**, which together foster coherence, collaboration, and creativity across the organization.

Encasing all of this is the sixth imperative: **Holistic Design Thinking Methodology**—the systems-design mindset that surrounds and unifies the entire framework. This methodology synthesizes systems thinking and human-centered design. It equips leaders to see interdependencies, surface leverage points, and craft solutions that are both structurally sound and socially resonant. In short, it helps leaders navigate complexity with care.

A Visual Overview

The following figure illustrates the IDT Strategy Framework as a network of interlocking gears—each essential, each reinforcing the others. At the center is the **Change Agent**, representing the individual or team driving transformation. Surrounding this hub are five gears: **Communication, Community, Branding, Empathy & Shared Language**, and **Design Thinking**.

Encompassing the system is the sixth imperative—**Holistic Design Thinking**—depicted as the engine and boundary that holds the mechanism together. It ensures that strategy remains rooted in both systemic understanding and human values.

As with any finely tuned machine, every cog must turn in harmony. If one falters —whether through breakdowns in communication or misaligned messaging—the system as a whole suffers. But when all six imperatives are engaged, the result is a resilient, adaptive, and generative pathway for leading change. Figure 8 visualizes how these elements are dependent on and work together as gears in a machine.

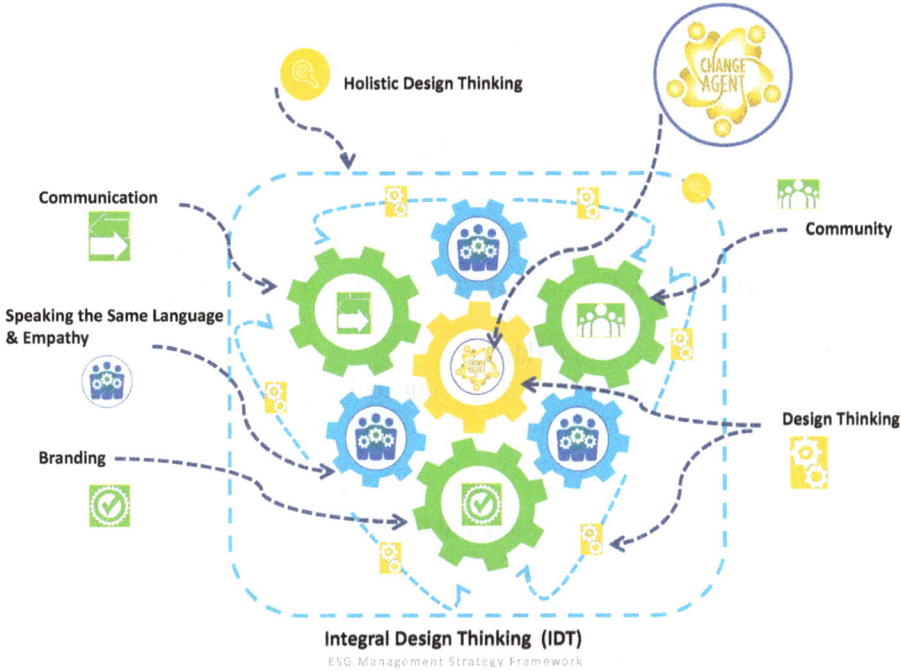

Figure 8: Integral Design Thinking (IDT) Strategy Framework (Source: Author).

Why IDT? Why Now?

In practical terms, IDT provides leaders and change agents with a flexible scaffolding— a way to understand where to begin, how to move forward, and how to adapt. It guides them to ask better questions, see connections that others may miss, and invite participation from the people who matter most.

The IDT framework was created in response to three persistent gaps in the sustainability space:

– The **lack of holistic, actionable models** for strategy and implementation.
– The challenge of aligning **vision with strategy**, and strategy with **culture**.
– The urgent need to integrate **empathy, innovation, and systems thinking** at the heart of organizational leadership.

What makes this framework *integral* is not just its interdisciplinarity, but its commitment to **wholeness**. It recognizes that sustainable transformation depends on aligning the parts—strategy and culture, leadership and participation, design and operations. It is to be used upon entering an organization, to assess if these mechanisms are working in the company. And making sure they do as these need to be working for any sustainability imperatives to be implemented. The IDT model is not only a lens for diagnosis but a structure for action. This framework exists to serve leaders who are navigating uncertain terrain—and who are ready to move from intention to architecture.

It is meant to be used—at the point of entry into an organization, during strategic pivots, and throughout ongoing transformation. It is a tool for assessing whether the internal mechanics of change—communication, culture, leadership, systems awareness—are in place and functioning. Because without them, no sustainability effort will endure.

This chapter is where I name the framework, define its purpose, and anchor its role in the journey ahead. The chapters to come will explore its components and applications in depth.

But for now, this is the guiding idea:

Change doesn't happen in silos. It happens in systems. And those systems must be designed—with care, courage, and clarity.

7.01 Foundations of the Research Aims and Objectives

At the core of this framework—and this book—is a guiding question:

How does meaningful, lasting change actually take hold inside organizations committed to sustainability?

Not just surface change. Not just performative strategy. But deep transformation that shifts how people think, work, relate, and lead.

This question didn't arise from theory alone. It grew from listening—closely—to sustainability professionals, design thinkers, and organizational leaders who were already doing the work. It emerged from the dissonance between big visions and stalled execution, between strategic plans and cultural realities. From this gap between intention and implementation, the **Integral Design Thinking (IDT)** framework began to take shape.

What became clear was that leaders weren't short on ambition. They were short on usable scaffolding—something holistic, human-centered, and adaptive enough to hold the complexity they faced daily. Something that could translate strategy into lived culture, and values into movement.

That need led to one central research question:

To what extent, and in what ways, can design thinking approaches and tools support inclusive, stakeholder-led innovation and culture change in sustainability management?

To answer it, the study was anchored in three research aims—each tied to real-world challenges and practical objectives.

Aim 1: Explore how design thinking supports innovation and culture change

- Can a methodology originally used in product design help shape values, norms, and leadership practice?
- Can empathy, iteration, and co-creation move beyond the workshop and into the fabric of an organization?

Objectives:
- Understand design thinking's value as a strategic and cultural tool
- Explore its influence on problem framing and creative leadership
- Examine its application in complex change environments

Aim 2: Critically assess the tools shaping sustainability innovation

- Are the approaches currently used by organizations truly serving the complexity of sustainability work?
- Where are the blind spots, and what makes a tool inclusive, flexible, and future-ready?

Objectives:
- Identify internal and external drivers of change
- Analyze the inclusivity and adaptability of current methodologies
- Surface which tools actually foster integration and collaboration

Aim 3: Identify strategies to embed cultural transformation into sustainability leadership

- What allows change to move beyond policy and become part of the organizational DNA?
- How can vision be translated into behavior, belief, and belonging?

Objectives:
- Clarify the role of design thinking and organizational learning in culture change
- Examine mechanisms for stakeholder engagement and ownership
- Understand the leadership conditions that enable implementation

These aims did more than guide the research—they shaped the framework itself. They became the compass for decision-making, for what was included, and for what mattered most.

Because in the end, the question behind every decision was this:

Will this help someone lead change more effectively—in the real world, under real constraints, with real people?

The IDT framework exists to answer *yes.* Not by prescribing steps, but by offering a structure that flexes. One that adapts to context, invites participation, and bridges the human and the systemic.

Next, we'll examine the landscape that makes this work more urgent than ever: the shifting sustainability terrain in the U.S. and the new pressures—and possibilities—that sustainability leaders now face.

7.1 Shifts in the U.S. and Global Sustainability Landscape

As the global dialogue around climate action, corporate responsibility, and stakeholder equity deepens, both the U.S. and international sustainability landscapes—particularly in the European Union—are undergoing significant transformation. This shift is more than a reaction to regulatory changes or consumer demands; it represents a fundamental rethinking of how businesses operate, innovate, and define success in a world of intersecting environmental, social, and economic crises.

The research underpinning this book identified **three key dimensions** (visualized in Figure 9) of this shift: the evolution of how sustainability is defined, the development of internal processes supporting sustainability, and the transformation of entire sectors. These patterns were especially evident in the U.S. and EU contexts, where regulatory, cultural, and market forces have created fertile ground for change. Together, they form the backdrop against which the Integral Design Thinking (IDT) framework was conceived.

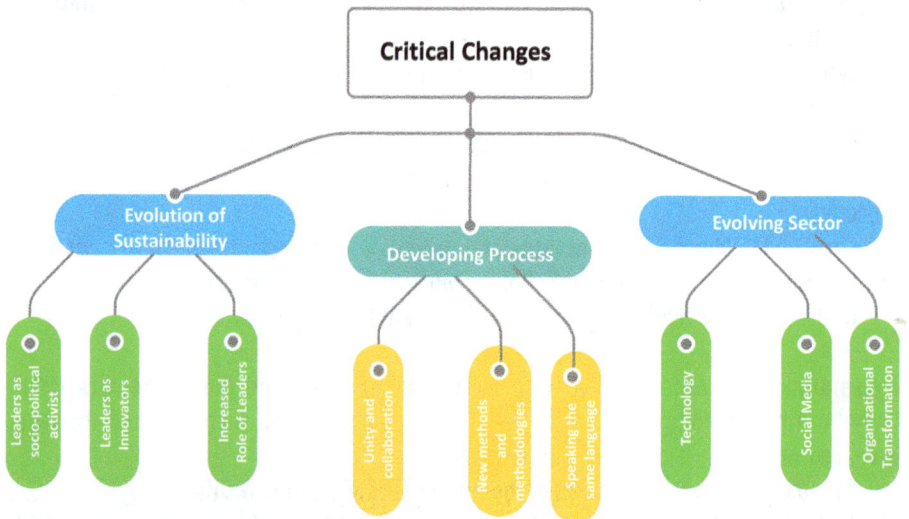

Figure 9: Interview Findings Critical Changes in the Sustainability Sector (Source: Author).

7.1.1 Evolution of Sustainability Defined

Sustainability is no longer a side initiative or a public relations talking point—it is increasingly seen as a strategic imperative. What once centered on environmental compliance has grown to include **Environmental, Social,** and **Governance (ESG)** priorities, stakeholder inclusion, and long-term resilience.

Across literature, interviews, and field practice, there has been a clear shift in how sustainability is framed. Terms like the "triple bottom line"—people, planet, profit—are now foundational, while newer paradigms like circular economy, carbon neutrality, net positive, and regenerative business are gaining traction. Leading organizations are asking deeper questions: *How can we create systems that regenerate, include, and evolve?* This broader, systems-oriented view is redefining corporate purpose and performance. These organizations are beginning to embrace the "quadruple bottom line," incorporating **purpose** as a guiding principle that integrates all other dimensions.

This shift is also re-shaping the role of sustainability leaders. Today's ESG leaders are not only strategists but **social-political activists and innovators.** They build internal communities, shape external partnerships, and champion inclusion, empathy, and stakeholder well-being. Their leadership style reflects a deeper understanding that sustainability isn't about fixing isolated problems—it's about transforming entire systems.

The European Union has been particularly catalytic in formalizing this shift. Policies such as the **European Green Deal**, the **EU Taxonomy for Sustainable Activities**[120], and the **Corporate Sustainability Reporting Directive (CSRD)**[121] push organizations toward more transparent, inclusive, and systemic sustainability practices. These efforts have global implications: U.S.-based companies with operations or investments in Europe are increasingly expected to meet EU standards, creating a harmonizing effect across regions.

This evolution has been shaped by increased regulatory scrutiny, investor activism, employee expectations, and shifting consumer behavior. Sustainability now informs everything from product development and hiring to supply chain strategy and corporate governance. It is no longer narrowly defined; it is now about **regeneration, inclusivity, accountability, and long-term adaptability**. And it's reshaping the purpose and structure of organizations at their core.

---

120 European Union, Eu Taxonomy for sustainability activities. Retrieved 2025, https://build-up.ec.eu ropa.eu/en/resources-and-tools/links/eu-taxonomy-sustainable-activities
121 European Union, Corporate Sustainability Reporting. Retrieved 2025, https://finance.ec.europa.eu/ capital-markets-union-and-financial-markets/company-reporting-and-auditing/company-reporting/cor porate-sustainability-reporting_en

7.1.2 Developing Process for Integration

As the definition of sustainability expands, so too does the need for structured, integrated processes. In earlier stages, organizations often relied on siloed departments or ad hoc initiatives. But today, the most effective sustainability efforts are those embedded across the enterprise—from **strategic planning and R&D to HR, finance, and operations**. Leading companies in the U.S. and Europe alike are embedding sustainability into **strategic planning cycles, innovation pipelines,** and **organizational performance metrics**. Notably, many of these organizations are turning to systems thinking and design thinking to guide this integration.

Interviews revealed that successful sustainability leaders are often "teams of one" or small, agile groups who must work cross-functionally, influencing others without formal authority. This requires strong collaboration skills, systems thinking, and a culture of learning. Design thinking tools—such as empathy mapping, journey mapping, and rapid prototyping—are now being used well beyond product development or for customer experience, but also for **internal change management, employee engagement**, and **policy innovation**. Some examples would be: redesigning employee engagement strategies, supply chains, and internal policies.

Systems thinking supports the identification of leverage points, feedback loops, and unintended consequences, allowing for more adaptive, resilient strategy-making. These methodologies enable companies to navigate complexity, engage diverse stakeholders, and prototype solutions before full-scale implementation. This shift demands **repeated cycles of reflection and redesign**. Leaders need to balance visionary ambition with practical application—building feedback loops, cultivating champions at all levels, and constantly recalibrating based on internal dynamics and external pressures.

Still, many organizations struggle to operationalize this mindset. Alignment gaps across departments, lack of leadership buy-in, and outdated incentive structures remain common obstacles. This is where holistic models like IDT become vital: offering not just process tools, but a way to think critically, inclusively, and holistically about transformation; not by replacing existing tools, but by helping leaders connect them in ways that are **inclusive, iterative, and adaptive**.

7.1.3 Sector-Level Transformation

Sustainability is no longer just about internal processes—it's transforming entire industries, from energy and agriculture to finance, fashion, manufacturing, and more. In the U.S., companies are developing **circular business models**, launching **ESG-focused investment funds**, and adopting **B Corp certification** to align profit with purpose. The European Union has gone further, rolling out **sector-specific regula-**

tions through programs like Fit for 55[122], the *EU Circular Economy Action Plan*[123], climate-aligned financial disclosure mandates and industry-level emissions targets that are reshaping global value chains.

Traditional sectors are responding by re-evaluating supply chains, investing in green innovation, and restructuring governance to include broader stakeholder representation. Financial institutions are reassessing risk models based on climate exposure. Manufacturers are redesigning products for disassembly and reuse. Retailers are responding to demand for ethical sourcing and transparency.

Across both regions, innovation is unfolding at every level:

- In finance, ESG data is informing lending decisions and portfolio strategies.
- In manufacturing, product design is being reimagined for disassembly, reuse, and lower embodied carbon.
- In public education, cross-district collaboration, such as the Urban School Food Alliance's[124] compostable tray initiative—demonstrates the power of collective procurement and shared purpose.
- In telecom, companies like Verizon have mobilized tens of thousands of employees through internal "green teams," including executive-level champions.

What these shifts reveal is that sustainability is no longer a reactive approach. It is **strategic, systemic, and deeply embedded in how organizations grow and adapt**. The evolving role of sustainability professionals—as change agents, community builders, and systems thinkers—reflects this new reality.

The evolution of sustainability is not linear or uniform. It reflects a dense web of policy, market, and cultural pressures. But across sectors and regions, the trend is clear: **sustainability is shifting from compliance to innovation, from intention to systemic integration, from reactive to regenerative.** This evolution —from definition to process to sector-wide impact—creates the context in which the *Integral Design Thinking (IDT)* framework was born.

As leaders across the U.S., Europe, and beyond seek to navigate complexity, they need more than compliance checklists. They need integrated, human-centered strategies that help them **lead with empathy, design for inclusion, and build for long-term resilience**. This landscape sets the stage for the next section: exploring the **key**

---

122 European Commission, Fit for 55: Delivering on the proposal. Retrieved 2025, https://commission. europa.eu/strategy-and-policy/priorities-2019-2024/european-green-deal/delivering-european-green-deal/fit-55-delivering-proposals_en

123 European Commission, Circular Economy Action Plan. Retrieved 2025, https://environment.ec.eu ropa.eu/strategy/circular-economy-action-plan_en

124 Urban Food Alliance came into existence to meet NYC's Zero Waste Initiative and targets. This non-profit organization was created as a collaborative by school food service professionals in 2012 to address the unique needs of the nation's largest school districts.

drivers of organizational transformation—and how IDT helps align them into a coherent, actionable path forward.

7.2 Key Drivers for Change

To understand how organizations can adapt and thrive in a rapidly shifting sustainability landscape, it is essential to identify the forces compelling them to act. These forces—both **external and internal**—do not merely pressure organizations into compliance; they present opportunities for redefinition, reinvention, and competitive differentiation. Figure 10, located at the end of this section, visualizes these drivers.

The IDT framework begins with the assumption that change is not just inevitable—it is already underway. The real question for leaders is whether they are prepared to respond to it with intention and coherence. Findings from this research, including literature reviews, interviews, and case studies, emphasize the critical drivers of transformation and the complexity of forces shaping them. These drivers reflect both external pressures and internal decisions, offering insight into the evolving role of sustainability leadership.

7.2.1 External Drivers for Change

External factors are accelerating the pace of transformation across industries, prompting organizations to adopt sustainability and ESG leadership roles. These drivers include: regulations, peer leadership, climate change resiliency strategies, and the drive of current generations' beliefs. The following sections will review each driver.

Regulations

Environmental and social legislation in the U.S. and globally is intensifying. From global frameworks like the EU Green Deal and CSRD to U.S.-specific regulations such as the Exchange Commission's (SEC) proposed climate risk disclosure rules to state-level mandates on emissions, organizations are increasingly held accountable for their environmental impact and social governance practices. Government mandates are pushing companies to reduce emissions, report on ESG metrics, and embed sustainability into their core strategy. Case studies such as NYC's PlaNYC and OneNYC illustrate how legislative actions have directly led to the creation and scaling of sustainability teams. Compliance is no longer optional—it is a threshold for market entry and reputational survival.

Industry Peer and Customer Influence

Organizations are responding not only to regulation but also to peer activity. Some strive to be first movers, adopting innovative technologies or ambitious targets to lead the market. Others follow trusted industry leaders. As commitments become public and methodologies are shared, a domino effect takes shape—transforming industry standards through collective leadership.

Today's consumers are not passive buyers—they are informed stakeholders who demand transparency, ethics, and sustainability. They want to know where products come from, how workers are treated, and whether a company's values align with their own. This shift is particularly prominent among Gen Z and Millennials, whose purchasing power and social media influence can amplify or dismantle brand reputations almost overnight.

Resiliency and Health

Climate change impacts—including extreme weather, rising sea levels, and supply chain disruptions—are elevating resilience as a strategic priority. These shifts have also expanded the sustainability conversation to include human and environmental health. Questions of how to foster healthy communities, develop resilient infrastructure, and ensure safe, equitable environments are now central to ESG planning.

Investors are seeing how sustainability builds healthier and more resilient organizations. This has created a doorway for Sustainable investing to move into the mainstream. ESG metrics are now a standard part of due diligence, and asset managers increasingly view sustainability performance as a proxy for long-term risk mitigation and innovation capacity. BlackRock's public calls for sustainability as a fiduciary responsibility underscore how ESG is reshaping capital markets.

Generational Thinking

Millennials and Gen Z are reshaping business expectations. Tech-savvy, purpose-driven, and vocal about their values, these generations are demanding transparency and ESG accountability from employers, brands, and institutions. Organizations that fail to adapt risk losing not only customers and investors but also their future workforce. As Laszlo (2005) asserts, the shift from shareholder to stakeholder thinking is no longer optional—it is imperative.

Global Crises and Collective Awareness

The COVID-19 pandemic, geopolitical instability, and growing awareness of systemic inequalities have spotlighted the fragility of existing systems. These events catalyze urgency and heighten expectations for businesses to act as a force for good. Organizations must now demonstrate resilience, equity, and long-term vision in response to compounding global risks.

Entire industries are being redefined by technological disruption and sustainability imperatives. Renewable energy, electric mobility, circular economy models, and regenerative agriculture are no longer fringe—they are gaining dominance. Businesses that fail to adapt risk obsolescence.

7.2.2 Internal Drivers for Change

While external forces may ignite the spark of transformation, it is often internal dynamics that determine whether the flame endures. These internal drivers, rooted in leadership intent, organizational culture, employee expectations, and brand identity—are not secondary influences. They are the levers from which lasting, meaningful change is built. As a sustainability leader, the question is not just what pressures exist outside your walls—but what potential lies within them.

Social Equity and Work–Life Balance

Today's workforce is redefining what it means to thrive at work. They are not simply seeking jobs—they are looking for purpose, respect, and balance. And they are bringing with them expectations that organizations foster fairness, inclusion, and well-being as core tenets of the workplace.

Social equity within an organization means more than checking boxes. It's about cultivating a culture where people feel safe to voice ideas, where pay is equitable, where leadership reflects diversity, and where a sense of belonging is real. It's also about transparent processes, inclusive hiring, and creating pathways for everyone to grow.

Work–life balance, too, has evolved. It is now seen as essential to organizational health. When employees are supported in managing stress, caring for their families, and taking space for personal restoration, productivity rises—and so does loyalty.

Pause and Consider: How are your internal policies communicating the message that your people matter? What story does your culture tell about balance, respect, and equity?

Change begins at the top. Organizations with leaders who embed sustainability into core vision and strategy are better equipped to align teams, integrate goals, and weather disruption. These leaders act not only as strategists but as cultural architects—**modeling behaviors and values** that shape the broader organizational ecosystem.

Organizational change begins with leadership that can see beyond the status quo. In companies where sustainability is core to the vision, we see stronger alignment across teams, more cohesive strategies, and better resilience in the face of disruption. Leaders who embed sustainability into their strategic intent shape culture, not just strategy.

Breaking Down Silos and Fostering Collaboration

Silos are not just organizational—they are mental models. They form when departments guard knowledge, when teams work in isolation, and when collaboration is treated as optional. Yet the challenges of sustainability do not respect boundaries. They are cross-cutting, messy, and interconnected.

Research findings reveal that organizations that succeed in transformation have made collaboration a norm, not a novelty. They build cross-functional teams, facilitate shared learning, and design processes that invite diverse inputs. Whether through community-building gatherings, "lunch and learn" events, or working groups that span departments, these organizations are breaking down barriers—not just between teams, but between mindsets.

Pause and Consider: Where do silos exist in your organization, and what beliefs uphold them? What could shift if those walls came down?

The complexity of sustainability challenges requires collaboration across disciplines—strategy, operations, design, HR, finance, and beyond. Internal silos must give way to integrated thinking and systems-level coordination. This push toward **transdisciplinary collaboration** is an internal driver with tremendous potential when harnessed effectively.

Brand Positioning and Influence

Sustainability is no longer a side story—it is central to brand identity. Internally, brand signals what the organization values. Externally, it tells customers, investors, and partners who you are. In today's market, positioning your brand around ESG values is not only a strategic necessity—it's a competitive advantage.

Younger generations, especially Millennials and Gen Z, are leading a cultural revolution in consumer and workplace behavior. They will spend more on brands they trust, sacrifice salary for alignment with purpose, and use their digital voice to elevate (or dismantle) reputations. This shift has made brand stewardship a shared responsibility across departments—not just marketing, but HR, sustainability, and leadership.

Case studies confirm this movement. Companies like Marlin Entertainment have rebranded their sustainability departments as "Being a Force for Good," embedding mission into both language and practice. Others, like Human Scale, publicly embrace mantras like "Less Bad Isn't Good Enough," signaling an authentic commitment to regenerative, not just sustainable, business.

Pause and Consider: What is your organization known for? What do you want it to be known for in five years—and what must change today to get there?

Employees increasingly want to work for organizations that reflect their values. **Purpose-driven work** is becoming a key retention strategy. Cultures that support inclusion, learning, and innovation are more adaptive to sustainability transformation. Conversely, cultures resistant to feedback and experimentation inhibit progress.

Strategic Necessity and Internal Resilience

For some organizations, change begins not with inspiration but with necessity. Rising resource costs, reputational risk, and supply chain vulnerabilities are forcing leaders to re-evaluate their business models. But when approached with intention, these pressures become catalysts for resilience.

Organizations that build adaptability into their culture—through agile teams, feedback systems, and learning mindsets—are better equipped to turn challenges into momentum. They shift from reactive firefighting to proactive, values-based planning.

> *Pause and Consider:* Where is your organization reacting to pressure—and where could it choose to lead instead?

Organizations that embrace **learning mindsets**, where failures are treated as learning opportunities, and iterative development is the norm—are **better positioned to adapt**. These internal capacities for reflection, experimentation, and responsive planning create the conditions for sustained innovation.

Whether you are beginning this work or deep in the trenches, these internal drivers matter. They are the soil in which all strategy takes root. Without attention to equity, collaboration, branding, and balance, even the most ambitious sustainability plan will struggle to grow. In both external and internal domains, the message is clear: change is not optional—it is fundamental. Leaders must learn to read the signals, understand their interconnections, and respond not with fragmented initiatives but with integrated, system-aware strategies.

Next, we'll explore the **challenges** these change agents face when trying to implement sustainability transformation.

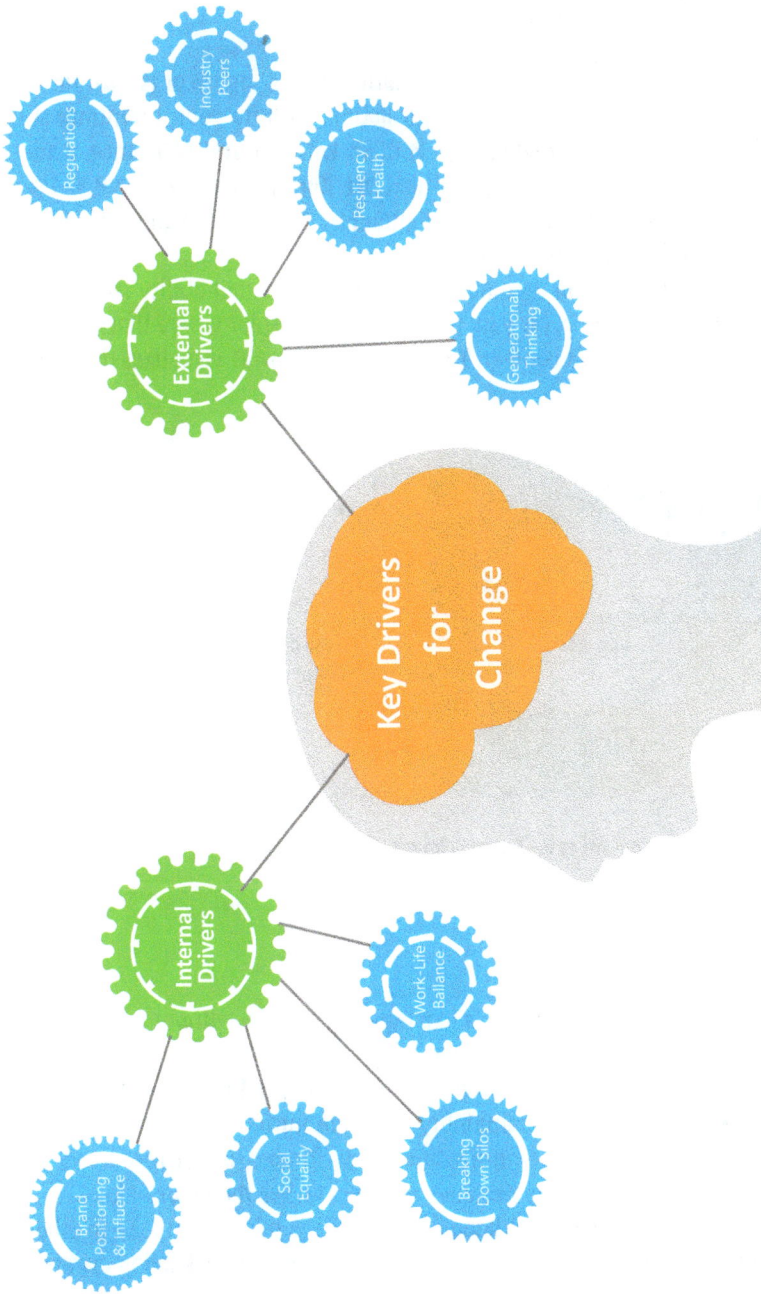

Figure 10: Interview Findings Key Drivers for Change (Source: Author).

7.3 Challenges for Change

Even as the urgency for sustainable transformation grows, many organizations remain stuck—trapped between aspiration and action. Despite good intentions and growing awareness, the road to real change is filled with cultural resistance, leadership hesitancy, and fragmented strategies. These are not just organizational snags—they are symptoms of deeper systemic misalignments. To move beyond the surface, we need to understand what's underneath.

This section will unpack the core obstacles that keep sustainability from taking root and offer reflection prompts for you, the reader, to consider where these barriers may be showing up in your own context. The following Figure 11 visualizes these challenges:

Figure 11: Interview Findings Challenges for Change (Source: Author).

7.3.1 Lack of Leadership Support

Sustainability without senior leadership is like building a house without a foundation. It might look promising at first, but it won't hold.

One of the most significant barriers to transformation is **insufficient buy-in at the top**. When executives treat sustainability as a side initiative, something nice to have rather than a strategic priority, it becomes underfunded, under-resourced, and ultimately, ineffective. Sustainability becomes a project rather than a principle.

Leaders must model the behavior, language, and vision they want to see in others. They are the culture-setters. Without visible commitment, efforts risk being dismissed as greenwashing or superficial compliance. There's also a mindset gap to confront: many traditional leaders are trained to optimize for short-term returns. But sustainability demands something more—an ability to hold long-term vision, systemic interdependence, and adaptive resilience.

Pause and Consider: How does leadership in your organization signal what matters? Is sustainability seen as central to success or a checkbox?

Leaders are the culture-setters. If they hesitate, so will the rest of the organization.

7.3.2 Cultural Barriers and Challenges

Culture shapes what people believe is possible. And in many organizations, the culture is still catching up to the sustainability imperative.

Cultural barriers often run deeper than policy. They show up in how people relate to change, how decisions are made, and how safe it is to speak up. Some of the most common obstacles include:

- **Fear of change:** Uncertainty can make people defensive. Sustainability, by nature, disrupts the status quo. Think of the following: Employees may fear job loss, increased workload, or the ambiguity of new expectations.
- **Siloed thinking:** Departments act as islands. Collaboration is rare. Opportunities are missed. If departments operate in isolation, it makes collaboration difficult and systems-level understanding rare.
- **Resistance to feedback:** Growth requires learning. But in rigid cultures, mistakes are punished, not explored. Remember: Sustainability requires iterative learning and accountability. Cultures that punish mistakes or ignore stakeholder input are incompatible with such openness.
- **Lack of psychological safety:** When employees don't feel safe to experiment or share ideas, innovation withers. Transformative change depends on shared trust and vulnerability.

Overcoming these barriers means cultivating a new kind of culture—one rooted in trust, shared purpose, and ongoing learning. It requires leaders and teams to rethink how they show up, how they listen, and how they co-create. To transform these cultural barriers, organizations must move beyond top-down mandates. They must build change from the inside-out—embedding new norms, rituals, and conversations at every level of the organization.

Pause and Consider: Where in your organization is it unsafe to question or innovate? What would it take to turn that around?

Think of culture like soil. If it's compacted, dry, or full of toxins, nothing new can take root. But when it's tended to—with care, nourishment, and openness—growth becomes inevitable.

7.3.3 Lack of a Holistic Strategy

Too often, sustainability work starts with energy audits or diversity workshops. These efforts matter, but when disconnected from a broader strategy, they rarely lead to transformation. This common stumbling block is the **absence of a unified, systemic approach**.

Without a holistic approach, organizations struggle to connect the dots between what they say and what they do. For example, if organizations cannot see how their operations, supply chains, governance structures, and stakeholder relationships interconnect, they may unintentionally create contradictions, promoting ethical sourcing while maintaining exploitative labor practices in other areas. This leads to:

–   **Contradictions** (ethical sourcing in one area, exploitative labor in another)
–   **Fragmentation** (multiple projects without alignment)
–   **Strategic fatigue** (teams lose energy when they don't see progress)

A holistic strategy integrates vision, culture, operations, and leadership into a single, coherent direction. It helps people understand the "why" and the "how."

What does a holistic strategy look like?

–   A clearly articulated purpose and set of values
–   Aligned internal systems and decision-making structures
–   Practical tools that bridge aspiration and execution
–   Mechanisms for reflection, feedback, and continuous learning

This is the space where the IDT framework becomes indispensable. It offers a system-aware, human-centered architecture for bridging what's missing—and making what matters truly actionable.

> *Pause and Consider:* Are your sustainability efforts connected to a shared purpose—or just a set of disconnected actions? What's one area where more strategic alignment could unlock progress?

Imagine trying to assemble furniture with pieces from different sets, no instructions, and missing screws. That's what fragmented strategy feels like. But with a clear design (and the right tools), everything clicks into place. When these challenges are named, they can be transformed. Instead of roadblocks, they become invitations—to reimagine leadership, re-center culture, and rebuild strategy from the inside out.

In the next section, we'll explore how to take these insights forward and begin preparing your organization—and yourself—for meaningful, sustained change through the application of the IDT framework.

7.4 Thoughts and Considerations

The journey toward sustainability is not just about implementing new systems or processes—**it's about transforming organizational consciousness**. As we've seen throughout this chapter, the path to change is riddled with complexity: competing priorities, cultural resistance, fragmented efforts, and shifting external expectations. But while the challenges are real, so too are the opportunities for redesign, renewal, and reinvention.

This is where the Integral Design Thinking (IDT) framework comes in—not as a step-by-step prescription, but as a **thinking system**. A scaffolding. A compass. It helps leaders navigate this complexity with clarity, coherence, and compassion.

From Fragmentation to Integration

One of the clearest insights from the research is the cost of fragmentation. We can see that there is a necessity to shift from **fragmented efforts** to **integrated systems**. When sustainability efforts are bolted onto existing structures rather than integrated into them, they often falter. Legacy systems resist new values. Well-intentioned strategies lack staying power.

True transformation means **weaving sustainability into the DNA of the organization**—from vision to culture, from governance to stakeholder engagement. The IDT framework provides a lens to explore this integration.

> *Pause and Consider:* Where do fragmentation and alignment show up in your current sustainability efforts? What systems are reinforcing silos? Where are the disconnections between our vision and our systems? How do our values show up in daily practices? Who is included in shaping and driving this change?

Think of your organization like a tapestry—if the threads of purpose, people, and process don't interlace, the weave won't hold. Sustainability needs to be part of the pattern, not an afterthought sewn on. The IDT framework offers a lens through which to explore these questions—focusing not only on external results, but also on internal alignment.

From Top-Down Control to Participatory Leadership

Sustainability cannot thrive through command-and-control leadership. It demands participation. It asks leaders to become facilitators of dialogue, not just distributors of direction. A critical consideration is the **shift in leadership model**. Sustainability requires more than hierarchical decision-making. It calls for **participatory leadership**—

the kind that invites collaboration, honors distributed expertise, and builds psychological safety.

The most resilient organizations co-create change. They build cultures of inclusion and shared purpose. They listen deeply, act collaboratively, and trust the wisdom that emerges from across levels and functions.

Pause and Consider: How are decisions made in your organization? Who gets to shape strategy—and who is left out of the room?

Think of leadership as tending a campfire. You may set the spark, but the fire only grows when others gather, feed it, and keep it alive. For organizations this involves:
- Encouraging dialogue across departments and levels
- Recognizing the power of bottom-up insight
- Training leaders to be facilitators and listeners, not just directors

Organizations that succeed in embedding sustainability are those that **co-create change**—they build coalitions of shared purpose, allowing ownership and accountability to take root across the system.

From Fixed Plans to Adaptive Learning

In a world where climate policy, public expectations, and market dynamics are constantly shifting, fixed strategies quickly become obsolete. In traditional change models, plans are set, timelines are followed, and deviation is discouraged. But sustainability exists in a rapidly evolving landscape. Climate, technology, regulation, and social expectations shift constantly. Instead, what's needed is a **learning mindset**—one that embraces iteration, experimentation, and feedback.

Design thinking reinforces this by replacing linear planning with prototyping, sensing, and discovery. It allows organizations to respond—not just react—and to do so with agility and intentionality.

Pause and Consider: Where are you holding onto certainty, where curiosity might serve you better?

Think of your strategy not as a map, but as a compass. It doesn't give you the path, it helps you navigate the unknown. Organizations must adopt a **learning mindset**—embracing agility, experimentation, and feedback.

The IDT framework integrates this philosophy. It encourages:
- Prototyping over perfection
- Iteration over linearity
- Discovery over assumption

Design thinking as a core methodology reinforces this adaptive approach. It helps leaders and teams stay connected to user needs, sense shifts in the environment, and continuously refine their strategies.

From Functional Success to Purposeful Impact

Perhaps the most vital consideration of all is **purpose**, and that compliance is not enough. Sustainability cannot be reduced to compliance, cost savings, or reputation management. At its heart, is about legacy—what we leave behind for future generations. It is a commitment to **future generations**, to **shared well-being**, and to **systems integrity**.

Purpose-driven organizations align strategy with values. They design experiences that matter. And they measure what counts: well-being, inclusion, resilience, and trust.

> **Pause and Consider:** What does "impact" mean in your organization? How do you know when you're creating value that matters?

A lighthouse doesn't chase ships—it stands anchored in its purpose, guiding others by the light it emits. Purpose must become your organization's north star. Organizations that lead with purpose:

= Align strategy with values
= Design experiences that matter
= Measure what truly counts (example: well-being, resilience, equity)

These organizations recognize that profitability and sustainability are not opposites— they are mutually reinforcing when grounded in authentic purpose.

Conclusion: Preparing the Ground for IDT

What the findings make clear—from case studies, interviews, and literature—is this: the sustainability landscape is shifting rapidly, and so must the mindset of organizations. The leaders who will thrive are those who can **adapt, integrate**, and **design with empathy**. They recognize that their people are not just implementers—they are the most vital resource in shaping the future.

This chapter has laid the groundwork for that shift. It has named the internal and external drivers, explored the barriers, and hinted at what a more integrated future could look like. The Integral Design Thinking (IDT) framework is offered as a dynamic tool to help guide that future.

In the chapters ahead, we'll bring the framework to life—through principles, tools, and applications. Together, we'll explore how to lead through complexity with greater coherence, compassion, and courage.

Because as we've seen, change doesn't start with a plan. It starts with a shift in how we think, listen, relate, and lead.

Change isn't a switch to be flipped—it's a landscape to be walked, step by intentional step, with a map you sketch as you go and a compass you learn to trust.

Let's keep walking.

8 Integral Design Thinking (IDT) Strategy Framework

From Knowing to Doing: Designing the Architecture of Change

Everything we've explored so far—design thinking, strategy, change management, systems thinking, and the evolving landscape of sustainability leadership—has been building toward this moment. If the earlier chapters were about tuning your awareness, challenging your assumptions, and expanding your lens, this chapter is about grounding all that insight into action.

Because insight without application is a missed opportunity. And in this space—where urgency meets possibility—we need both.

This is where the **Integral Design Thinking (IDT) Holistic Strategy Framework** steps in. Not as a silver bullet, but as a blueprint for how real change takes hold. Developed through research, lived experience, and pattern recognition across literature and practice, IDT is designed to meet sustainability leaders exactly where they are—navigating complexity, pushing against resistance, and seeking coherence in a sea of competing priorities.

If you're here, chances are you're trying to lead in a space where the rules are still being written. Maybe you're building something from scratch. Maybe you're trying to transform what already exists. Either way, the path likely feels unclear. You may be wondering:

How do I start? Where do I focus? And how do I make change stick when the system keeps pushing back?

You're not alone. One of the biggest barriers I've seen in sustainability and culture change work is the lack of a shared roadmap. Too often, change agents are tasked with leading transformation—but aren't given the language, tools, or organizational permission to do it well.

That's why this framework exists.

What IDT Is (and Isn't)

The IDT Strategy Framework is more than a diagram—it's a way of thinking. A way of acting. A way of designing systems that are both structurally sound and socially resonant. It's built around six interconnected imperatives (visually represented in Figure 12) that support transformation at both strategic and human levels:
1. **Design Thinking – Core Imperative 1**
2. **Communication – Core Imperative 2**

https://doi.org/10.1515/9783111705286-009

3. **Community = Core Imperative 3**
4. **Branding = Core Imperative 4**
5. **Empathy and Shared Language = Core Imperative 5**
6. **Holistic Design Thinking Methodology = Core Imperative 6**

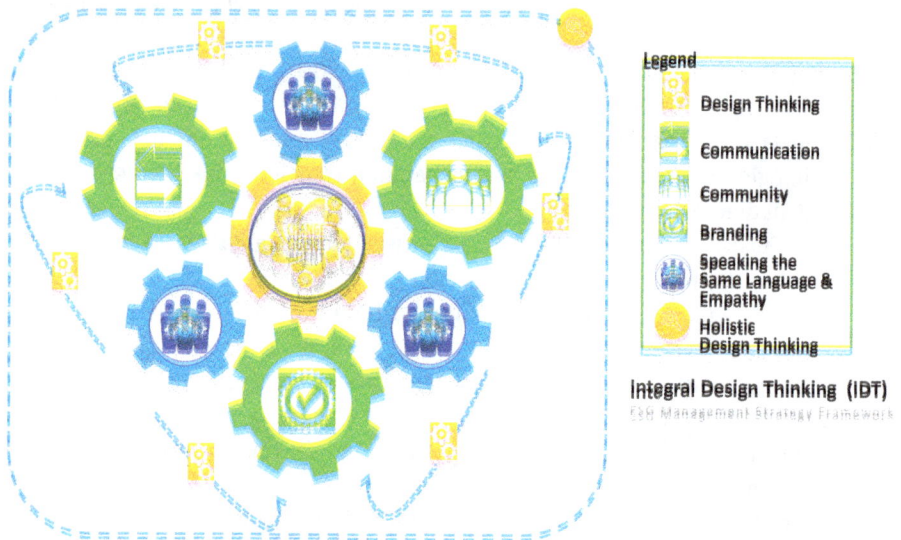

Figure 12: Final areas of the Integral Design Thinking Strategy Framework (Source: Author).

Together, these imperatives form a system—like the interlocking gears of a well-tuned machine. Each part reinforces the others, and when one falters, the whole system feels it. But when aligned, they create a resilient, responsive pathway to culture change that's as practical as it is purposeful.

Pause and Consider: Which of these elements already exists in your organization's change efforts? Which ones feel overlooked or underused? (Use the template to help in the assessment.)

A Framework Designed for Practice

This framework wasn't created in isolation. It was built to address real-world constraints and challenges—those raised by ESG leaders, change agents, and practitioners

navigating barriers like siloed thinking, cultural resistance, and the overwhelming demand for proof before action. It's informed by the gaps they voiced:
= A lack of holistic, actionable tools
= Disconnection between values and operations
= A desire for integration, not fragmentation

The IDT framework responds by offering not just a structure, but a strategy—and not just a strategy, but a shift in mindset. Figure 13 aids in the visualization of how IDT framework can support ESG integration.

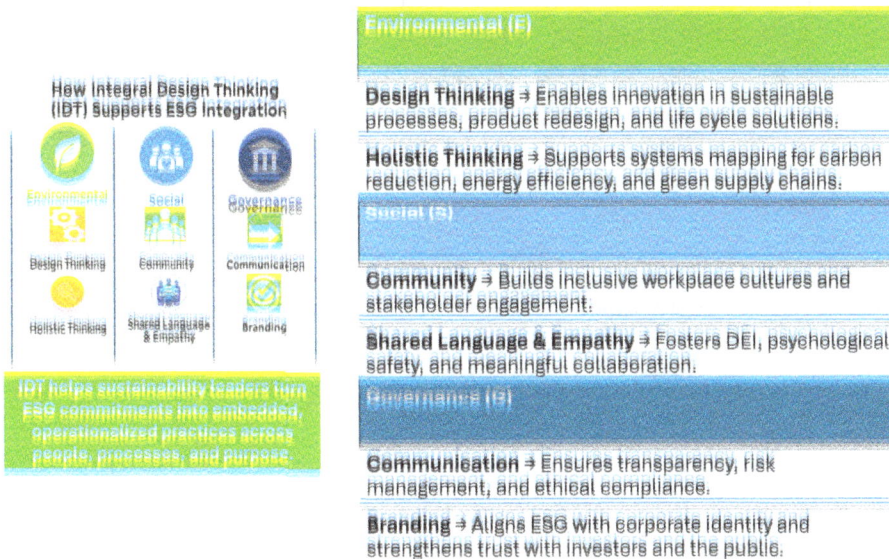

Figure 13: How IDT Supports ESG Integration (Source: Author).

Each phase of the framework is supported by tools drawn from the best thinking in the field (These will be discussed in chapter 9), including:
= The **Interaction Matrix**, adapted from Wilber's *Integral Vision*
= The **Building Purpose** tool, drawn from Scharmer's *U Theory*
= The **Intervention Map**, inspired by Doppelt's *Seven Interventions for Sustainability*
= The **Design Value Creation Canvas**, based on Laszlo's *Eight Disciplines of Value Creation*

These tools don't stand alone—they are embedded within the framework, aligned with the change journey of an organization and its people.
Think of the IDT framework as a loom. The imperatives are the warp and weft—the vertical and horizontal threads—while the tools are your shuttle, weaving together intention, insight, and action into a fabric strong enough to hold transformation.

Why This Framework Matters Now

What this research found—what practitioners confirmed again and again—is that sustainable transformation isn't just about what you do. It's about **how** you do it. It's about seeing the system, naming the barriers, and designing a strategy that brings people along, not just pushes them forward.

Most sustainability initiatives fail not because they lack vision—but because they lack coherence.

The IDT framework fills that gap. It's a bridge between knowing and doing. Between theory and reality. Between aspiration and integration.

And it's meant to be used—by you.

In the pages ahead, we'll walk through each of the six imperatives. You'll learn what they mean, why they matter, and how to bring them to life in your context. You'll also find examples, questions for reflection, and tools to support your work. Because frameworks don't work unless people do—and people don't move unless they see themselves in the process.

> *Pause and Consider:* What would it take for your organization to become truly "integral" in its approach to sustainability? Where might you begin?

So let's begin—by laying the foundation for something not only functional, but transformative.

8.1 Design Thinking and Holistic Design Thinking Methodology (HDTM)

In today's interconnected world, sustainability challenges don't show up neatly labeled or confined to a single department. They ripple—through climate, culture, infrastructure, leadership, and lived experience. Addressing them demands more than a toolkit. It demands a shift in how we see, think, and engage. This is where **Design Thinking (Core Imperative 1)** steps in—not just as a process but as a mindset (visualized in Figure 14).

Design Thinking is a human-centered methodology that emerged from the intersection of design and business strategy. It helps organizations tackle "wicked problems"—the kind that don't have one right answer, but require iterative discovery, dialogue, and co-creation. But here's the catch: traditional DT, while powerful, isn't always enough when it comes to the multilayered demands of sustainability transformation.

Design Thinking was born at the crossroads of innovation and empathy—helping teams navigate ambiguity through iteration, collaboration, and user insight. But as I observed in my research and case studies, when it comes to large-scale cultural and sustainability transformation, traditional DT often doesn't go far enough. It is a neces-

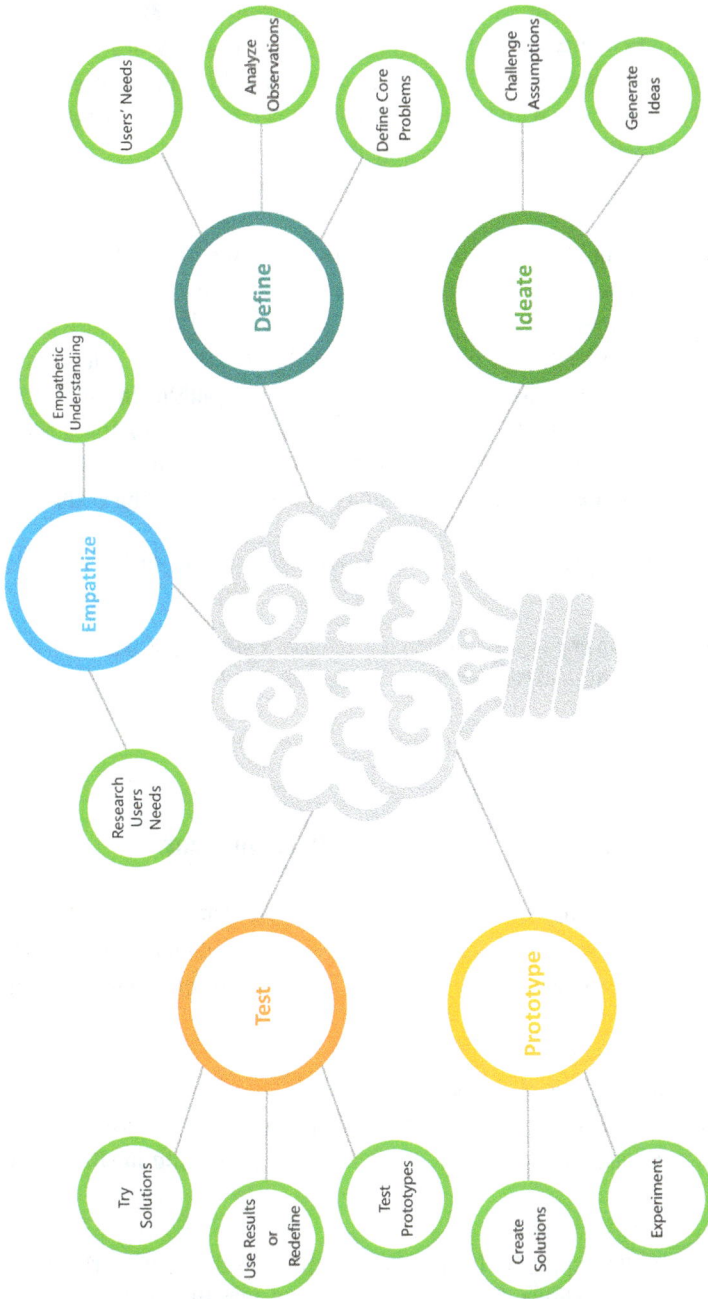

Figure 14: Design Thinking Methodology (Source: Author).

sary mindset that everyone needs to embrace, but as a methodology, it needs to evolve. **Design Thinking (DT)** is not just a methodology, but as a way of being. And yet, even this celebrated approach, with its creative agility and human-centered lens, sometimes falls short when faced with the scale and entanglement of ESG transformation. That's why this framework takes things a step further.

It's one thing to prototype a product. It's another to reimagine systems of power, voice, and value.

That realization led to the development of the **Holistic Design Thinking Methodology (HDTM = Core Imperative 6)**—a next-generation approach that weaves together the best of design thinking, systems theory, and action learning. HDTM was born from practice: from case study work across sectors, from gaps that real leaders voiced, and from the need for a method that could hold complexity without defaulting to simplification. HDTM isn't just about solving problems creatively. It's about aligning those solutions with the deeper purpose and operational DNA of the organization, especially when the stakes include climate resilience, social equity, and long-term cultural change.

> *Pause and Reflect:* Are you solving problems in isolation—or are you seeing how those problems are connected to something deeper?
>
> Think of traditional Design Thinking as a spotlight—it helps you illuminate a specific issue. Holistic Design Thinking is a constellation—it connects stars into a system, showing you how everything relates.

Let's pause here. Because this distinction matters.

What Makes Holistic Design Thinking Methodology (HDTM) Different?

HDTM (visualized in Figure 15) begins where DT ends: by looking at the system before diving into the solution. While conventional DT moves from problem to prototype, **HDTM** zooms out before it zooms in. and **asks three grounding questions before any ideation begins**:

= *What system are we a part of?*
= *Whose voices are missing from this process?*
= *How do our internal culture, leadership structures, and external pressures interact to shape what's possible?* Then—and only then—do we move into ideation and intervention.

This isn't just a philosophical upgrade. It's a necessary recalibration for working inside complex, adaptive organizations. The HDTM is reflective, iterative, and rigorously grounded in three lenses:

1. **Design Science Research (DSR)** = Guides the creation of tangible tools and frameworks that address real-world challenges, not just theoretical ones. This guides the development of practical, testable tools that respond to real organizational challenges.
2. **Action Research (AR)** = Centers learning by doing—engaging practitioners in a cycle of reflection, experimentation, and adaptation, which brings learning-by-doing into the heart of strategy development.
3. **Complex Adaptive Systems (CAS)** = Recognizes that change is nonlinear, organizations are ecosystems, and success often lies in emergence—not control thinking; we need to embraces the messy, dynamic nature of organizations navigating sustainability transitions.

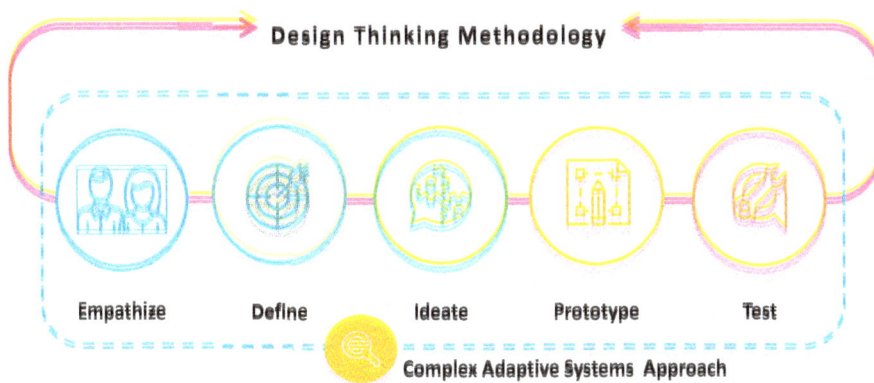

Figure 15: Holistic Design Thinking Methodology (Source: Author).

Together, these perspectives enable a form of design that sees the whole organization, values every stakeholder, and anticipates the unexpected. This approach is about co-creating change rather than imposing it. It's about moving from "fixing" problems to cultivating new capacities—within people, systems, and culture. It honors the messiness of reality, while still striving toward coherence and purpose.

In HDTM, empathy isn't a soft add-on; it's the strategic core. Not only do we empathize with the end-user (as traditional DT encourages), but we extend that empathy to employees, leadership, communities, and even the planet itself. That's what makes it integral.

Pause and Reflect: What if your organization's next solution didn't start with "fixing a problem" but with asking: What's the deeper pattern we're part of?

The Five Core Stages—Still Present, Now Evolved

HDTM retains the essential logic of the five-stage DT process—*Empathize, Define, Ideate, Prototype, and Test*—but stretches it into a broader arc of systems engagement. Each step is deepened, contextualized, and connected to organizational culture.

Here's how HDTM reimagines the DT journey:

– **Empathize** becomes more expansive: not just about users, but employees, communities, ecosystems.
– **Define** includes mapping root causes and systemic feedback loops, not just problem statements.
– **Ideate** is enriched with stakeholder voices across the organization—not just the design team.
– **Prototype** honors lived experience, co-creation, and culture readiness.
– **Test** embraces iteration as ongoing transformation—not a one-off event.

When implemented, HDTM becomes a practical guide for navigating the turbulence of organizational change. It has been successfully piloted through case studies in both public and private sectors—from winegrowers on Long Island to sustainability offices in New York City schools, to real estate firms rethinking their ESG positioning.

What I learned across all these contexts is this: Leaders are ready for transformation, but they need a map—and HDTM offers one. Not as a rigid formula, but as a compass pointing toward a more adaptive, participatory, and purposeful way of designing strategy. And perhaps most importantly, **HDTM encourages returning to the beginning as new information surfaces**.

> *Try This:* As you read, sketch your current sustainability challenge as a system. Where does it begin? Where are the tensions? Who's affected?

In the next sections, we'll dive deeper into the strategic elements that support HDTM in practice: from communication and branding to community engagement and empathy. But it all begins here—with a design methodology that sees the whole picture, values people at every level, and guides organizations not just to do better, but to *be* better.

8.2 Communication, Branding, and Community

Communication, Branding, and Community are the Trinity of Transformation. Let's start with the first with **Communication (Core Imperative 2).**

If strategy is the map, then **communication is the terrain**—the living, shifting landscape through which people find meaning, direction, and belonging. It's how we navigate complexity, make meaning, and build trust. And in sustainability leadership, no amount of visionary planning will matter if no one can *see* themselves in the story.

Let's start with a truth: **Communication is not just messaging—it's meaning-making.**

It's the alchemy that turns jargon into clarity, values into action, and abstract concepts like ESG into something you can feel in the hallway or see in how meetings are run. Effective sustainability leaders understand this. They don't just broadcast; they listen, translate, and co-create understanding across silos, departments, and mindsets. They understand that this isn't just about talking *at* people. It's about creating feedback loops, honoring different forms of knowledge, and building dialogue.

Pause and Reflect: When was the last time your organization felt aligned—not just on what to do, but why it matters?

Communication: From **Transmission** to **Transformation**

In the interviews and case studies, communication consistently emerged as a barrier—or a breakthrough. Initiatives stalled when communication was fragmented, unclear, or overly top-down. But when leaders created genuine *channels*—two-way, iterative, inclusive communication—things changed.

In one case, sustainability champions across departments were trained not just in the content of an initiative, but in how to tell its story. They weren't told *what* to say—they were invited to find their voice within a shared purpose. That's how internal buy-in was built: through ownership, not compliance.

Communication in sustainability is like irrigation in a garden—you don't just water one part and hope for growth. You need consistent flow, all the way to the roots.

Consider and Reflect: All the imperatives rely on each other, try to understand and connect how these cogs work together.

Branding (Core Imperative 3) is the culture you can see. In the Integral Design Thinking framework, branding isn't about colors or logos. **It's about identity.** Who are we as an organization? What do we *stand for*—and how is that reflected in what people experience every day? It is both **internal and external to the organization**.

Branding becomes a powerful internal compass when it aligns with values, tone, and lived behaviors. A sustainability brand done well acts like a cultural artifact—it tells a story that reinforces strategic priorities, makes values visible, and builds emotional connection. It fosters internal alignment and signals to the outside world: *this is what we care about, and here's how we show up.* Microsoft's transformation under Satya Nadella is a perfect example. The redefined mission—*"to empower every person and every organization on the planet to achieve more"*—wasn't just a rebranding effort. It was **a re-anchoring of purpose**. From there, communication strategies, leadership alignment, and reporting structures followed.

Pause and Reflect: *If someone walked into your organization today, would your sustainability ethos be obvious in what they see, hear, and feel?*

Strong branding creates **psychological safety**. It says: *we know who we are.* And that consistency helps people trust the journey—even when the terrain gets rough. Think of it this way: when your sustainability team speaks, do they sound like the rest of the organization? Do their actions, tone, and initiatives align with your broader strategy? If not, there's a gap—and your brand can help close it.

If Brand is the culture you can see, then **Community (Core Imperative 4) is the culture you can feel**. Community is often misunderstood as "outreach." I am not talking about the external "community outreach" sense (though that matters too), but internally—your teams, departments, and leadership need to feel like part of something greater. Building community means cultivating spaces for co-creation, feedback, and participation. In organizations applying IDT, **community is practice.** It's the way culture becomes tangible, this transformation happens in the **spaces between people:**

= The lunchroom conversation where someone first hears about a pilot initiative.
= The cross-functional working group where a skeptical manager becomes an unlikely advocate.
= The internal storytelling event that helps someone feel seen—and, maybe for the first time, hopeful.

Building these spaces requires intention. It means designing feedback loops, inviting dissent, and elevating lived experience alongside data. **Community** doesn't just support transformation—it *is* **transformation**. In my research this came up again and again: initiatives succeeded where communities were engaged early and often, and where communication was designed to *include*, not just inform. Leaders who embraced branding as a cultural exercise, not just a marketing function—were able to shift perception and behavior more effectively. And those who built internal communities of practice created resilience and adaptability, even in moments of uncertainty.

So, what does this mean for you, as a sustainability leader or change agent?

= **Make communication two-way:** Use tools like feedback loops, open Q&As, and internal listening sessions to deepen understanding. **Communication** is how people know what's happening and why.
= **Develop a values-based brand:** Let your sustainability work become a visible, experiential expression of what matters most. **Branding** is how people recognize your identity and feel proud to be part of it.

= **Foster internal communities**: Build cross-functional working groups, storytelling hubs, and informal spaces for dialogue and peer learning. **Community** is where people belong, contribute, and grow.

Together, these three forces form the social fabric of transformation. They make strategy tangible. They anchor vision in daily life. And when woven through the IDT framework, they become not just methods, but *mindsets*.

> **Try This**: *Start a "sustainability storytelling circle" in your organization.*
>
> *Once a month, invite employees to share small moments where they saw sustainability in action—whether in a decision made, a conversation had, or a challenge overcome. Notice how your culture begins to shift.*

8.3 Speaking the Same Language and Empathy

Speaking the Same Language and Empathy (Core Imperative 5) are the emotional infrastructure of change. These two need to be considered as one unit at all times, and just like a Design Thinking mindset, these need to be in part of the behavior and mindset of all in the organization.

Have you ever been in a room where everyone nodded in agreement—only to walk away realizing that no two people shared the same interpretation?

Welcome to one of the most overlooked challenges in organizational change: **language**.

In sustainability work, misalignment in language isn't just a communications hiccup—it's a strategic barrier. When we say "systems thinking," "resilience," "ESG," or "net-zero," do we mean the same thing? Do we understand how those terms land with someone in finance versus facilities? With the executive team versus front-line staff?

In the Integral Design Thinking (IDT) framework, **"speaking the same language"** doesn't mean using identical words—it means **building shared meaning**. It's about crafting a common vocabulary grounded in clarity, inclusion, and purpose. It's about understanding who you're talking to, how to craft the messaging, and what information they need to become champions of the organization. And in the messy, high-stakes world of sustainability transformation, this kind of clarity isn't optional. It's foundational.

> **Pause and Reflect**: *What terms in your sustainability strategy could mean five different things to five different people?*

I want to stress the importance of **shared language** as it is the **invisible Glue** in an organization. When a team shares language, it shares **expectations**, **understanding**, and **ownership**. But this doesn't happen by accident. It's created—through dialogue, reflection, and the courage to pause and ask:

What do we mean when we say that?

In the IDT framework, shared language becomes the **invisible infrastructure** that allows communication, branding, and community to function. It ensures that your messages are not just heard—but understood, internalized, and acted upon.

In **Case Study 2**, over 50 stakeholders from nonprofits, government, and education came together under the Innovation Council to co-define what sustainability meant for the New York City Department of Education. Only after that shared definition was created could they begin aligning programs, metrics, and communications.

Shared language is the operating system of transformation. If it's glitchy or incompatible, even the best apps—your strategies—will crash.

And then there's **empathy, the strategic core** for transformation. Too often misunderstood as "being nice" or "soft," empathy in this work is **strategic muscle**. It's how we discover what isn't being said. It's how we understand not just what needs to change—but why it's hard to change. Empathy is what transforms strategy from something **done to people**, into something **co-created with them**.

Within the IDT and HDTM frameworks, empathy is both a **starting point and a system-wide practice**. We use it not just to connect with end users, but to deeply understand internal stakeholders, operational realities, emotional climates, and institutional history.

We ask:
– What are our people afraid of?
– What invisible pressures shape how they show up?
– What kind of support do they need to say "yes" to change?

This is more than listening. It's **sensemaking with care**.

In **Case Study 3**, the creation of the *Global Citizen Pledge*—signed by 90% of headquarters staff—was an act of shared language *and* empathy. It clearly communicated what sustainability meant in that specific context, and it asked people to make a personal connection to shared values. That's not policy. That's culture.

Together, They Build Trust and Coherence

When empathy and shared language work together, something remarkable happens:
Trust forms. Walls lower. And change takes root.

This doesn't mean everyone agrees on everything. But it does mean they understand each other and that creates space for authentic dialogue, better decision-making, and inclusive innovation.

As a leader or change agent, this means:

- Don't assume understanding—**create it**.
- Don't just empathize with end users—**practice empathy internally**, across all levels of your organization.
- Use tools like **empathy maps**, **story circles**, and **co-definition exercises** to create shared meaning and emotional resonance.

Pause and Reflect: Where in your organization is the language misaligned? Where might a little more empathy unlock understanding, reduce resistance, or build trust?

In Summary:

- **Shared language** is the bridge between strategy and implementation.
- **Empathy** is the engine that makes that bridge walkable.
- Together, they form the emotional infrastructure of change—ensuring that transformation is felt, not just planned.

These may seem like "soft skills," but in systems transformation, they are your most powerful tools.

8.4 Applying the IDT Framework in Practice

In my framework, **alignment is both a process and an artifact**. It is something we facilitate—through dialogue, workshops, and creative interventions—and it is something we represent visually, so stakeholders can literally see how everything connects.

You've now explored the foundational components of the Integral Design Thinking (IDT) Framework—how design thinking becomes holistic, how communication, branding, and community work together, and how shared language and empathy are critical levers for transformation. But here's the truth: none of these parts mean much without alignment.

Alignment is what transforms ideas into motion.

Alignment in Integral Design Thinking (IDT) doesn't just mean agreement. It means **coherence across levels**—from leadership vision to day-to-day practice, from organizational values to the behaviors that reinforce them. It's the connective tissue that ties strategy, people, systems, and purpose together. Without alignment, even the most beautifully crafted sustainability strategy can feel like it's working *against* the organization rather than through it. Too often in sustainability and ESG leadership, strategy lives in slides while culture lives in hallways.

The IDT framework seeks to close that gap. Again, alignment within this model is not just about organizational consensus—it's about creating *coherence*. From internal beliefs to external behaviors. From individual mindsets to systemic structures. It is, in essence, the connective tissue that allows everything we've discussed to move as a living system.

Pause and Reflect: Where in your organization do people feel the values but not see them in practice?

The IDT Alignment Model: From Fragmentation to Flow

At the heart of this framework lies a visual and strategic model of alignment. It maps coherence across three nested domains (visualized in Figure 16):
1. **Inner Alignment** = Individual purpose, values, and behaviors.
2. **Relational Alignment** = Team norms, collaboration patterns, and communication practices.
3. **Structural Alignment** = Organizational systems, policies, leadership behavior, and cultural rituals.

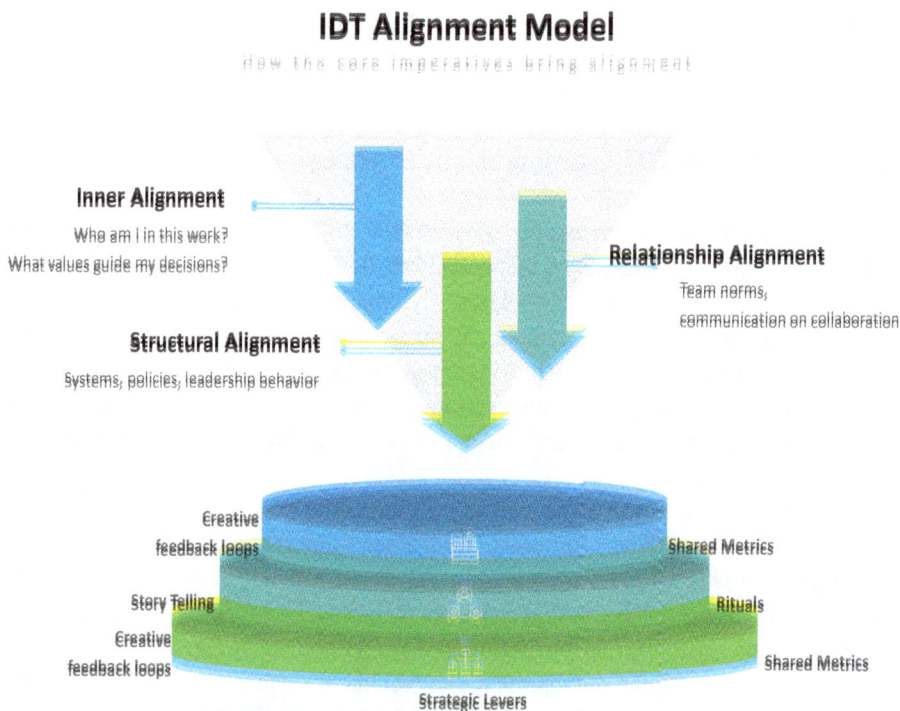

Figure 16: IDT Alignment Model (Source: Author).

Think of your organization like a symphony. Inner alignment is each musician knowing their part. Relational alignment is their ability to listen and play in tune. Structural alignment is the score and conductor bringing them together in harmony. When these layers are aligned, something powerful happens: resistance softens, collaboration increases, and transformation feels natural—not forced. I call this **strategic flow** as seen in Figure 16:

Imagine a series of three concentric circles:
=   The **innermost ring** is *Inner Alignment*, prompting questions like:
    =   "Who am I in this work?"
    =   "What values guide my decisions?"
=   The **middle ring** is *Relational Alignment*, asking:
    =   "How do we collaborate?"
    =   "Where are trust or clarity breaking down?"
=   The **outermost ring** is *Structural Alignment*, addressing:
    =   "Are our systems designed to reinforce our values?"
    =   "Does leadership behavior match the message?"

At the intersections between these rings are the *strategic levers*: **storytelling, rituals, measurements (shared metrics), and creative engagements (Creative feedback loops)**. These tools allow teams to "pulse check" their alignment in real-time.

These become the tools through which alignment is *felt*, not just mapped. As we build the strategic components of the IDT framework, we also need to concurrently make sure these gears are aligned. The IDT Alignment Model enables us to understand the connections and critically analyze these alignments.

Case Examples: Alignment in Action

The real-world application of the IDT alignment model was demonstrated across diverse contexts—from corporate sustainability teams to government agencies and education systems. In my case studies, organizations that used visual alignment tools—like purpose maps, quadrant models, or cross-functional flow charts—found that people understood the "why" behind the change more quickly and could locate themselves *inside* the strategy. Visuals brought coherence. They served as common reference points, especially across departments with different priorities or ways of thinking.

In **Case Study 3** of my research, for instance, alignment was achieved through:
=   A **Global Citizen Pledge** that defined shared sustainability values.
=   Cross-functional **communication channels** that ensured transparency at every level.
=   A rebranding effort that embedded **organizational identity** with purpose and values.

These initiatives weren't isolated—they worked together, nested within the IDT framework, to move the organization from fragmentation to integration. Review Case Study 3- IDT Map for more information. This can be seen in Figures 17, 18, & 19.

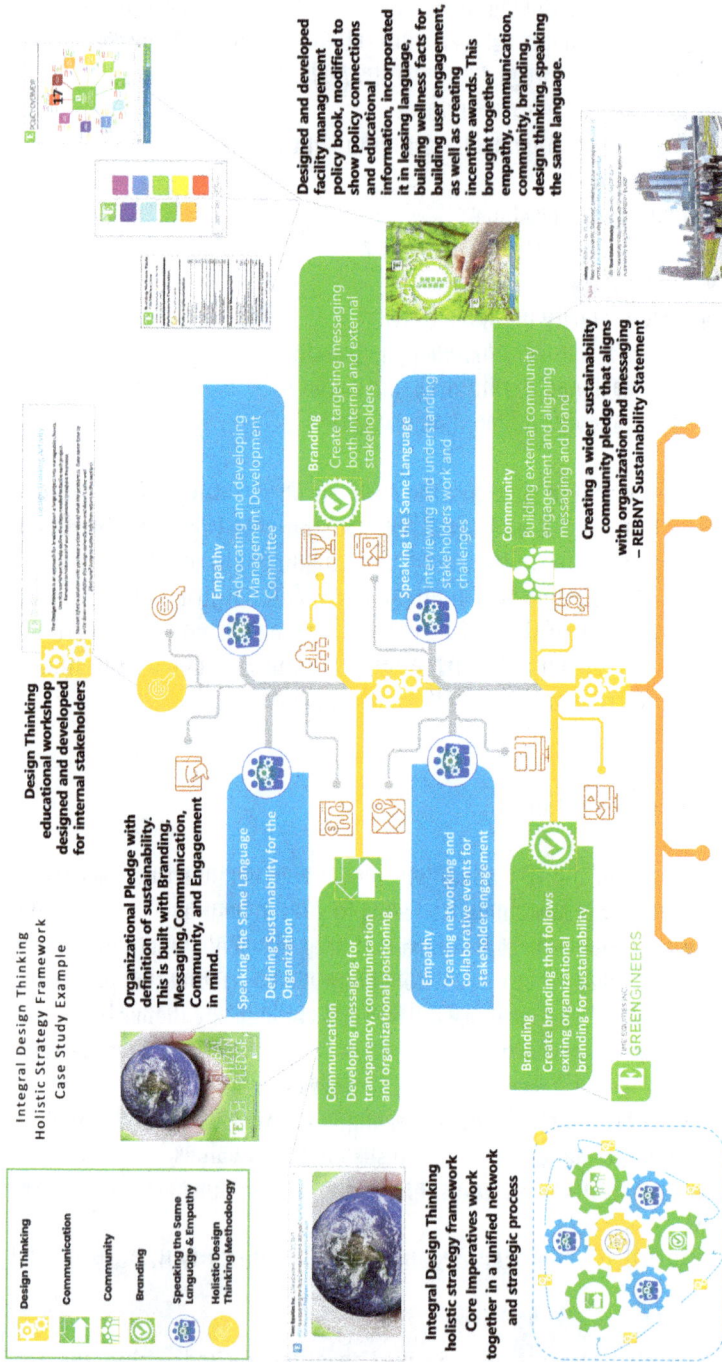

Figure 17: Case Study 3 IDT Map (Source: Author).

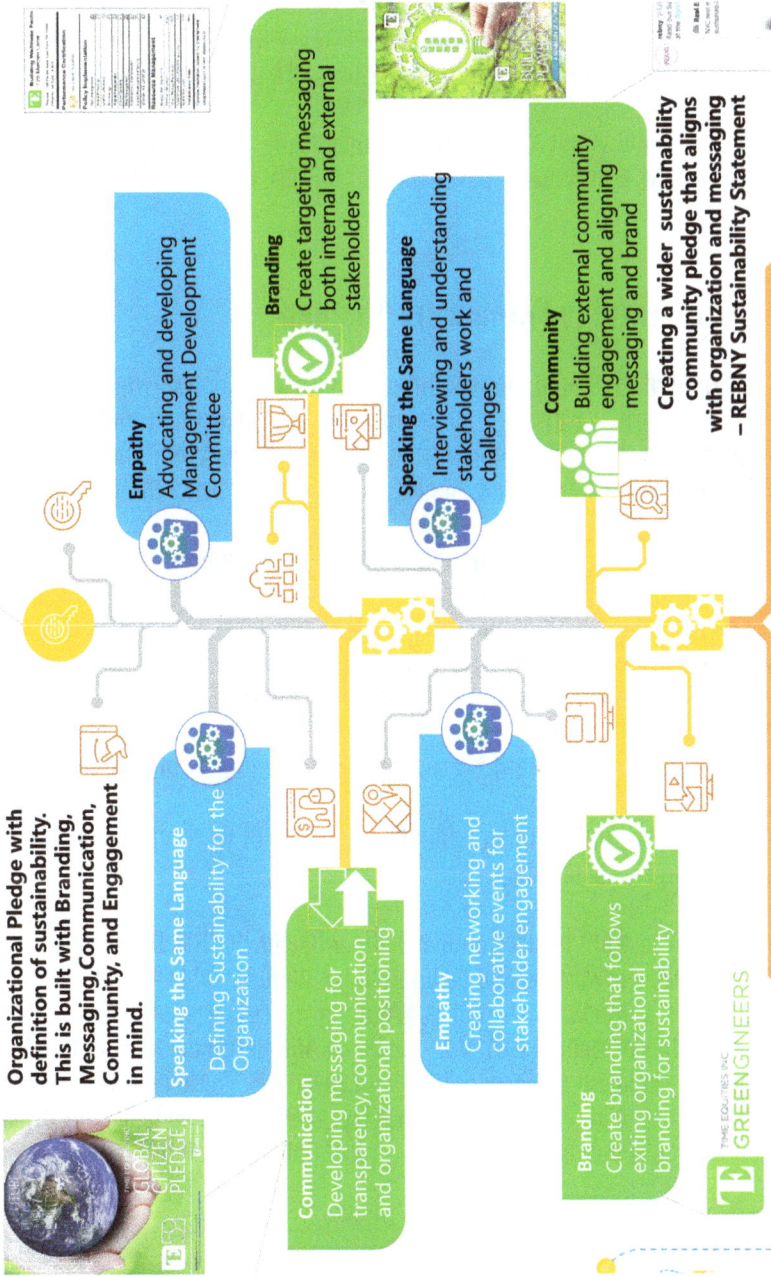

Figure 18: Case Study 3 IDT Map - part 1 (Source: Author).
Figure 19: Case Study 3 IDT Map - part 2 (Source: Author).

By mapping your organization onto this framework, you can identify misalignments—places where people feel disconnected from the vision, where collaboration breaks down, or where policies contradict stated values. And more importantly, you can start to repair those gaps—together.

This alignment model is not a one-and-done diagnostic. It's a living mirror. And when used consistently, it becomes a powerful tool for sustainable cultural transformation.

8.5 IDT Holistic Strategy Framework Toolbox

By now, we've explored the foundations of Integral Design Thinking—what it is, why it matters, and how it creates strategic coherence. But insight without tools is like a compass without a map. That's why this section offers a practical **toolbox**: a curated collection of frameworks, prompts, and models you can use to bring the IDT Holistic Strategy to life in your organization.

Think of this toolbox as a **guide for transformation in motion**. These tools are not plug-and-play solutions. They're designed to be adapted, reinterpreted, and co-created by teams. Their power lies in how they help people make meaning together.

At its heart, the toolbox supports three essential goals:

1. **Making strategy tangible** = Helping teams visualize, test, and adapt strategic ideas in real-time.
2. **Fostering participation** = Creating space for diverse voices to engage meaningfully in change efforts.
3. **Building capacity** = Equipping individuals and teams to work more creatively, empathetically, and systemically.

Each subsection (8.5A to 8.5F) focuses on a specific pillar of the IDT framework and provides relevant tools, worksheets, and facilitation techniques. Table 9 gives an overview of the IDT Core Toolbox. Each tool is grounded in research and field-tested through the case studies presented earlier in the book. And here's the most important thing: this toolbox is not about perfection. It's about **progress**. These tools are here to help you *get started*, not to get it right on the first try. They're here to help your organization move—from fragmentation to alignment, from talking to doing, from aspiration to action.

Table 9: IDT Core Imperative Toolbox Overview.

Section	Focus Area	Outcome
Toolbox Overview		
8.5A	Design Thinking Support Tools	Clarify challenges, prototype solutions, and foster creativity.
8.5B	Communication Support Tools	Align messaging, deepen transparency, open dialogue.
8.5C	Community Support Tools	Build trust, co-create with stakeholders, and foster belonging.
8.5D	Branding Support Tools	Shape identity, express values visually and emotionally.
8.5E	Shared Language & Empathy Support Tools	Build understanding, reduce resistance, strengthen alignment.
8.5F	Holistic Design Thinking Methodology Tools	Integrate systems thinking, design science, and reflection.

8.5A IDT = Design Thinking Support Information

Design Thinking is the entry point to creativity, empathy, and innovation—but it can't just live in theory. It is the front door to possibility. It's where curiosity meets complexity and where sustainability leaders step beyond incrementalism into true transformation. But here's the truth: it's not enough to know *about* Design Thinking. For it to reshape systems, it must become part of everyday conversations, decisions, and culture. That's where this section comes in.

This section offers **practical support tools** that help organizations activate the design thinking mindset across all levels, from identifying root problems to prototyping and iterating solutions. These support tools are designed to make Design Thinking real—not abstract. They are field-tested, human-centered, and flexible enough to meet organizations where they are, whether you're working on ESG strategy, culture change, or reimagining team dynamics. An example of this can be seen in Figure 20, which is a one pager that can be downloaded and utilized to support teams' understanding the intent of this imperative and some considerations to aid in the implementation.

Purpose of These Tools
Use these exercises and prompts to:
- **Empower teams** to think creatively and act courageously in the face of uncertainty.
- **Create structured moments** for reflection, experimentation, and continuous learning.
- **Foster collaboration** across traditional silos and hierarchies.

– **Align innovation** with deeper organizational purpose and sustainability goals.

Pause and Reflect: Where in your organization are solutions being designed without first deeply understanding the problem?

Core Tools and Exercises

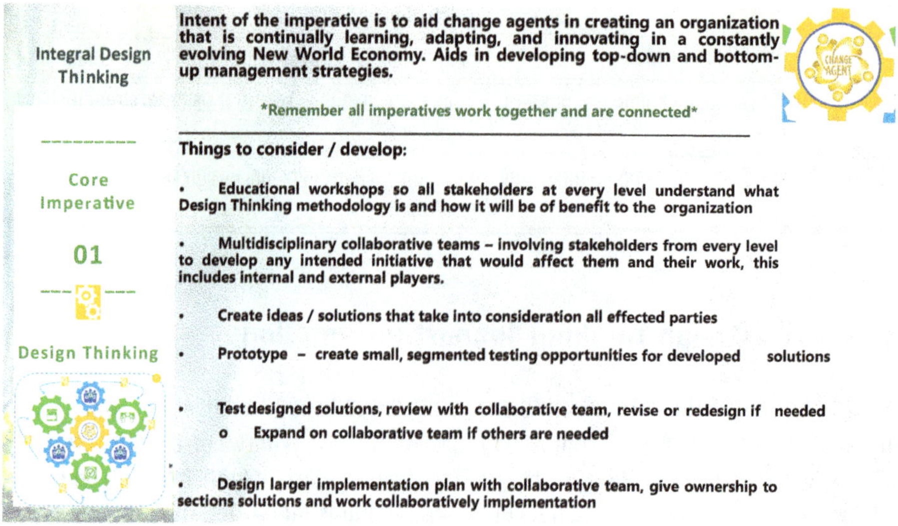

Figure 20: IDT – Design Thinking support information (Source: Author).

The intent of the Design Thinking imperative is to aid change agents in creating an organization that is continually learning, adapting, and innovating in a consistently evolving New World Economy. It will aid in developing top-down and bottom-up management strategies. When looking to implement consider avenues that will educate the organizations' population in the process and methodology. An example would be creation of educational workshops so all stakeholders at every level understand what it is and how it will be of benefit.

In this process, multidisciplinary collaboratives need to be created. These teams should involve stakeholders from every level to develop any intended initiative that would affect them and their work, this should include internal and external players. This way all solutions that are created would have the foresight and understanding of needs and challenges. Also, when testing solutions they should be prototyped in small increments and tested, this way it can be seen if changes need to be made or if other voices need to be brought into a re-ideation stage. This process should give ownership to all involved.

As already stated, Figure 20 was designed help teams start the process and can be used in professional development workshops or for team reflections as strategies are being built. There will be one for every core imperative that can be used individually of with the others to aid in the alignment of all. The following are sample exercises that can be done on an individual level, with a small team, or a larger working group. Remember these are a small example of the creative exercises that can aid organizations.

Sample Exercises
1. **The Challenge Reframing Canvas**
    Use when: Teams are stuck in a solution mindset or misaligned on the real issue.
    Goal: Help people shift from symptoms to root causes.
    Purpose: Surface root causes and shift perspective.

Prompt questions:
–   What problem are we *really* trying to solve?
–   Who feels this issue most directly?
–   What assumptions are we making that might not hold?

Tip: Ask each stakeholder to define the problem from their perspective, then synthesize patterns.

---

2. **Empathy Mapping for Organizational Personas**
    Use when: You want to bring stakeholder voices into strategy design.
    Purpose: Surface root causes and shift perspective.
    Goal: Understand users, employees, or community members on a deeper level.

Map quadrants:
–   What are they hearing?
–   What are they thinking/feeling?
–   What are they seeing?
–   What are they doing?

Adaptation: Compare maps for different stakeholder groups (e.g., frontline staff vs. executives) to uncover disconnects and invisible barriers.

---

3. **Co-Creation Workshop Framework**
   Use when: You need to engage diverse teams in ideation.
   Purpose: Generate aligned, participatory ideas for change.
   Goal: Generate ideas that are desirable, feasible, and aligned with strategic goals.

Structure:
- Warm-up + Context Setting
- Lightning Interviews or Stakeholder Insights
- Brainstorming with time-boxed rounds
- Clustering and voting
- "What would it take?" feasibility mapping

Output: A shortlist of ideas ready for low-risk prototyping.

---

4. **Rapid Prototyping Sprint**
   Use when: You have ideas and need to test them quickly and cheaply.
   Purpose: Learn fast, adapt faster.
   Goal: Learn fast, fail smart, iterate continuously.

Cycle:
- Select 1–2 concepts.
- Create a low-fidelity prototype (paper, storyboard, roleplay).
- Test with 3–5 users or team members.
- Collect insights.
- Adapt and re-test.

Remember: Prototypes are not solutions—they are *questions made tangible.*

---

5. **Reflective Design Retrospectives**
   Use when: You complete a phase or pilot and want to extract learning.
   Purpose: Embed learning into your culture.
   Goal: Institutionalize learning and adjust direction as needed.

Facilitation Guide:
- What worked?
- What didn't?
- What surprised us?
- What succeeded, and why?
- What should we leave behind?
- What's our next best experiment?

Facilitator tip: Invite reflections not just on tasks, but on how people *felt*. This builds psychological safety and trust over time.

═══

Implementation Guidance

Here's how to move from one-off workshops to a living, evolving culture of design:

- **Start small, go deep:** Pilot in one team or department, then scale organically. Normalize experimentation through pilot programs. Use design tools in regular operations—don't isolate them in "innovation teams."
- **Reward learning over perfection:** Normalize smart risk-taking and experimentation. Reward learning (not just results).
- **Visualize insight:** Use whiteboards, murals, or digital canvases to make process and learning visible. Document insights visually to make learning shareable across the organization.
- **Bridge silos:** Mix roles, departments, and perspectives in all DT sessions.
- **Ground in purpose:** Keep asking, "What matters most to the people this will affect?"

These tools are most effective when paired with leadership sponsorship and cross-functional buy-in. They become cultural signals—ways of saying, *"We value curiosity, empathy, and action."*

Real-World Insight: Design Thinking = Case Study 3

In *Case Study 3*, the "Lunch and Learn" initiative became a gateway for embedding DT thinking across the organization. These sessions introduced new frameworks, including sustainability and design thinking, to stakeholders from *every* department—breaking down silos, opening communication, and building new internal alliances.

This led to the formation of an Education Committee and sparked unexpected collaboration between departments that rarely interacted. It wasn't just knowledge sharing—it was culture shaping.

"Design Thinking was our way of seeing each other again—not just as roles, but as people." = [Interviewee from Case Study 3]

8.5B IDT = Communication Support Information

In the landscape of sustainability transformation, communication is more than how we speak—it's how we **align, connect, and lead**. In the Integral Design Thinking (IDT) framework, communication is not treated as a static output, but as a **living system** that evolves in rhythm with the organization. It shapes meaning, influences behavior, and acts as the bridge between values and action.

But here's the key insight: communication isn't one strategy—it's an ecosystem. It stretches across formal messaging, visual design, leadership voice, informal peer dialogue, storytelling, and the unspoken norms that live in organizational culture. When communication breaks down, strategy does too.

If design thinking is how we unlock creative, human-centered solutions, then communication is how we make those solutions **stick, spread, and scale**.

This section provides practical tools to help leaders and teams **design communication as a strategic asset—not an afterthought**.

Communication Tools & Practices

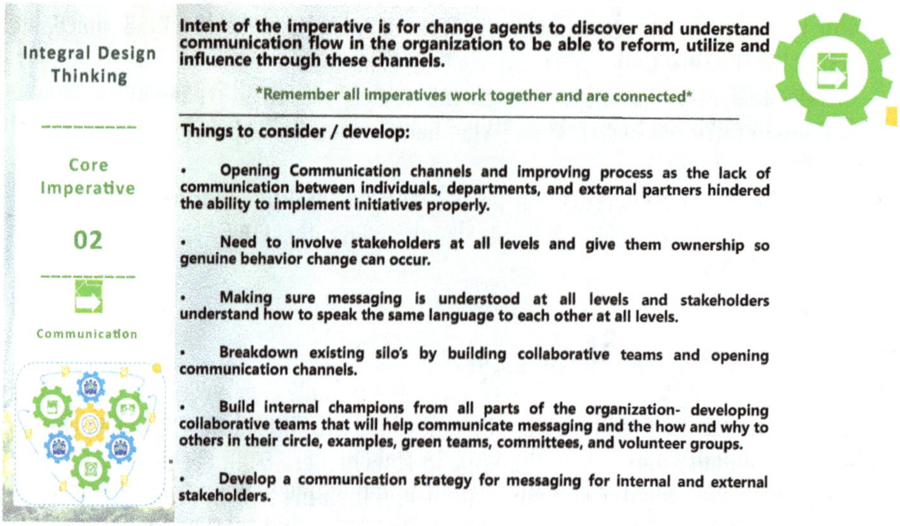

Integral Design Thinking

Core Imperative

02

Communication

Intent of the imperative is for change agents to discover and understand communication flow in the organization to be able to reform, utilize and influence through these channels.

Remember all imperatives work together and are connected

Things to consider / develop:

• Opening Communication channels and improving process as the lack of communication between individuals, departments, and external partners hindered the ability to implement initiatives properly.

• Need to involve stakeholders at all levels and give them ownership so genuine behavior change can occur.

• Making sure messaging is understood at all levels and stakeholders understand how to speak the same language to each other at all levels.

• Breakdown existing silo's by building collaborative teams and opening communication channels.

• Build internal champions from all parts of the organization- developing collaborative teams that will help communicate messaging and the how and why to others in their circle, examples, green teams, committees, and volunteer groups.

• Develop a communication strategy for messaging for internal and external stakeholders.

Figure 21: IDT – Communication support information (Source: Author), pg 168.

The intent of the communication imperative is for change agents to discover and understand communication flow in the organization to be able to reform, utilize, and influence through these channels. Change agents will need to open communication channels and improve if there is a lack of communication between individuals, departments, and external partners, as this would hinder the ability to implement initiatives properly.

As you move into each section remember that all imperatives are connected and have synergies. For example, connection from Design Thinking process of collaboration, bringing a multidisciplinary team together from all levels not only will give them ownership, it will bring understanding of need, the how and the why. These individuals will become the internal/external champions that will help communicate messaging in their departments or area of work. These teams will aid in developing solutions for systems to support proper communications strategies for their area of work.

Figure 21 will be available to be used in professional development workshops or for team reflections as strategies are being built. The following are sample exercises that can be done on an individual level, with a small team, or a larger working group. Remember these are a small example of the creative exercises that can aid organizations.

Sample Exercises
1. **Messaging Alignment Matrix**
   Use when: Teams or departments are using conflicting language or misaligned messaging.
   Goal: Ensure clarity, consistency, and strategic coherence.

How it works:
– Identify key messages (e.g., sustainability goals, culture change intentions).
– Map how these are communicated across audiences (internal, external, leadership, community).
– Spot gaps, inconsistencies, and misalignments.
– Co-develop unified language and adapt per audience.

Tip and Reflection: Revisit this matrix quarterly as your strategy evolves. Where in your organization are different teams saying the same thing . . . differently? Where does this create confusion or mistrust?

---

2. **"Narrative Threads" Storytelling Framework**
   Use when: You need to inspire buy-in or communicate change.
   Goal: Humanize the message and emotionally engage your audience.

Core elements:
– **Start with why** – What's the emotional driver behind the strategy?
– **Show the challenge** – What's at stake? What problem are we facing?
– **Share the vision** – What future are we working toward?
– **End with a call to participation** – How can others contribute to this vision?.

Application: Use in town halls, newsletters, onboarding, and leadership communication. Think of storytelling as the "thread" that stitches values into the fabric of the organization.

3. Visual Language Style Guide
Use when: You want to align the look and feel of sustainability communications.
Goal: Ensure that visual cues reinforce the tone and message of your strategy.

Includes:
= Color palette aligned with core values (e.g., greens for regeneration, neutrals for equity, blues for trust).
= Iconography or visuals for key pillars (ESG, IDT, community, etc.).
= Templates for slides, reports, and internal communications.

Why it matters: Visual consistency builds **cognitive trust** and makes abstract strategies feel concrete and actionable.

4. Feedback Loop System Map
Use when: Communication is flowing one-way, you're missing stakeholder input, and you need deeper engagement.
Goal: Build feedback mechanisms to gather input, respond, and adapt in real time.

Component Examples:
= Pulse surveys with space for narrative responses
= Real-time anonymous suggestion tools (digital or in-person)
= Quarterly listening sessions with executive sponsors
= Regular feedback summaries shared back with action updates; Example "you said / we did" transparency.

Facilitator Tips and Outcome: Co-design this system with multiple departments—don't build it in isolation. This will build trust, transparency, and a culture of responsiveness. Think of your communication system like a circulatory system—are ideas flowing or getting blocked?

5. Communication Pulse Audit
Use when: Engagement is lagging or confusion is high. You suspect communication isn't landing, or engagement is low.
Goal: Rapidly assess the health of your communication system.

Audit Questions:
- Are we clear on our sustainability vision and why it matters? Is it understood at all levels?
- Where is communication strongest? Where is it weakest? Can staff articulate our goals in their own words?
- Are we using language that resonates or alienates? Where is information flowing easily? Where is it blocked?
- Are we listening as much as we're speaking?

Facilitator's note: Host this as a workshop or roundtable with cross-functional reps to uncover blind spots.

Implementation Guidelines

To truly integrate communication into your IDT strategy:
- Make it **co-owned**: Communication shouldn't sit only with HR or Comms—it belongs to everyone. **Co-owned** by both leadership and employees.
- Keep it **iterative**: As your strategy evolves, so must your communication. **Iterative**, not static—adjusted as the organization learns and grows.
- Make it **accessible**: Avoid jargon, use visuals, and translate complex concepts into everyday language. **Accessible**, meaning free of jargon, visually inviting, and translatable across roles and departments.
- Link it to **rituals**: Embed key messages into team meetings, onboarding, performance reviews, and annual events.

Remember, communication is a *relationship*. These tools are designed to strengthen that relationship—so that strategy doesn't just live in documents, but lives in conversation.

Real-World Insight: Design Thinking = Case Study 2 & 3

In Research Case Studies 2 and 3, communication silos stifled the early adoption of sustainability efforts. Success came when communication became two-way—when "hallway conversations" were seen as valuable as all-staff emails. Working groups, interdepartmental learning sessions, and peer storytelling helped shift communication from transactional to transformational.

*Pause and Reflect: Before you move on, consider: Where is your organization communicating **about** change, but not creating space to **listen** to it? What hidden assumptions live inside your language that could be clarified, reframed, or reimagined?*

Remember: In IDT, communication isn't just an enabler of strategy—it *is* strategy. It's how culture is built in real time.

8.5C IDT – Community Support Information

If sustainability is the **goal**, and strategy is the **path**, then **community** is the engine that carries us forward.

In the **Integral Design Thinking (IDT)** framework, community is not an afterthought. It's not just something you build around an initiative—it *is* the initiative. Community is a mindset. It's the connective fabric of relationships, values, participation, and trust that holds transformation in place long enough to take root.

Whether you're working with employees, partners, board members, or customers, transformation doesn't happen in isolation. It happens through **relationships**—through the conversations in hallways, the informal Slack threads, the celebratory rituals, and the shared sense that *we're in this together*.

And here's the truth: **community is not built once. It is continually cultivated.** That's what makes it a practice.

This section offers tools and structures to help you foster internal and external communities that are resilient, participatory, and aligned with your sustainability purpose—because in a world full of uncertainty, **community is the strategy that endures.**

Community Engagement Tools

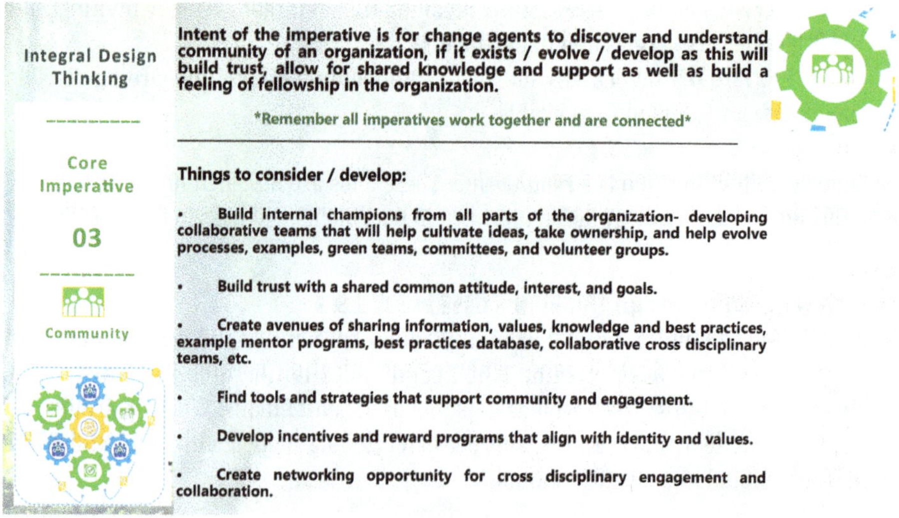

Integral Design Thinking

Intent of the imperative is for change agents to discover and understand community of an organization, if it exists / evolve / develop as this will build trust, allow for shared knowledge and support as well as build a feeling of fellowship in the organization.

Remember all imperatives work together and are connected

Core Imperative

03

Community

Things to consider / develop:

- Build internal champions from all parts of the organization- developing collaborative teams that will help cultivate ideas, take ownership, and help evolve processes, examples, green teams, committees, and volunteer groups.

- Build trust with a shared common attitude, interest, and goals.

- Create avenues of sharing information, values, knowledge and best practices, example mentor programs, best practices database, collaborative cross disciplinary teams, etc.

- Find tools and strategies that support community and engagement.

- Develop incentives and reward programs that align with identity and values.

- Create networking opportunity for cross disciplinary engagement and collaboration.

Figure 22: IDT – Community support information (Source: Author).

The intent of the community imperative is for change agents to discover and understand community of an organization if it exists or where it stands. Does it need to be developed or evolved? Creating of a solid community will build trust, allow for shared knowledge, and support, as well as builds a feeling of fellowship in the organization. This will help build avenues for sharing information, values, knowledge, and best practices. Some examples of these are: mentor programs, best practices data base, collaboration/networking across multi-disciplinary teams, and incentive and reward programs that align with identity and values.

Figure 22 will be available to be used in professional development workshops or for team reflections as strategies are being built. The following are sample exercises that can be done on an individual level, with a small team, or a larger working group. Remember these are a small example of the creative exercises that can aid organizations.

Sample Exercises
1. **Community Mapping Matrix**
   Use when: You're unclear who your stakeholders are or how they connect.
   Goal: Visualize the web of relationships surrounding your initiative.

Map Dimensions:
– Who is impacted?
– Who influences success or failure?
– Who holds key knowledge, data, or decision-making power?
– Who is often excluded or unheard?

Outcome and Reflection: A shared understanding of who needs to be involved, when, and how. Where might you be designing *around* people instead of *with* them?

---

2. **Stakeholder Persona Cards**
   Use when: You need to step into the shoes of diverse community members and meet people where they are.
   Goal: Build empathy, tailored communication, and design engagement strategies personalized to real human needs.

Elements to define:
– Role and influence in the system
– Needs and concerns
– Hopes and fears
– Preferred ways to receive and share information

Application and reflection: Use these personas during strategy sessions, policy development, or communication planning to avoid one-size-fits-all assumptions. Remember, strategy doesn't land in abstract; it lands in *people*. Persona thinking helps us design for that.

---

3. **"Design With, Not For" Co-Engagement Sessions**
   Use when: You want to avoid top-down decisions and increase buy-in.
   Goal: Invite diverse stakeholders to co-create the path forward from the start.

Structure:
=   Frame the shared challenge
=   Break into mixed-role working groups
=   Co-create ideas and interventions
=   Collect insights and share next steps collectively

Facilitator Tip: Always end with recognition—thank people publicly, share what they contributed, and show how their input will be used. Think of this as a community potluck—you provide the table and structure, but the richness comes from what everyone brings.

---

4. **Community Health Pulse Survey**
   Use when: You want to measure how connected and engaged your internal/external communities feel.
   Goal: Uncover hidden disconnects, engagement gaps, or signs of momentum. Identify areas of strength, disconnect, or fatigue.

Sample Questions:
=   I feel part of a larger purpose at this organization.
=   I know where to share my ideas, questions, or concerns.
=   I believe leadership values a range of voices and perspectives, and trust that feedback leads to action.
=   I have seen actions taken based on community input, and leadership values diverse voices.

Best Practice: Keep the survey short and repeat quarterly. Share back results and next steps.

---

5. **Recognition & Ritual Design Toolkit**
   Use when: You want to build culture, celebrate progress, and embed values into everyday moments.
   Goal: Use intentional rituals and recognition to strengthen identity, belonging, and momentum to reinforce values and celebrate progress.

Ideas include:
- Storytelling events where staff share moments of impact
- Peer-to-peer recognition boards or digital "shout outs"
- Community-led mini-grants for grassroots sustainability ideas
- Sustainability birthdays: Celebrate initiative anniversaries or milestones

Why this matters: Rituals build meaning and emotional connection. They turn strategies into *shared experiences* as they make culture *visible* and values *tangible.*

Case Insight: The Power of Micro-Moments

In Case Study 3, Employees embraced this mindset by introducing a *Sustainability Pledge Experience.* Held during Earth Month, the initiative invited employees to meet the sustainability team, sign a symbolic pledge, and receive a plant and a branded pen as gentle reminders of their commitment. It was intentionally designed as both a **ritual and a relationship builder.** The experience made the department feel visible. It made sustainability personal. And it created cross-departmental connections that outlasted the event.

These kinds of engagements are not just nice-to-haves—they are **culture changers.**

Implementation Reflection

To cultivate a meaningful community, sustainability leaders must create:
- **Belonging** = People feel seen, heard, and part of something meaningful.
- **Agency** = Everyone sees how they can contribute and influence.
- **Resilience** = Communities can hold each other through tension, change, or ambiguity.

In your organization, this might mean stepping back from the task list and asking:
- Who needs to be at the table—but isn't yet?
- What small rituals can we introduce to turn strategy into shared experience?
- Where can we build new bridges—not just between roles, but between values?

When communities are strong, **culture becomes self-sustaining.** And that's when transformation moves from effort : : : to flow.

8.5D IDT = Branding Support Information

Let's get something clear from the start:

Branding is not decoration. It's declaration.

Branding is often misunderstood as a surface-level concern—logos, fonts, color palettes. In the Integral Design Thinking (IDT) framework, branding isn't just about how something *looks*—it's how it **feels**, how it **lives**, and how it **leads**. It's how we express who we are, what we value, and why we exist. It is *strategy made sensory*.

A brand is identity made visible. It's how your organization signals to the world— *and to itself*—what it stands for. In sustainability transformation, where values and vision are your true north, branding becomes your **emotional compass**. It helps people see, feel, and *believe* that the change is real.

Done well, branding connects people to purpose. It creates clarity, trust, and coherence. Done poorly—or ignored entirely—it creates confusion, fragmentation, and cynicism.

So, let's flip the script:

Branding is not the polish after the strategy. It is the strategy's voice, wardrobe, and handshake.

Branding Tools & Elements

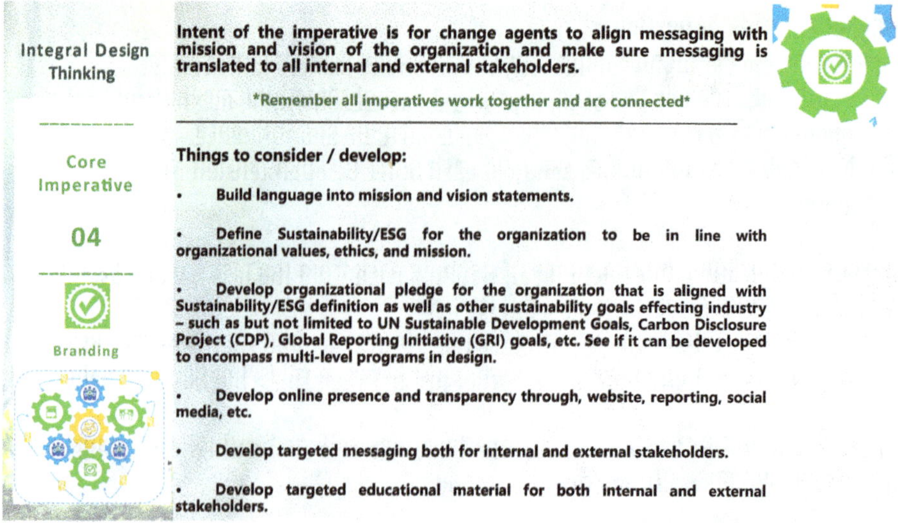

Integral Design Thinking

Intent of the imperative is for change agents to align messaging with mission and vision of the organization and make sure messaging is translated to all internal and external stakeholders.

Remember all imperatives work together and are connected

Core Imperative

04

Branding

Things to consider / develop:

• Build language into mission and vision statements.

• Define Sustainability/ESG for the organization to be in line with organizational values, ethics, and mission.

• Develop organizational pledge for the organization that is aligned with Sustainability/ESG definition as well as other sustainability goals effecting industry – such as but not limited to UN Sustainable Development Goals, Carbon Disclosure Project (CDP), Global Reporting Initiative (GRI) goals, etc. See if it can be developed to encompass multi-level programs in design.

• Develop online presence and transparency through, website, reporting, social media, etc.

• Develop targeted messaging both for internal and external stakeholders.

• Develop targeted educational material for both internal and external stakeholders.

Figure 23: IDT – Branding support information (Source: Author).

The intent of the Branding imperative is for change agents to align messaging with mission and vision of the organization and making sure messaging is translated to all internal and external stakeholders. For sustainability it is critical to build supportive language into the mission and vision of the organization, as well as defining sustainability/ESG for the organization that aligns with values, ethics, and mission. These definitions then need to be communicated and branded to internal and external stakeholders. For example develop an organizational pledge that is aligned with Sustainability/ESG definitions as well as other sustainability goals effecting current market, such as UN Sustainability Development Goals (UN SDG) and have them developed to encompass multi-level programs. Through these targeted messaging, educational materials, and transparency through website, reporting, social media, etc. can be built.

Figure 23 will be available to be used in professional development workshops or for team reflections as strategies are being built. The following are sample exercises that can be done on an individual level, with a small team, or a larger working group. Remember these are a small example of the creative exercises that can aid organizations.

Sample Exercises

1. **Brand Narrative Blueprint**
    Use when: Your organization lacks a cohesive story about its sustainability journey.
    Goal: Craft a compelling, values-driven narrative that guides all messaging.

Core elements:
– **Origin story** – Why did we begin this work?
– **Purpose** – What change are we here to create?
– **Voice** – How do we speak about our mission?
– **Call to action** – How can others join?

Application and Reflection: Use for external communications, onboarding, website messaging, stakeholder engagement, employee communications, and partner presentations. Consider, does your sustainability story feel lived-in . . . or left behind?

---

2. **Tone & Voice Guide**
    Use when: Messaging sounds inconsistent across teams or channels.
    Goal: Create a shared, recognizable language for your sustainability identity.

Guide Components:
– Tone qualities (e.g., bold but humble, transparent, hopeful, optimistic, grounded, transparent)
– Do/Don't examples (e.g., Do say "climate resilience"; don't say "eco-washing")
– Keywords and preferred terminology to anchor vision
– Language inclusivity and accessibility guidance

Outcome: When tone is aligned, people know *who* is speaking—even if the speaker changes. This builds connections without losing professionalism or credibility. Think of tone as your musical key. No matter who picks up the instrument, the sound stays familiar.

---

3. Visual Identity Alignment Kit
Use when: Your sustainability work looks generic or disconnected.
Goal: Build consistency and recognizability in your visual presence.

Includes:
- Color codes tied to core values (e.g., green = regeneration, blue = trust, orange = innovation)
- Typography that reflects tone (e.g., modern serif = thoughtful/trusted)
- Icons/symbols for IDT pillars
- Templates for slide decks, reports, internal signage

Design Tip: Use real photos from your organization's efforts—not just stock images. **Authenticity is the ultimate aesthetic.** When someone sees your sustainability report, do they see *you* in it?

---

4. Brand Touchpoint Audit
Use when: You're not sure if your brand shows up consistently across the organization.
Goal: Ensure alignment between what you *say* you value and what people *experience.*

Audit touchpoints:
- Website and social media
- Employee onboarding materials
- Internal newsletters and signage
- Office space/environment
- Events and community presence

Process: Map each touchpoint, rate consistency and impact, then identify areas for alignment. This should be done in a managed schedule (e.g., every quarter)

---

5. "Living the Brand" Workshop
Use when: You want branding to move from vision to behavior.
Goal: Help people personalize and act on brand values in daily decisions.

Workshop flow:
- Share the brand story
- Map personal/team connections to values
- Scenario role-play: "What does this look like in action?"

Team commitments: What's one thing we'll do to live this brand?

Why it works: Because branding is *not* just what you publish. It's how you show up—*in every room, every meeting, every moment.* Branding becomes a lived experience, not a marketing exercise.

Case Insight: Brand as Connection

In **Case Study 3,** the sustainability team used a clever brand activation to build internal community and emotional resonance. During Earth Month, they launched a **Sustainability Pledge** campaign. Employees received a pen with the new sustainability logo and a desk plant with the logo on the pot—symbolic, tangible tokens of their commitment. The experience was personal, interactive, and communal. It reinforced values while breaking down silos. It made the brand real. And it seeded culture change—one conversation, one signature, one green plant at a time.

Implementation Strategy

A powerful brand is:

- **Rooted in authenticity** = Reflect *who you are* and *what you are becoming,* not who you think people want you to be.
- **Emotionally resonant** = People remember how your brand made them *feel.*
- **Visually consistent** = Familiarity breeds trust.
- **Flexible** = Adaptable across contexts while staying anchored in your core.

When integrated into IDT, branding becomes more than a marketing function. It becomes a **cultural mirror and a strategic compass**—showing who you are and **who you're inviting others to become.**

> *Pause and reflect:* Where in your organization is your sustainability identity *clear, felt, and shared*—and where is it still silent or uncertain?

8.5E IDT = Speaking the Same Language and Empathy Support Information

In complex, dynamic organizations, misalignment rarely happens because people disagree on *values.* It happens because they don't share the **same meaning behind the words.** One person says "resilience," another hears "efficiency." Someone says "culture shift," and others think "rebranding." These aren't communication problems— they're *translation* problems.

If communication is the connective tissue of strategy, then **shared language and empathy** are the heartbeat that keeps it alive.

In the **Integral Design Thinking (IDT)** framework, *speaking the same language* is about building **coherence**, not conformity. It's about intentionally creating shared definitions and meanings that act as bridges between people, departments, and disciplines. When people truly understand one another, they move faster, trust deeper, and create more meaningful change.

And this is where **empathy** becomes essential—not as a "soft" add-on, but as a **strategic amplifier**. Empathy helps us hear not just what's said, but what's meant. It reveals motivations, hesitations, and the silent signals that shape behavior. In IDT, empathy and language clarity are deeply interwoven—and indispensable to transformation.

Shared Language & Empathy Tools

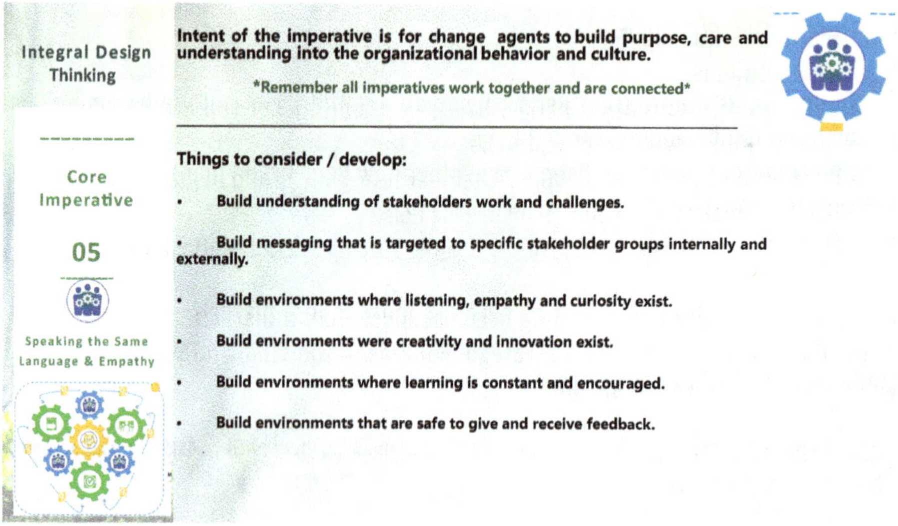

Integral Design Thinking

Intent of the imperative is for change agents to build purpose, care and understanding into the organizational behavior and culture.

Remember all imperatives work together and are connected

Core Imperative

05

Speaking the Same Language & Empathy

Things to consider / develop:

- Build understanding of stakeholders work and challenges.
- Build messaging that is targeted to specific stakeholder groups internally and externally.
- Build environments where listening, empathy and curiosity exist.
- Build environments were creativity and innovation exist.
- Build environments where learning is constant and encouraged.
- Build environments that are safe to give and receive feedback.

Figure 24: IDT – Speaking the Same Language and Empathy support information (Source: Author).

The intent of the Speaking the Same Language and Empathy Imperative is for change agents to build purpose, care, and understanding into the organizational behavior and culture. For this imperative we want to build environments:
- Where listening, empathy, and curiosity exist.
- Where creativity and innovation exist.

- Where learning is constant and encouraged.
- Where stakeholders feel safe to give and receive feedback.

Here change agents need to empathize with stakeholders to understand their work and challenges. They will need to target messaging for select stakeholders both internal and external to the organization. Take a moment to reflect on synergies for this imperative, to accomplish this communication, branding, and community need to be aligned and understood holistically. Similarly, information needs to be gathered and understood from this imperative to guide the strategies for the others.

Figure 24 will be available to be used in professional development workshops or for team reflections as strategies are being built. The following are sample exercises that can be done on an individual level, with a small team, or a larger working group. Remember these are a small example of the creative exercises that can aid organizations.

Sample Exercises

1. **Organizational Lexicon Canvas**
   Use when: Confusion arises around key terms, especially across functions or roles.
   Goal: Co-create a shared language that supports strategic clarity.

Steps:
- Identify 10–12 commonly used—but inconsistently understood—terms (e.g., sustainability, equity, innovation, impact, stakeholders)
- Break into small cross-functional groups
- Ask: *What does this word mean to us? How/Where is it misunderstood? What does it look like in practice?*

Collect insights and synthesize into a **living lexicon**.
   Output: A shared language document used in onboarding, meetings, and communications.

---

2. **Empathy Mapping for Internal Stakeholders**
   Use when: You're facing resistance or need to build better internal buy-in.
   Goal: Reveal the unspoken pressures, needs, and perspectives shaping stakeholder behavior.

Use prompts:
- What are they worried about?
- What pressures (political, personal, professional) are influencing them?
- What does success *look like* and *feel like* for them?
- How can we support their experience, and what support would actually matter?

Application: Ideal before launching new initiatives, policy changes, or restructuring. Think of this as "emotional user research"—you're mapping the internal terrain before building your road.

---

3. "Say-Think-Feel-Do" Mapping
Use when: You need to align communication with human psychology.
Goal: Anticipate behavior and design communication that connects.

Quadrants:
- What do they *say* publicly?
- What do they *think* privately?
- What do they *feel* emotionally?
- What do they *do* behaviorally?

Insight: Helps design strategy that addresses the real (not just surface-level) experience. You get below the surface to design messages that resonate with lived experience—not just organizational goals.

---

4. Empathy Circles
Use when: Trust is low or people feel unheard. You want to create safe, inclusive spaces for people to share their stories.
Goal: Build psychological safety, trust, and inter-team empathy. Create emotionally safe spaces to build connection and understanding.

Format:
- Small group (4–6 people)
- Facilitator-led time structured sessions
- Structured prompts (e.g., "Tell a story about a time you felt unheard," or "What does sustainability mean to you personally?")
- No interruptions, no "fixing," just listening
- Group reflection at the end

Impact: Builds emotional insight, relational depth, breaks down hierarchy, and fosters genuine collaboration—especially valuable during times of change.

---

5. Language Audit Mini-Workshop
Use when: Organizational language feels dense, disengaging, or confusing.
Goal: Make communication clearer, more inclusive, and more human.

Steps:
= Collect real communication samples: emails, web copy, slide decks, reports
= Assess using criteria: Is this clear? Inclusive? Jargon-heavy? Emotionally engaging?
= Rewrite a few examples together
= Document learnings and apply across departments

Tip: Pair this with your brand tone and voice guide from the Branding section for full alignment.

Integration insights
When teams pause to build shared language and lead with empathy:
= **Resistance decreases**
= **Engagement increases**
= **Collaboration deepens**

And when empathy is embedded into communication, community-building, and leadership practices, organizations begin to **feel different**. More connected. More human. More whole. Empathy and language clarity are not soft skills. They are *strategic capacities*. And when practiced intentionally, they unlock deeper, faster, and more lasting change.

Case Insight
And most importantly, **strategies stick**.

Case Study 3 demonstrated this beautifully through the **sustainability pledge**. By co-defining sustainability internally and communicating it through consistent, emotionally resonant language (even down to gifts like pens and plants), the pledge didn't feel like an initiative. It felt like a **movement**. Employees signed not just because they were asked—but because they *understood*. The message was internalized. And from that internal coherence, external engagement followed.

> **Pause and Reflect:** *Where in your organization is language creating friction instead of flow? Where is empathy needed—not as kindness, but as clarity?*

Implementation Strategy
Empathy and shared language must be:
= **Modeled by leadership** – If execs aren't clear and compassionate, others won't be either.

- **Practiced across silos** – These tools are bridges between departments, not just within them.
- **Integrated into change** – Use these before, during, and after transitions—not just when things go wrong.

Empathy isn't just emotional intelligence. It's *strategic intelligence* in human-centered systems.

And when we speak the same language with care and coherence, we stop forcing change—and start inviting it.

8.5F IDT – Holistic Design Thinking Methodology (HDTM) Support Information

If design thinking is the doorway to creative strategy, then **Holistic Design Thinking Methodology (HDTM)** is the architecture of the house itself.

HDTM sits at the very heart of the **Integral Design Thinking (IDT)** framework. It is not a linear process—it is a dynamic ecosystem. It integrates the structure of systems thinking with the responsiveness of human-centered design. It is both intentional and emergent. It is a strategic cycle that helps leaders move from reflection to action, with empathy, creativity, and complexity-awareness as guiding principles.

It doesn't just ask, *"What's the solution?"*—it asks, *"What's the deeper pattern that created the need for a solution in the first place?"*

In other words: **HDTM helps you see the forest, the trees, and the soil beneath.**

Where traditional design thinking focuses on solving problems creatively, HDTM goes a step further: it helps organizations understand *why* those problems exist in the first place—within the cultural, relational, and systemic layers that shape every action and outcome. It focuses on **understanding context, surfacing assumptions**, and **designing with complexity in mind**. It helps leaders move from reactive improvement to proactive, adaptive transformation.

With this methodology, a three-step evaluation process was designed to create consistency throughout the analysis process and make sure that all aspects are considered holistically. This section provides support tools to apply HDTM's full cycle in organizational settings.

HDTM Process: Three Core Phases (Visualized in Figure 25)
1. **Identify the Problem (Discovery + Diagnosis)**
2. **Design the Solution (Ideation + Intervention)**
3. **Evaluate and Reflect (Learning + Adaptation)**

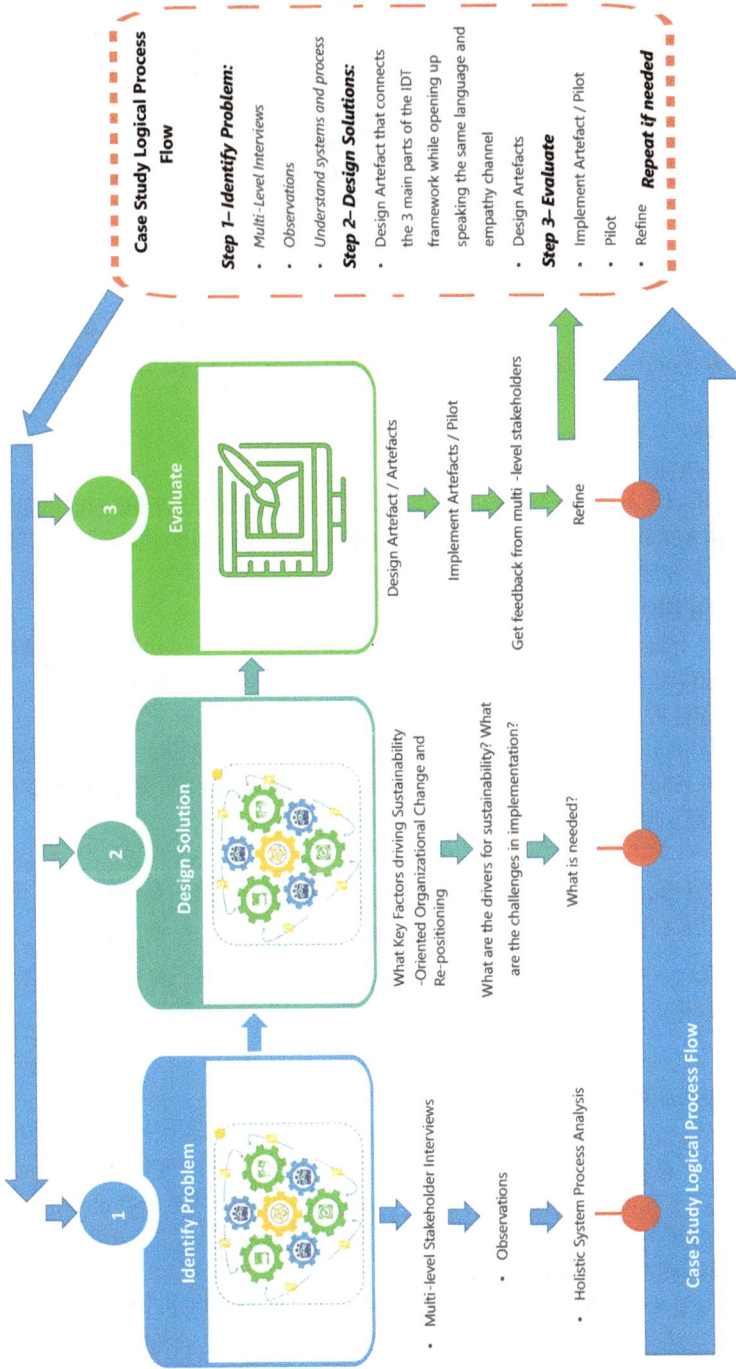

Case Study Logical Process Flow

Step 1– Identify Problem:
- *Multi-Level Interviews*
- *Observations*
- *Understand systems and process*

Step 2– Design Solutions:
- Design Artefact that connects the 3 main parts of the IDT framework while opening up speaking the same language and empathy channel
- Design Artefacts

Step 3– Evaluate
- Implement Artefact / Pilot
- Pilot
- Refine ***Repeat if needed***

Identify Problem
- Multi-level Stakeholder Interviews
- Observations
- Holistic System Process Analysis

Design Solution
- What Key Factors driving Sustainability -Oriented Organizational Change and Re-positioning
- What are the drivers for sustainability? What are the challenges in implementation?
- What is needed?

Evaluate
- Design Artefact / Artefacts
- Implement Artefacts / Pilot
- Get feedback from multi -level stakeholders
- Refine

Case Study Logical Process Flow

Figure 25: IDT – Holistic Design Thinking Methodology (HDTM) – Process Flow Guide (Source: Author).

The **Holistic Design Thinking Methodology (HDTM)** process is both a diagnostic and design cycle—moving organizations from fragmented assumptions to integrated solutions. This visual model outlines how to apply HDTM within real-world sustainability transformation efforts.

Each phase is essential, and although they flow sequentially, they should also be viewed as iterative. Change is rarely linear. You may find yourself returning to earlier stages as new data and insight emerge.

Step 1 = Identify the Problem

This phase begins with **deep listening and systemic inquiry**. The aim is to understand the organizational landscape through multiple lenses—not just what is visible on the surface.

Activities include:

= **Multi-level Stakeholder Interviews**

Engage individuals across the organization—executives, middle management, frontline staff, and external partners—to hear how they perceive the system, the challenges, and the opportunities.

= **Organizational Observation (Action Research)**

Change agents take on the role of embedded observers—tracking workflows, communication patterns, informal norms, and bottlenecks in real time.

= **Holistic Systems Process Analysis**

Map how systems interact: how decisions are made, where feedback loops exist (or don't), and what cultural narratives shape behaviors. Use system diagrams, stakeholder maps, or quadrant assessments.

Pause and Reflect: What assumptions are being made about the problem—and by whom? Where do those assumptions diverge?

This should give the team a clear articulation of the root challenges, grounded in evidence, lived experience, and systems insight, not surface-level symptoms.

Step 2 = Design the Solution

Once the problem is understood in context, the team shifts to co-creating interventions. But in HDTM, design isn't just about generating ideas—it's about ensuring they are **aligned**, **inclusive**, and **embedded** within the real workings of the organization.

Activities include:

= **Identify Key Drivers and Barriers**

What's pushing the organization toward sustainability? What's holding it back? Name the forces shaping current dynamics (cultural, structural, relational).

= **Co-Create Design Artefacts**
  Develop tools, rituals, communications, or system adjustments that respond to the insights gathered. These artefacts should activate the **three IDT pillars**:
  = Strategic Communication
  = Community Connection
  = Branding Strategies
  = While opening up Shared Language & Empathy Channels
= **Position Interventions within the Ecosystem**
  Consider how the new solutions fit within existing processes and identities. Who needs to champion them? What unintended consequences could arise?
  Think of the solution as a **keystone** in an arch. It's not a separate piece—it holds everything else in place.

Step 3 = Evaluate

Design thinking without learning is just decoration. In this phase, we test, reflect, and refine. This is where ideas meet reality.

  Activities include:
= **Implement Design Artefacts or Pilot Programs**
= Start small. Roll out prototypes in safe-to-fail environments. Ensure cross-functional feedback loops are in place.
= **Gather Feedback Across Stakeholder Levels**
= Use pulse surveys, listening sessions, or observation journals to learn how the interventions are received, adopted, or resisted.
= **Refine Based on Data and Dialogue**
= Don't just ask, *"Did it work?"* Ask, *"What did we learn about ourselves, our system, and our culture?"*
= Treat evaluation not as a verdict, but as a **mirror**—one that helps the organization see itself more clearly.

Looping Back: Repeat If Needed

As the graphic illustrates, this process is **iterative**. You may uncover deeper issues during evaluation that require returning to the discovery phase. This is a sign of progress, not failure.

Key Takeaway:

HDTM invites us to work **with complexity**, not against it. It's about finding coherence, not control.

HDTM Tools & Structures

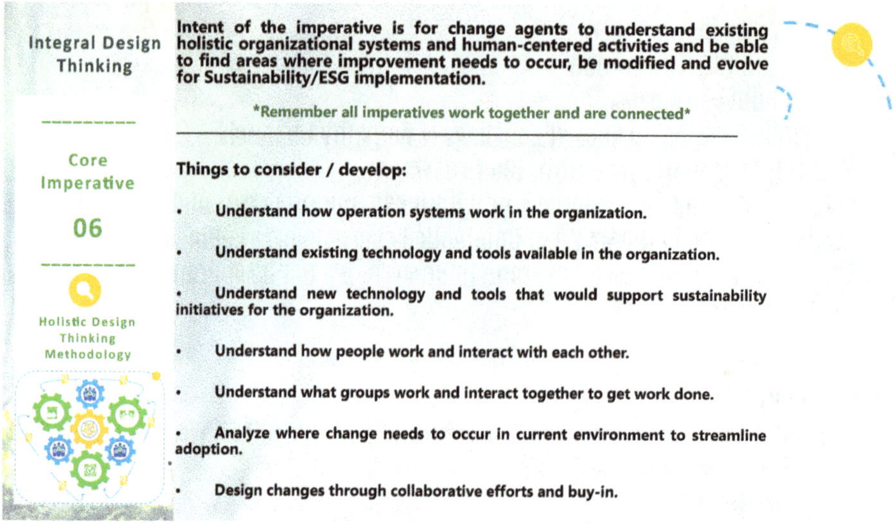

Integral Design Thinking

Intent of the imperative is for change agents to understand existing holistic organizational systems and human-centered activities and be able to find areas where improvement needs to occur, be modified and evolve for Sustainability/ESG implementation.

Remember all imperatives work together and are connected

Core Imperative

06

Holistic Design Thinking Methodology

Things to consider / develop:

- Understand how operation systems work in the organization.

- Understand existing technology and tools available in the organization.

- Understand new technology and tools that would support sustainability initiatives for the organization.

- Understand how people work and interact with each other.

- Understand what groups work and interact together to get work done.

- Analyze where change needs to occur in current environment to streamline adoption.

- Design changes through collaborative efforts and buy-in.

Figure 26: IDT – HDTM support information (Source: Author).

The intent of the Holistic Design Thinking Methodology (HDTM) imperative is for change agents to understand existing holistic organizational systems and human-centered activities. This helps them find areas where improvements need to occur, be modified, and evolved for sustainability/ESG implementation. Some examples of areas that need to be researched and analyzed are:

- Understanding of operation systems.
- Understanding of existing technologies and tools.
- Understanding of how people work and interact.
- Understanding of what groups work and interact together (current state and future state).

Change agents will have to analyze where change needs to occur in current environment to streamline adoption and then design change through collaborative efforts and buy-in.

Figure 26 will be available to be used in professional development workshops or for team reflections as strategies are being built. The following are sample exercises that can be done on an individual level, with a small team, or a larger working group. Remember these are a small example of the creative exercises that can aid organizations.

Sample Exercises

These exercises bring HDTM to life in team meetings, strategy offsites, and system-wide interventions.

1. **Systemic Root Cause Mapping**
   Use when: You suspect the surface problem is just a symptom.
   Goal: Uncover the deeper forces driving current challenges.

Approach:
- Start with a core issue or visible problems (e.g., lack of ESG adoption).
- Ask: *Why is this happening?* Repeat "why?" 3–5 times to reach deeper causes.
- Explore internal (culture, systems) and external (market, regulatory, community) contributors.
- Map relationships and identify **leverage points** for change.

Best for: Leadership retreats, cross-functional teams, strategic planning workshops. Think of this as tracing the roots beneath the surface, not just trimming the leaves.

---

2. **Adaptive Ideation Matrix**
   Use when: You need to generate ideas that fit the complexity of your ecosystem.
   Goal: Balance creativity with real-world constraints and system complexity.

Matrix Columns:
- **Desirable** (human-centered)
- **Viable** (financially/logically sound)
- **Feasible** (organizationally possible and realistic)
- **Sustainable** (aligned with long-term impact/purpose)

Facilitator Tip: Encourage wild ideas (Dream Big) in early rounds, then iterate and converge. Consider ⸞ *Which quadrant does your organization over-prioritize? What's getting neglected?*

---

3. **Prototyping & Interventions Design Sheet**
   Use when: You're ready to turn ideas into action.
   Goal: Move from "talk" to "test" using design-based experimentation.

Template Includes:
- What change are we trying to make?
- What does success look like?
- Who needs to be involved?
- What's our first experiment?
- What data will we collect?

Reminder: Prototypes should be low-risk, low-cost, and high-learning.

Prototypes = hypotheses made tangible. They are tools for learning, not polished solutions.

---

4. Reflexive Evaluation Framework

Use when: You want to reflect deeply—not just on *what* happened, but on *how* and *why*.

Goal: Reflect on assumptions, shifts, and surprises.

Structure:
- What did we assume going in?
- What actually happened?
- What surprised us or challenged us?
- What changed as a result—about us, the system, or the strategy?
- What would we do differently?
- What is next?

Adaptation: Use this after pilot projects, strategy launches, or policy shifts. Invite both emotional and analytical responses. Truth lives in both.

---

5. Learning Loop Tracker

Use when: You want to institutionalize learning, not just log outcomes.

Goal: Create a habit of collective reflection and adaptive action.

Tracker Elements:
- What phase of the HDTM cycle are we in? Phase tracking log
- What have we learned? Insight capture form.
- What decisions or adaptations resulted? Decision log.
- Who else needs to know? Culture check: are we sharing this learning?

Why it works: Helps organizations build muscle for adaptive change, not just one-time improvement. Post this tracker in shared spaces—make learning visible and communal.

HDTM Integration Guidance

To embed HDTM in your organization:
- **Position it as a way of working**, not a special project.
- Use it in strategic planning, program design, team development, change initiatives, and even onboarding.

= Combine it with earlier IDT tools—like communication mapping, brand narrative, and empathy circles—for full alignment.
= Model it at the leadership level. How leaders reflect, iterate, and learn signals whether it's truly part of culture.

HDTM is not meant to replace existing systems—it's meant to **reveal the gaps** and help you design more conscious, inclusive, and adaptive ones.

It's not just a toolkit. It's a practice of **thinking integrally, acting creatively, and leading holistically**.

Case Study Insight

In both research **Case Studies 2 and 3**, HDTM principles were applied from the moment the change agent entered the organization. Using semi-structured interviews, they didn't just ask for information—they mapped **how the system actually worked**, who influenced what, and what barriers quietly shaped behavior. They weren't solving *for* people—they were learning *with* them.

This led to changes that weren't just strategic—they were culturally embedded. Leaders didn't impose solutions. They discovered them, together.

Pause and Reflect: *Where are you solving symptoms instead of systems? What would change if you shifted from reacting to redesigning?*

8.6 Synthesis of Tools = Conclusion and Reflection

Let's pause here and take a breath.

We've just journeyed through one of the most practical—and potentially transformational—chapters in this book. But let's be clear: this toolbox isn't just about tactics. It's about transformation. Each section—from design thinking to branding, from community to empathy—has offered you tools not just to *plan* better, but to *lead* better. To lead with more clarity, more coherence, and more care.

What makes these tools powerful isn't just their structure—it's their **intent**. They aren't designed to control change. They're here to help you *navigate* it. They don't prescribe fixed answers. They invite *better questions*. They don't assume your organization is a machine. They recognize it as a *living system*. And in living systems, transformation cannot be imposed. It must be cultivated, and co-created.

What You've Built with This Toolbox:

You now hold a modular, adaptable strategy toolkit designed to support integral, sustainable change. Together, we've explored how:

- **Design Thinking**, when applied holistically, becomes more than a creative exercise. It becomes a system for organizational reflection, experimentation, and alignment.
- **Communication** evolves from broadcasting to bridging—from messaging to meaning-making.
- **Community** is no longer just a stakeholder group. It becomes the connective tissue of resilience and belonging.
- **Branding** shifts from aesthetic to *authentic*. It becomes a cultural story that people feel, not just see.
- **Empathy and Shared Language** become strategic capacities, not soft skills. They enable clarity in complexity and connection across difference.
- And all of it is grounded in a methodology—**HDTM**—that honors systems thinking, iteration, and the wisdom of reflection.

This isn't just a toolbox.

It's a **transformation toolkit**.

A Final Reflection

Before we move forward, take a moment. Ask yourself:
- *Where in your organization is this work already alive, even if informally?*

- *Where are the tensions—between values and behavior, or vision and execution—that these tools could help illuminate?*
- *And perhaps most importantly:*

What might change if every team member felt seen, heard, and connected to a shared purpose?
Because that is the quiet power—and radical promise—of **Integral Design Thinking**:
To help organizations not only perform better, but become more *human*, more *whole*, and more *courageous* in the face of change.
Let this chapter be a beginning, not a blueprint.
Adapt it. Expand it. Make it your own.
The next chapter will take us deeper into the **creative-thinking tools** that bring transformation to life. But everything you need to begin is already in your hands.
Now, it's time to use it.

Takeaway Summary: The IDT Holistic Strategy Toolbox

What This Chapter Gave You:
- A practical, modular **toolkit** to support holistic strategy in complex organizations.
- Tools to activate **Design Thinking** not just for innovation—but for **culture and systems change**.
- Communication methods that foster **transparency, alignment, and trust**.
- Community-building approaches that deepen **participation and resilience**.
- Branding frameworks that express **authentic identity and shared purpose**.
- Exercises for creating **shared language** and embedding **strategic empathy**.
- A methodology (HDTM) for **designing, testing, and evolving** sustainable interventions.

Core Insights to Carry Forward

- Transformation doesn't happen through strategy alone—it happens through people.
- Communication, branding, and community are not support functions—they are strategic levers.
- Empathy and shared language are not soft—they are structure.
- Tools don't create change. People using tools—with intention, reflection, and courage—create change.

Try This
At your next strategy session, ask:

"Which of these tools can help us see the system more clearly—and engage with it more humanely?"

You don't have to use everything at once. Pick one. Pilot it. Reflect. Adapt. That's what Integral Design Thinking is about.

9 IDT Strategy Framework Creative-Thinking Tools

If Chapter 8 was about tools for alignment, then Chapter 9 is about tools for **transformation**.

This is where the heart of **Integral Design Thinking (IDT)** comes alive—not just as a framework, but as a *creative way of seeing and shaping the world*. Here, we focus on **creative-thinking tools**—not in the arts-and-crafts sense, but as serious, strategic instruments for imagining what doesn't yet exist and for holding space in uncertainty until something new can emerge.

In today's sustainability landscape, creative thinking is not a luxury—it's a leadership imperative. We are working in systems that are too complex, too interdependent, and too rapidly evolving to be navigated with linear logic alone. What we need is **generative thinking**—the ability to design in uncertainty, to iterate in ambiguity, and to sense what the future might be calling us to create.

That's what this chapter offers.

What Makes These Tools "Creative" Thinking Tools?

These tools:

= Invite **reflection and imagination**, not just planning.
= Encourage **emergence** over prescription—welcoming what wants to unfold.
= Help leaders and teams design for **wholeness**: integrating mind, heart, culture, and system.
= Are built on **design science, systems theory, and reflective practice**, anchored in real-world organizational change.

They are structured enough to guide you, but open enough to let your organization breathe into its own voice and values.

What This Chapter Delivers:

= Tools grounded in the **Design Science Management Framework** (9.1).
= A curated suite of **creative-thinking instruments** for visioning, reflection, prototyping, and narrative-building (9.2–9.6).
= Methods to support long-term **cultural alignment and regenerative strategy**.
= Flexible formats you can use in leadership retreats, team design sessions, or moments of strategic pause.

What We're Really Doing Here:

We're shifting from asking, *"What's the plan?"* to asking, *"What wants to emerge here— and how do we support it with intelligence, empathy, and structure?"*

This is design thinking as a **life practice**. As a leadership orientation. As a methodology for healing fragmentation and catalyzing purpose.

Let's begin with the foundation: how **Design Science** connects to strategic sustainability work in real time.

https://doi.org/10.1515/9783111705026-010

Note: *I will be using the word researcher but this is representation of the change agent at the center of the IDT framework. Place yourself in the researcher's shoes working as an investigator, like a detective solving a mystery—gathering clues, asking questions, and piecing together evidence to uncover the truth.*

9.1 Design Science Foundations & Management Framework

It's one thing to talk about transformation. It's another to design it.

To implement change that sticks, especially in the complex arena of sustainability, we need more than good intentions or strong values. We need **methodologies that are as adaptive and layered as the systems we're trying to change**. That's where **Design Science** comes in.

Design science is not theoretical hand-waving. It's practical. It's tested. It's built for messy, human-centered realities. In the context of the Integral Design Thinking (IDT) framework, design science provides the foundation for **developing actionable, evidence-based tools**—tools that don't just describe the world, but reshape it.

What is Design Science?

At its core, **Design Science Research (DSR)** is about producing knowledge through *design and iteration*. It's a form of inquiry that's rooted in doing—not just observing. Where traditional science seeks to explain, design science seeks to **create and evaluate solutions** to real-world problems.

In the IDT framework, this approach is especially powerful because:
- It embraces complexity rather than avoiding it.
- It values collaboration with practitioners and stakeholders.
- It builds tools (called *artefacts*) that are piloted, refined, and adapted to context.

In sustainability work, this is gold. Because change is not static—it evolves. And our thinking must evolve with it.

Integrating Design Science with Management Practice

In IDT, I combine design science with management frameworks in a **three-phase process**, adapted and field-tested through real-world case studies (this was first brought up in 8.5F IDT – Holistic Design Thinking Methodology (HDTM) Support Information):

Phase 1: Identify the Problem
- Use sensemaking, stakeholder interviews, and systemic mapping to understand the root issue.
- Ask: *Where is the breakdown? What are we not seeing? What layers (personal, cultural, structural) are involved?*

Phase 2: Design the Solution
- Ideate, co-create, and prototype with those impacted.
- Build artefacts—tools, models, communications, policies—that reflect the organization's unique ecosystem.
- Embed empathy and co-ownership into the design.

Phase 3: Evaluate the Intervention
- Test. Reflect. Learn. Adjust.
- Measure not just outcomes, but *process quality*, adoption behavior, and unintended consequences.
- Repeat the cycle with new insight.

This cycle mirrors how **living systems adapt**—which makes it uniquely effective for managing the evolving nature of sustainability in organizations.

Figure 27 gives a visual image of the process. Remember we have to consider the connections of everything we do and make sure they are working together, nothing lives in isolation. As we identify the problem (Phase 1), we will need to understand what is happening in the organization, outside the organization and what has been written. This should be in-depth research that is holistic.

Moving to Designing Solution (Phase 2) – there should be continued research, analysis, and assignment of its value to the identified problem as a solution (called Artefacts) is developed. When working in these phases, the lead practitioner needs to act as an **Action Researcher**. An *action researcher* is someone who studies a real-world problem by working directly with the people involved to both understand it and help solve it. Instead of standing on the sidelines, action researchers roll up their sleeves, get involved, test ideas, and learn along the way. Their goal is to create practical, meaningful change—while also gaining deeper insights through the process. Think of them as a combination of guide, partner, and investigator—learning by doing, and improving as they go.

The important part of wearing an action researcher hat is that you do not give direction/orders, you have the group make the decisions, solve the problems, you provide insight to challenges that might be faced for a found solution, then sit back observe and analyze everything holistically to understand what the challenges are in the Evaluate (Phase 3) step of the process.

Note: Don't let the word research scare you off, research is gathering information, this can be done in many ways – Consider what ways have you gathered information?

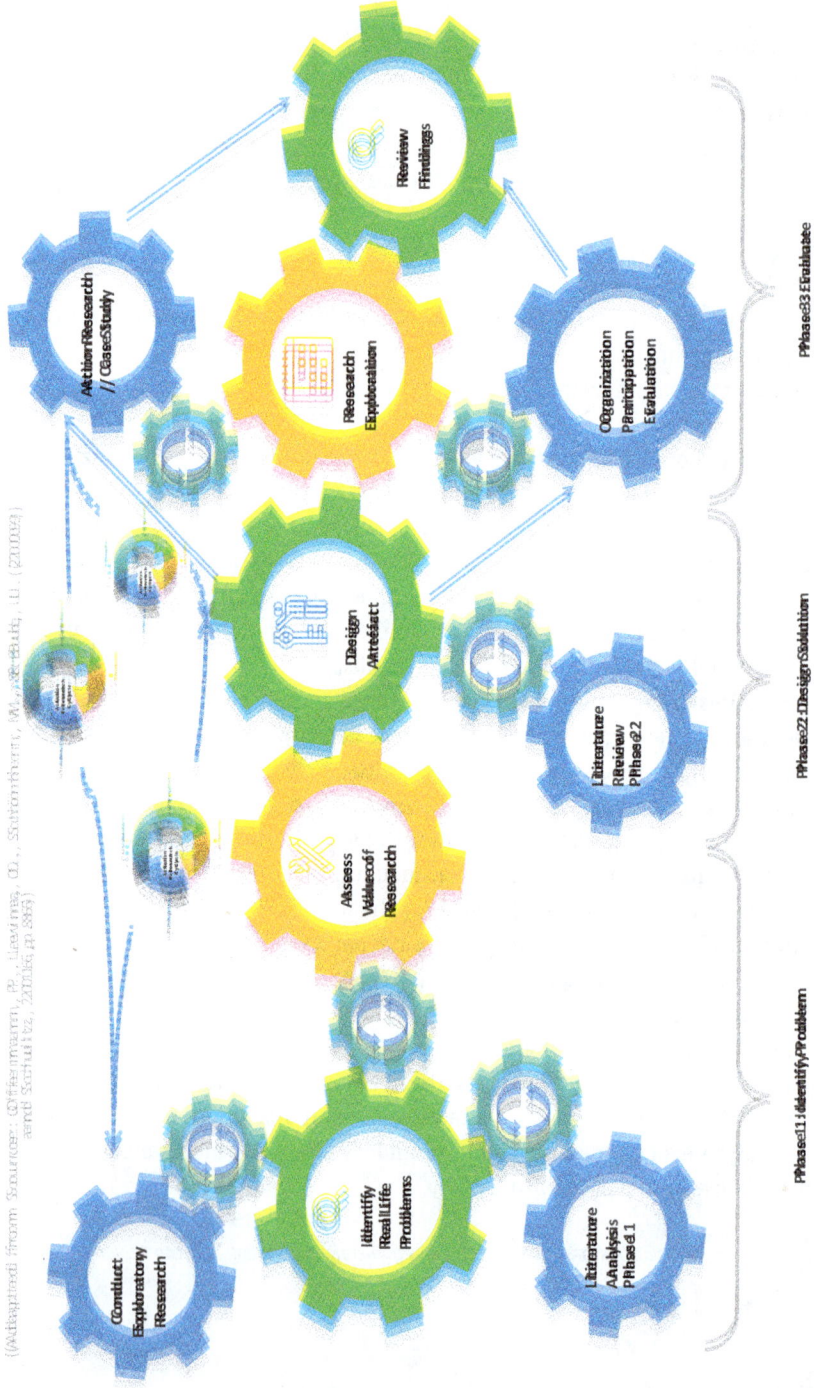

(Adapted from Source: Offermann, P., Levina, O., Schönherr, M., & Bub, U. (2009))

Figure 27: IDT Three Phase process (Source: Author).

Phase 3 Evaluate

Phase 2 Design Solution

Phase 1 Identify Problem

Management Framework Alignment

To anchor this methodology in practice, we align it with **three strategic capacities** every organization must develop to lead change holistically:

1. **Strategic Foresight** = Seeing patterns, anticipating shifts, staying flexible.
2. **Cultural Intelligence** = Understanding internal dynamics, beliefs, and behavioral norms.
3. **Creative Capacity** = Turning insight into interventions through inclusive design.

In IDT, each tool introduced in the following sections of this chapter maps back to this foundation. They are not "one-size-fits-all" instruments, but **modular elements** you can adapt, remix, and evolve as your organization grows.

Integral Design Thinking (IDT) is not just a philosophy—it is a *discipline of practice*. And behind that practice is a strong methodological backbone rooted in **Design Science Research (DSR)** and **Action Research (AR)**. These are not abstract academic traditions. They are living, breathing frameworks that guide how we *build, test,* and *refine* solutions in complex, human systems.

In this chapter, we walk through how these research traditions inform the IDT approach to organizational transformation and sustainability strategy. We explore the foundations of design science, how research models are developed, and how iterative, participatory methods like action research enhance both rigor and relevance.

Note: *Understanding these foundations will help you understand the why and how to use the tools I am giving you. So take your time in seeing the connections.*

9.1.1 Design Science Research Methods, Foundations, and Research Model Development

Design Science Research (DSR) is built on a deceptively simple premise: knowledge is not only something we discover—it's something we **create**.

Unlike traditional research, which seeks to explain or predict, DSR is about **intervention and learning**. It involves designing artefacts (tools, processes, models) that address real-world problems, and then refining those artefacts through rigorous, reflective testing.

In the context of IDT, DSR serves three essential purposes:

1. **Grounding innovation in inquiry** = We don't design from assumptions; we design from insight.
2. **Connecting theory to practice** = Our strategies are not conceptual—they're contextual.
3. **Embedding learning into design cycles** = Every tool is an opportunity to learn, adapt, and evolve.

In short, we don't design to finish—we design to understand.

This approach allows us to create research models that are iterative, participatory, and deeply rooted in context. In IDT, these models evolve alongside the organizations using them. They are not static frameworks; they are **living systems of inquiry**.

9.1.2 Design Science Research Guidelines and Framework

To ensure rigor and replicability, DSR is guided by a clear set of principles. In my application of DSR within IDT, I draw from well-established guidelines and adapt them to fit the specific needs of organizational sustainability and culture change.

Key Guidelines of DSR in IDT:
- **Problem relevance** – Address a real and significant organizational challenge.
- **Design as an artefact** – Create usable outputs: tools, systems, models, narratives.
- **Design evaluation** – Implement and test the artefact in a real-world setting.
- **Research rigor** – Ground the work in both theory and practical methods.
- **Research contribution** – Add to both knowledge and practice.
- **Design as a process** – Iterative cycles of build → test → reflect → refine.
- **Communication of results** – Make findings useful for both scholars and practitioners.

In IDT, this framework is **embedded**, not external. It informs how tools are developed (e.g., empathy maps, brand narratives), how they are tested (e.g., piloting interventions), and how learning is captured (e.g., through retrospectives and reflective journals).

What makes this powerful is that DSR in IDT is never just academic. It's **relational**. It happens *with* people, not to them. And it values emotional insight as much as strategic data.

9.1.3 Action Research and Methodology Framework

While DSR gives us the structure to design and evaluate, **Action Research (AR)**, visualized in Figure 28, gives us the relational wisdom to do so *with integrity and inclusion.*

AR is participatory by nature. It is based on the belief that those closest to the issue are also closest to the solution. It blurs the lines between researcher and participant, between strategy and story.

In IDT, AR strengthens the methodology by:
- Centering **co-creation** rather than top-down implementation.
- Making reflection part of the work, not an afterthought.
- Building a culture of learning through real-time action.

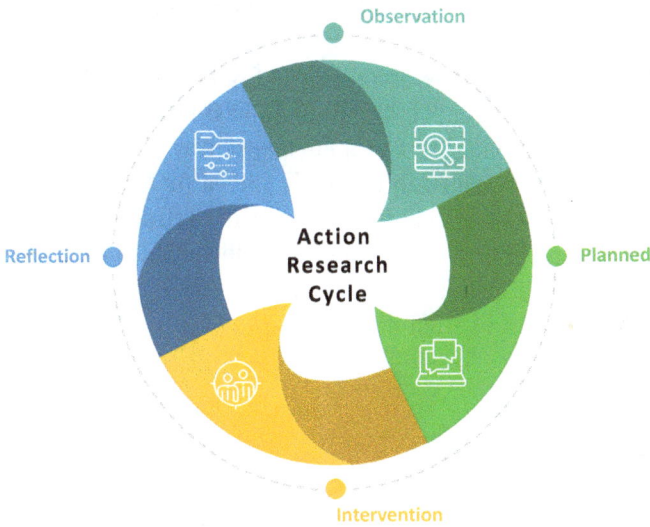

Figure 28: Action Research Cycle (Source Author).

The Action Research Cycle (as applied in IDT):
1. **Observe:**
   – **Diagnose** – Identify and describe the issue from multiple perspectives.
2. **Planned:**
   – **Design** a collaborative intervention, informed by diverse input.
3. **Intervention:**
   – **Act** – Implement the strategy or artefact with shared ownership.
4. **Reflect:**
   – Capture learning at individual, team, and system levels.
   – **Adapt** – Adjust based on what's working and what's not.

This recursive cycle fosters trust, surfaces tacit knowledge, and builds the emotional infrastructure for sustained change. It also makes invisible dynamics—like resistance, power, or fear—available for compassionate inquiry and strategic response.

Together: A Methodology for Holistic, Adaptive Change
Design Science and Action Research are not competing approaches—they are **complementary lenses**. Together, they offer a grounded, adaptive, and humane way to lead transformation in complex systems.

Design Science provides the **structure and discipline**. Action Research provides the **participation and empathy**. And Integral Design Thinking weaves them together—into a methodology that is not only intelligent, but also wise.

9.2 Integral Design Thinking (IDT) Creative-Thinking Tools

When people hear "creative thinking," they often picture brainstorming sessions, sticky notes, and sudden bursts of inspiration. But in the context of Integral Design Thinking (IDT), creativity is something deeper—it's a disciplined way of seeing, sensing, and synthesizing. It's a practice rooted in curiosity, guided by empathy, and sharpened by thoughtful analysis. This section explores how IDT reframes creative thinking—not as a loose or random process, but as a powerful, intentional method for making sense of complexity. Through reflective inquiry, systems awareness, and tools that make the invisible visible, we move from imagination to insight—and from insight to impact.

9.2.1 Approach to Analysis

Creative thinking often gets framed as spontaneous, unstructured, or intuitive. And while creativity absolutely calls on imagination and emotion, it also requires something more: **analysis**. In the IDT framework, creative thinking is a disciplined, reflective, and systems-aware process. It's not just about ideas—it's about *insight*.

Analysis in IDT isn't linear or reductionist. It's **integrative**. It connects the dots between what is seen and what is sensed, between the data and the dynamic, between parts and the whole.

In this section, we explore how the IDT creative process approaches analysis—bridging the rational and the intuitive to generate strategies that are bold, empathetic, and grounded in context.

What Do We Mean by "Creative Analysis"?

In IDT, creative analysis is the process of making meaning from complexity. It helps teams and leaders:

- **Surface hidden patterns** within systems and culture.
- **Understand relationships** between issues, actors, and actions.
- **See root causes**, not just symptoms.
- **Identify leverage points** for action and intervention.
- **Hold paradoxes** without rushing to resolve them.

This is not about simplifying the world—it's about engaging with its complexity more skillfully.

Key Characteristics of the IDT Approach to Analysis
1. **Multi-perspectival** = We analyze from multiple lenses (individual, team, system, environment). No single view tells the whole story.
2. **Non-linear** = Creativity moves in spirals, not straight lines. We circle back, reframe, and evolve understanding.
3. **Empathy-informed** = Data doesn't live in spreadsheets alone. Lived experience is a valid and vital form of insight.
4. **Pattern-driven** = We look for coherence and dissonance across stories, signals, and symbols—not just metrics.
5. **Reflective** = Insight arises not just from thinking, but from *pausing, sensing, and feeling*.

Analytical Methods Used in IDT Creative Work
Here are a few examples of how creative analysis is practiced in the field:

= Thematic Clustering
Thematic clustering is a method used to organize and make sense of qualitative information—like interviews, reflections, or stories—by grouping similar ideas, patterns, or insights together into meaningful themes. This helps identify where alignment exists—and where fragmentation might be hiding. Think of it as gathering puzzle pieces that share a color or shape. When clustered, they start to reveal a bigger picture about what people are experiencing, feeling, or focusing on. It's especially useful in identifying alignment, tension, or hidden patterns within complex systems or cultures.

= Empathy-Based Synthesis
Empathy-based synthesis is the process of making sense of what people share—not just by analyzing their words, but by tuning into their emotions, tone, and lived experiences. It goes beyond facts to ask: *How did this feel? What truly mattered to them? What wasn't said, but was clearly felt?* In Integral Design Thinking, this approach helps teams design solutions that are not only smart, but deeply human and resonant with those they aim to serve.

= Systems Mapping
Systems mapping is a visual method used to understand the relationships, patterns, and dynamics within a complex system. Instead of looking at problems in isolation, systems mapping shows how different parts—people, policies, behaviors, and environments—are interconnected. It helps teams see root causes, feedback loops, and leverage points for change. In IDT, it's not just about drawing connections—it's about adding meaning, emotion, and context to these connections so organizations can navigate complexity with is the practice of exploring the deeper, often subconscious patterns that show up in language, behavior, and culture—through the lens of recurring characters, metaphors, or symbols. greater clarity and purpose.

– Archetypal & Symbolic Analysis

Archetypal and symbolic analysis In organizations, this might look like noticing when someone always takes the "hero" role, or when the team describes change as a "battle" or a "journey." These patterns reveal hidden mindsets, fears, or power dynamics that shape how people show up and respond to change. In IDT, this kind of analysis helps uncover what's beneath the surface—so leaders can address not just the visible issues, but the emotional and cultural currents driving them.

– Silence & Absence Analysis

Silence and absence analysis is the practice of paying attention to what's *not* being said, who's *not* in the room, and what data, feelings, or perspectives are consistently overlooked. In IDT, this approach helps uncover blind spots, gaps in inclusion, or avoided truths within an organization. It asks: *Whose voice is missing? What emotions are being suppressed? What patterns are we ignoring?* By listening to the quiet spaces, this analysis brings awareness to what may be quietly shaping— or stalling—transformation.

Why This Matters

In a world where complexity is the norm, not the exception, organizations can no longer afford surface-level thinking. What makes the IDT approach to analysis so essential is its ability to hold space for nuance, emotion, and contradiction—without losing clarity. These creative methods aren't just tools for innovation; they are practices for deeper awareness, wiser decision-making, and more human-centered leadership. When teams engage in this kind of analysis, they don't just generate solutions—they cultivate the insight, empathy, and adaptability needed to lead real transformation. This is why it matters: because how we make sense of the world shapes what we're able to change in it.

> **Pause and Reflect:**
> Traditional analysis asks: *What do we know?*
> IDT asks: *What are we learning—and how are we changing as we learn it?*
> This subtle shift is powerful. It allows your organization to make sense of complexity not by simplifying it—but by learning how to move through it more wisely.
> Creative thinking becomes not just idea generation—it becomes **strategic sensemaking.**

9.2.2 Overview of the Tools

Now that we've explored how Integral Design Thinking approaches creative analysis— with its emphasis on reflection, empathy, and systemic insight—it's time to bring those principles to life. These tools are not prescriptions; they are invitations to explore, sense, and build together. Each one is rooted in the core principles of IDT—to help teams see more clearly, feel more deeply, and act more wisely in the face of complexity. They support every phase of transformation: from sensing and diagnosing, to visioning, aligning, acting, and reflecting.

They help make the invisible visible, whether that's emotion, system dynamics, or cultural undercurrents and they provide structure without rigidity. Most importantly, they create space for meaningful dialogue, collective intelligence, and the emergence of new possibilities. Whether you're leading a workshop, guiding a change process, or seeking deeper insight within your team, these tools can be adapted to meet the moment. Use them to bring clarity to complexity, spark new ideas, and strengthen the human connection at the core of sustainable change.

Now that we've established how IDT approaches creative analysis—as a reflective, multi-layered process—it's time to introduce the **suite of creative-thinking tools** that put this analysis into action.

Each of these tools is designed to help organizations:
– Navigate complexity with clarity.
– Make the invisible (emotions, patterns, systems) visible.
– Foster team reflection, creativity, and co-creation.
– Move from insight to possibility—and from vision to iteration.

These tools are **flexible by design**. Use them in workshops, team offsites, leadership retreats, or as part of your ongoing change management process. Each one supports a different mode of transformation: sensing, visioning, prototyping, reflecting, and adapting.

Guiding Principles for Using These Tools
1. **Facilitate, don't prescribe** – Let teams make the tool their own.
2. **Hold space for ambiguity** – These tools are not about control, but emergence.
3. **Honor the emotional field** – Real insight includes what people are feeling, not just what they're saying.
4. **Use visuals to support clarity** – Most tools benefit from large-format boards, drawing, or post-it collaboration.
5. **End with reflection** – Each tool should generate insight, not just output.

This chapter is not about giving answers. It's about building the **capacity to hold better questions**, and the creativity to explore what might be possible.

The next sections 9.3, 9.4 & 9.5 will look at tools in each of the IDT Three Phases of the process, visualized in Figure 29.

Figure 29: IDT = Holistic Design Thinking Methodology Three-Phase process flow.

9.3 Phase 1: Identify the Problem

Every sustainable transformation begins with one essential—and often overlooked—step: **seeing clearly**.

It sounds simple. But in complex systems, clarity is not obvious. Problems present themselves in tangled layers. Symptoms masquerade as causes. Stakeholders disagree about what's broken, or why it matters. And without realizing it, organizations rush into action before they've aligned on purpose.

In the Integral Design Thinking (IDT) framework, **Phase 1 is about diagnosis—but not in the clinical sense**. This is diagnosis that is empathic, participatory, and system-aware. It's about **asking better questions**, not finding fast answers.

9.3.1 Mapping Relationships: The IDT Interactions Matrix (Phase 1)

When you step into an organization as a change agent—especially in the context of sustainability and culture work—one of the most important things you can do is map the terrain. Not just the technical systems or official processes, but the human web of connections that either enable or block transformation. That's what the IDT Interactions Matrix is here to help you do.

In Phase 1 of the Integral Design Thinking process—*Sense & Diagnose*—we begin by understanding who's connected to whom, and how. The Interactions Matrix (visualized in Figure 30) is a creative thinking tool designed to help you visualize and analyze these relationships across four dimensions:

= **Internal Department** (your immediate team and collaborators)
= **Internal Company** (wider departments and leadership within the organization)
= **External Partners** (vendors, consultants, allies outside the organization)
= **External Community** (citizens, NGOs, advocacy groups, etc.)

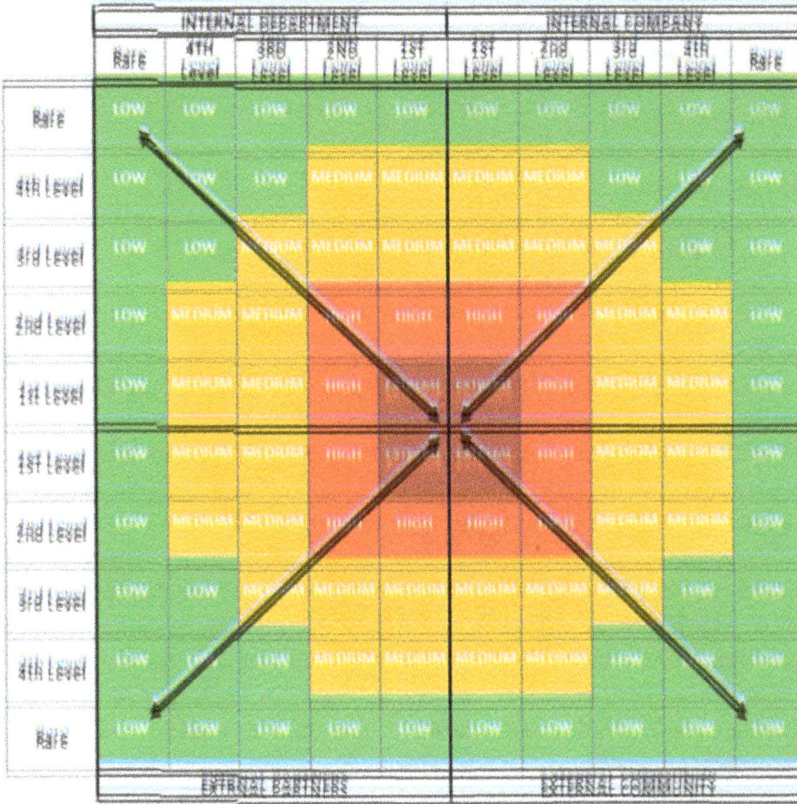

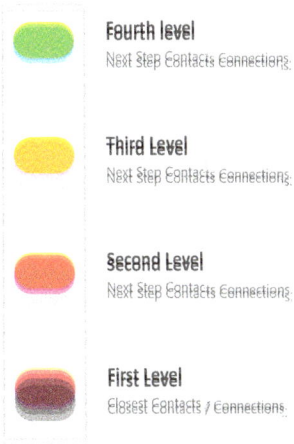

Figure 30: IDT Interactions Matrix (Source Author).

These four quadrants echo Wilber's (2001) Integral Theory, which emphasizes that a full systems view must account for internal and external dynamics, both individual and collective (see Section 2.3.3[125]). The matrix is more than a contact map. It's a visual strategy tool to help you:
- See where influence and support currently live
- Surface overlooked stakeholders
- Spot gaps, blockers, or hidden power nodes
- Strategically shift relationships to support the change effort

How It Works
As you fill in the matrix, you're encouraged to classify connections based on both **proximity** and **intensity**:
- **Proximity:** First-level (closest), Second-level, Third-level, Fourth-level (farthest), or Rare.
- **Intensity of Interaction:** Extreme, High, Medium, or Low.

A first-level contact with *extreme* interaction might be a daily collaborator who deeply influences your project. A fourth-level, low-contact connection might be a community voice or distant executive who is barely in the picture—but could become a critical champion with the right outreach.

The matrix color-coding (as shown in Figure 28) helps quickly visualize where your strongest influence lies, and where new connections need to be nurtured or restructured. Green zones indicate low-intensity relationships, yellow shows moderate connection, orange and red signal critical players or potential blockers with high influence.

Why This Matters
Change doesn't happen in a vacuum. It happens through relationships. And too often, we assume those relationships are already understood or well-formed. This tool slows us down enough to *see* the system we're working within—not just in terms of people, but in terms of influence, trust, visibility, and alignment.

By using this matrix, leaders can:
- Identify who needs to be brought closer into the process
- Strategically reposition stakeholders based on their influence or potential impact
- Understand which relationships need strengthening to reduce friction or resistance
- Build inclusive, multi-stakeholder working groups or advisory committees

---

125 Jaber, M., 2021. Integral Design Thinking: A Novel Cross-national Framework for Sustainability Management, PhD Thesis, BCU, UK.

In case study 2, for example, leadership team used this model to design multi-level committees that supported strategy roll-out. Understanding which voices to elevate—and which ones to invite in—was central to gaining internal alignment and external credibility. Some questions that can be asked are:

- What are we really trying to change?
- Who defines the problem—and who's excluded from that definition?
- What deeper patterns are holding this problem in place?
- What assumptions are we carrying without realizing it?
- What values are quietly shaping our framing?
- What purpose might be emerging through this challenge?

Remember, this is where strategy becomes relational. This is where culture speaks—if we're listening.

This tool also supports ongoing reflection. Over time, as your initiative evolves, your network of influence should, too. The matrix can be revisited regularly to evaluate what's shifted, what needs adjustment, and where new allies can be engaged.

> **Pro Tip: Use It in Layers**
> One powerful variation of this exercise is to complete *separate* matrices for different focus areas: e.g., internal communication, external branding, community engagement. Then compare them side-by-side. Where are the overlaps? Where are the blind spots? Where are the leverage points?
>
> Figure 30 also offers an even more rapid version for quick ideation or team-based brainstorming. Use a single quadrant layout to quickly focus on one relationship field. This can spark fast insights about where to deepen, bridge, or even release certain relationships.
>
> **Time for Reflection**
> The IDT Interactions Matrix is not just about who you know—it's about understanding how systems of relationship and influence shape your ability to create change. It gives you a map. And with that map, you can begin to navigate with more intention, clarity, and power.

In the next section, we explore how to transition from sensing and mapping into the act of visioning. Now that you know who's at the table, the question becomes: *What future are you inviting them to co-create?*

9.3.2 IDT – Building Purpose (Phase 1)

Once you've mapped the landscape of relationships and influence through the IDT Interactions Matrix, the next step is to ask yourself: **What are we truly designing for?**

Before jumping into building strategies or rolling out initiatives, we pause—and reconnect to purpose.

That's where the **IDT = Building Purpose** tool comes in.

Adapted from Otto Scharmer's **Theory U**, this tool supports change agents in moving from analysis to alignment. It invites you to slow down and connect with a deeper intention—one rooted not just in performance metrics, but in meaning, humanity, and collective growth.

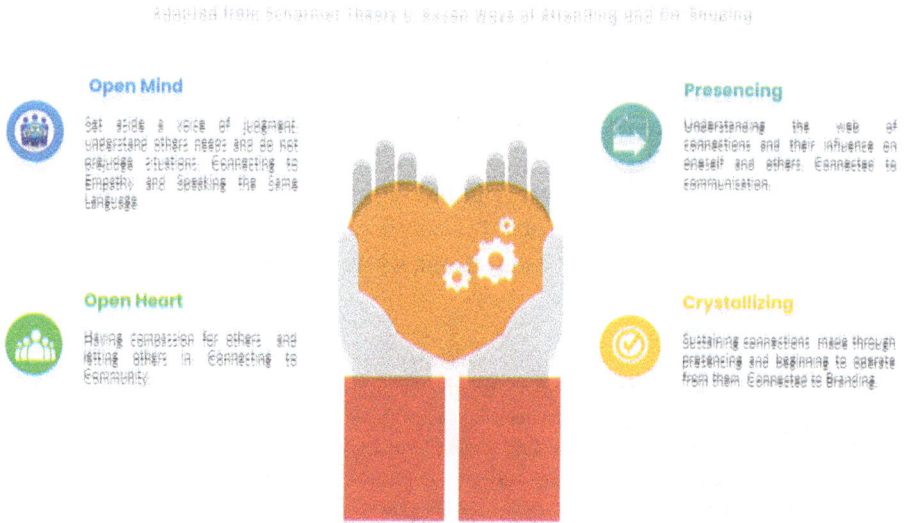

Open Mind

Set aside a voice of judgment. Understand others needs and do not pass judgment. Connecting to Empathy and speaking the same language.

Presencing

Understanding the web of connections and their influence on oneself and others. Connected to communication.

Open Heart

Having compassion for others and letting others in. Connecting to Community.

Crystallizing

Spotting connections made through presencing and beginning to operate from them. Connected to Branding.

Figure 31: IDT Building Purpose (Source Author), pg 226.

As shown in Figure 31, the process moves through four powerful modes of attention:

= **Open Mind** = Set aside the inner voice of judgment and listen openly. What are others saying, needing, or experiencing? This step is about empathy and developing a shared language for change.
= **Open Heart** = Let compassion in. This is where connection happens—not just on a strategic level, but on a human one. Community, care, and inclusion are at the center.
= **Presencing** = Become aware of the web of connections you're part of—and how your presence shapes the system. This is about sensing into what wants to emerge.
= **Crystallizing** = Let that sensed purpose begin to take form. Start making decisions and designing next steps not just from intention, but from alignment with your values and insights.

How It Works

The Building Purpose tool can be used individually or in teams. Set aside time and space for reflection. Use visual prompts, journaling, dialogue circles, or storytelling to explore each phase:

1. **Begin with an open-ended prompt** such as, "What are we being called to do?"
2. **Guide reflection** using the four attention modes.
3. **Capture insights** as they emerge—these become the seeds of vision and strategy.
4. **Revisit the process** throughout the project lifecycle to stay grounded in purpose.

Why This Matters

In complex systems, it's easy to get caught in action mode. But purpose gives direction. It filters out noise, aligns teams, and builds energy around what truly matters. Without it, we risk solving the wrong problems—or solving the right ones in disconnected, surface-level ways.

This tool is especially useful:
= At the beginning of a project to anchor vision
= In team retreats to build alignment
= When navigating resistance or ambiguity
= As a reflective practice to stay connected to meaning

The invitation here is simple, but profound: **Don't just move forward—move inward first.** The clarity you cultivate now will shape every decision you make later.

Pro Tips for Practice
= **Create a safe space** for this work. Vulnerability and depth require psychological safety.
= **Use storytelling or metaphor** to access deeper layers of insight.
= **Bring in diverse voices**—especially those often excluded from strategic conversations.
= **Don't rush the process.** Insight emerges at its own pace.

Time for Reflection
= What am I really designing for?
= What kind of future do I want to help create?
= Who is this for—and how do I stay connected to them?
= What does success *feel* like, not just look like?

This tool reminds us: Strategy without purpose is noise. When we build with intention, we don't just make change—we make it matter.

9.3.3 Phase 1 Summary and Reflection

Phase 1 of the IDT framework invites us to do something radical in a culture of urgency: **slow down and look more deeply**. Not just at the problems on the surface, but at the relationships, values, and assumptions that shape how we see those problems in the first place.

This phase isn't about diagnosing symptoms. It's about surfacing systems. It asks us to pause, listen widely, and hold the complexity of an organization, not to control it, but to understand it more clearly. But here's what this phase gives in return:
- Clarity without oversimplification.
- Alignment without coercion.
- Purpose that feels *felt*, not just stated.

Through interaction mapping, systems thinking, reflective tools, and purpose discovery, organizations begin to see the *whole system*—not just the symptoms they're trying to solve. And more importantly, they begin to see **each other**. The people behind the roles. The emotions behind the language. The values that may have gone unspoken for too long.

We began this phase with **Mapping Relationships** through the **IDT Interactions Matrix**, a tool designed to reveal who's influencing the system, where power lives, and where meaningful collaboration must happen. By making these often-invisible dynamics visible, change agents gain a clearer sense of where to focus attention, and who must be included to build trust and momentum.

Next, we turned inward with the **IDT – Building Purpose** tool. Here, the goal is not strategy—it's alignment. This reflective process grounds teams in the deeper why behind their work. Through the four modes of attention—**Open Mind, Open Heart, Presencing, and Crystallizing**—leaders begin to design not just with intention, but with integrity. This is where transformation becomes personal, collective, and values-aligned.

Together, these tools remind us that clarity is not about simplicity—it's about seeing the whole picture. And from that perspective, we can begin to design more thoughtfully, more inclusively, and more powerfully.

Key Insights from Phase 1:
- **Problems are not isolated.** They live in networks—of people, power, process, and perception. They are *interdependent* and *relational*.
- **Relationships are strategy.** Influence, trust, and collaboration shape what change is possible.
- **Purpose is not a tagline.** It's a felt sense of meaning that guides decisions and unites people. It is an *organizing intelligence*—a source of alignment, energy, and clarity.
- **Systems resist being changed without being understood.** Listening is as strategic as acting.

– **The real work is often invisible.** And yet, it's this inner work that sets the tone for what follows.
– **Co-creating** the problem definition is just as important as solving it.

Reflective Prompts for Practitioners & Teams
Use these as journaling or group reflection exercises before entering the design phase:
– What shifted in our understanding of the problem?
– What perspectives did we hear that we hadn't considered before?
– Where are we still uncertain—and what might we need to sit with a little longer?
– How do we want to move forward: with urgency, or with integrity?
– What's calling to emerge through this challenge—not just what needs to be fixed?
– What relationships need strengthening—or reimagining?
– Where did we feel the most resistance, and what might that be teaching us?
– What purpose emerged as most meaningful—and how do we stay rooted in it?
– Are we solving the right problem—or reframing it in a more powerful way?

What Comes Next
With a clearer understanding of the challenge—and of ourselves—we are ready to move into **Phase 2: Design the Solution**. This next phase is not about jumping to answers. It's about **designing with care, creativity, and alignment**, using everything we've surfaced in this first phase as fertile ground.

Because when we begin with truth and clarity, the solutions that follow don't just solve problems.

They *transform systems.*

9.4 Phase 2: Design the Solution

At the heart of Phase 2 is the **IDT Interventions** tool, inspired by **Doppelt's Seven Interventions of Sustainability**. These interventions have been adapted and visually restructured to align directly with the IDT framework (see Figure 32). Together, they form a creative-thinking tool that supports the design of regenerative, participatory solutions.

Change agents should hold these seven strategic lenses in mind when shaping interventions:
– **Change the Dominant Mindset** – Get buy-in from people across the organization. This isn't about top-down mandates—it's about building trust and shared belief.
– **Rearrange the Parts** – Look at your current structures. What can be simplified or shifted to improve flow and coherence?

Figure 32: IDT Intervention (Source Author).

= **Change Goals by Crafting an Ideal Vision and Guiding It** – Embed purpose by reframing goals and creating shared direction.

= **Restructure the Rules of Engagement by Adopting New Strategies** – Encourage collaboration through updated protocols, clear roles, and psychological safety.

= **Shift Information Flows** = Open up communication channels so information travels up, down, and across—honestly and effectively.

= **Correct Feedback Loops** = Make learning continuous. Educate teams, create honest feedback structures, and track what matters.

= **Adjust the Parameters by Aligning Systems and Structures** – Design interventions holistically, aligning messaging, operations, branding, and partnerships.

How It Works

The IDT Interventions tool can be used in design sessions, strategic retreats, or cross-functional workshops. It works especially well when facilitated with outputs from Phase 1:

1. **Bring together representatives** from across the four quadrants mapped earlier (Internal Department, Internal Company, External Partners, and External Community).

2. **Review each of the seven interventions** using Figure 29 as a guide.

3. **Ask targeted questions**, such as:
    - How do we get real engagement from our people?
    - What needs to shift in our structures or messaging?
    - What feedback systems do we need to build?
4. **Map existing initiatives** to the seven puzzle pieces—then assess gaps.
5. **Co-design actions** that embody both the values from the Building Purpose tool and the system insights from the Interactions Matrix.

This tool also encourages the use of integrative design workshops—where diverse perspectives meet to co-create the path forward. For example, in Case Study 2 (see Section 5.3.3[126]), an Innovation Council of 52 people from various stakeholder groups helped unify vision and define artifacts that would anchor transformation.

Why This Matters

Without structure, purpose can drift. And without strategy, relationships can stall. This tool translates deep insight into sustainable action by aligning systems with values. It helps:
- Prevent fragmentation of efforts
- Build coherence across teams and departments
- Connect top-down vision with bottom-up insight
- Encourage systems thinking over quick fixes

The IDT Interventions tool is where design begins to feel tangible—and powerful. It gives leaders and teams a shared architecture to work from.

Pro Tips for Practice
- Use this tool **after you've completed Phase 1 outputs** to ensure interventions align with purpose and context.
- **Don't try to do all seven interventions at once.** Start where there is traction and grow from there.
- **Engage skeptics early.** They often hold key insights about systemic resistance.
- Consider **hosting co-design workshops** that use each puzzle piece as a station or theme.

Time for Reflection
Designing the solution isn't about rushing to action—it's about **designing with care, creativity, and clarity.** These tools are your bridge between insight and implementation. Use them to ask bold questions, involve the right voices, and shape structures that are alive with shared purpose.
- Which intervention feels most urgent for us right now?
- Where might we be reinforcing the very patterns we want to change?

---

126 Jaber, M., 2021. Integral Design Thinking: A Novel Cross-national Framework for Sustainability Management, PhD Thesis, Section 5.3.3, pg 135.

- What relationships or systems need to be restructured—not just tweaked?
- How can we design with both empathy and accountability?

By engaging with the IDT Interventions tool, you move from purpose to practice. You begin not just to imagine change—but to architect it.

Applying the Tools in Practice

The research and case studies behind IDT show how powerful these tools can be when grounded in real contexts. In Case Study 2, for example, an "Innovation Council" of 52 cross-sector representatives (city agencies, unions, principals, parents, sustainability officers, and more) came together to co-create the NYC DOE's Sustainability Pledge and Framework. This wasn't just good design—it was good *engagement*, rooted in shared purpose and the seven interventions.

To apply these tools effectively, consider these prompts:

- What systems need to shift to reflect our emerging purpose?
- Who needs to be brought into the conversation now (refer to your Phase 1 Interactions Matrix)?
- What interventions will remove barriers and create better conditions for success?
- What practices (e.g., educational workshops, feedback mechanisms, integrative councils) can build trust, alignment, and sustained momentum?

In the next phase, we shift from design to evaluation. Because in complex systems, the work doesn't stop with rollout—it evolves. And evaluation in IDT isn't just about measurement—it's about learning.

9.5 Phase 3: Evaluate, Align, and Scale

Once interventions have been designed and implemented, the work doesn't stop. In fact, it enters one of its most crucial stages: **evaluating impact, aligning systems, and scaling sustainable value**. Phase 3 of the Integral Design Thinking (IDT) process focuses on creating *regenerative momentum*—making sure that the change you've initiated actually works, and that it can grow.

This is where the **IDT Design Value Creation** tool comes in.

Adapted from **Laszlo's Eight Disciplines of Value Creation** (2005), this creative-thinking tool ensures that every strategy, artefact, or initiative is designed not just to solve a problem—but to **generate lasting value** across systems.

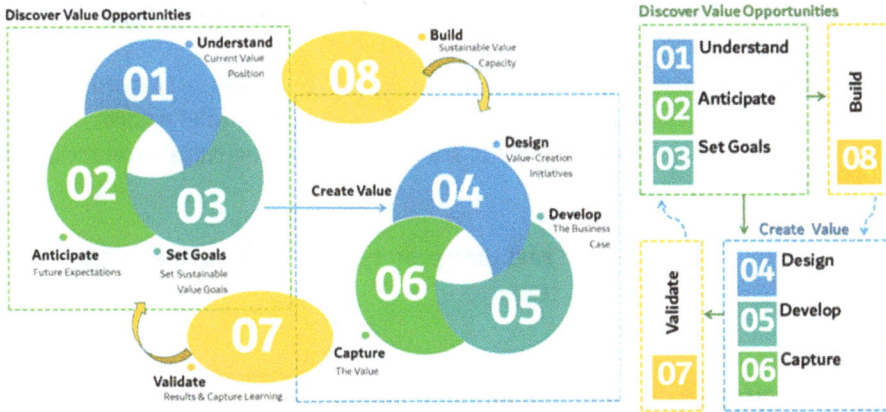

Figure 33: IDT Design Value Creation (Source Author).

As seen in **Figure 33**, the process is broken into **three interconnected phases**:

1. **Discover Value Opportunities**
   Understand the current value position, anticipate future expectations, and set sustainable value goals.

2. **Create Value**
   Design initiatives, develop business cases, and capture the value generated through pilots or prototypes.

3. **Validate & Scale**
   Test impact, refine based on feedback, and build internal capacity to scale the effort organization-wide.

How It Works

Think of this as a cycle—not a one-time event. The steps are iterative and designed to support continuous learning and refinement.

1. **Understand** – Where are we now? What value are we already delivering (or failing to deliver)?
2. **Anticipate** – What will stakeholders need tomorrow? What's shifting in our environment?
3. **Set Goals** – What does success look like? What values and outcomes will we prioritize?
4. **Design** – What initiatives, systems, or artefacts will deliver that value?

5. **Develop** – What business case or strategic framing will ensure feasibility and alignment?
6. **Capture** – What value is being created—and for whom? How is it experienced?
7. **Validate** – Test assumptions, gather results, and determine what works.
8. **Build** – Strengthen your capacity to scale: through partnerships, resources, and institutional learning.

These eight steps can be used in **real-time prototyping cycles**, strategic planning, or post-implementation evaluation sessions.

Why This Matters

It's not enough to implement a good idea. Without evaluation, even the most inspired intervention can drift—misaligned, misunderstood, or underutilized.

This tool helps leaders and teams:

- Make the **invisible visible**—especially in terms of impact and perceived value
- Align change efforts with **measurable outcomes**
- Build a **shared language** for defining success
- Avoid premature scaling by ensuring **readiness and resonance**
- Evolve interventions through a **feedback-informed process**

Just like in the case studies, it becomes clear that successful change agents **don't just launch initiatives—they learn from them.** This model builds that learning into the DNA of every project.

Pro Tips for Practice

- **Co-define value with stakeholders** – Don't assume you know what matters. Ask.
- **Visualize success early** – Use simple graphics or metrics to make value tangible from day one.
- **Pilot with intention** – Small-scale implementation helps surface friction points before full rollout.
- **Build in validation loops** – Make time to pause, reflect, and adapt.
- **Tell the value story** – Use both data and narrative to share outcomes with diverse audiences.

Time for Reflection

- What value are we trying to create—and who defines it?
- Are we measuring what really matters—or just what's easy to count?
- What evidence do we have that this change is working?
- What lessons emerged from testing—and how will they shape our path forward?
- How can we scale without losing meaning or momentum?

This phase is where **intention becomes integrity.** It's where transformation proves its worth—not only to funders or leaders, but to the communities it's meant to serve. And when value is clear, shared, and validated, it invites others to join, invest, and expand the effort.

9.6 Overview and Tips: Implementing Integral Design Thinking (IDT) in Practice

If Chapter 8 gave us the compass—**strategic alignment**—then Chapter 9 gave us the wings. This chapter is where Integral Design Thinking (IDT) comes alive. Not just as a model or methodology, but as a way of thinking, a way of sensing, and a way of being in relationship with complex systems.

We didn't just talk about transformation here—we practiced it. Through creative-thinking tools, deep reflection, and iterative strategy work, we've built a flexible, yet grounded pathway for navigating real-world sustainability challenges with intelligence, empathy, and resilience.

And now, before we close this chapter, we zoom out.

This is your chance to connect the dots, to reflect across phases, and to see how everything interrelates—from visioning and relationship mapping to designing, testing, and scaling initiatives that matter.

How It All Connects

At the center of IDT is a deceptively simple question: **"What wants to emerge—and how do we support it with intelligence, empathy, and structure?"**

To answer that, we've walked through a **three-phase process**:

1. **Phase 1: Identify the Problem**
   - Mapping relationships, seeing systems, and surfacing purpose.
   - Tools: Interactions Matrix, Building Purpose.
2. **Phase 2: Design the Solution**
   - Translating insight into coherent interventions.
   - Tool: The Seven IDT Interventions.
3. **Phase 3: Evaluate, Align, and Scale**
   - Validating value, capturing learning, and growing what works.
   - Tool: IDT Design Value Creation (based on Laszlo's 8 Disciplines).

But beyond the phases and tools, something deeper is unfolding.

The Six Core Imperatives: Your Strategic System for Transformation

Each tool you've encountered is mapped—either implicitly or explicitly—to one or more of IDT's **Six Core Strategic Imperatives** introduced in Chapter 8. These are the gears that drive not only your strategy, but your organizational culture:

1. **Design Thinking** – Your core practice of iteration, empathy, and innovation.
   → Most evident in Phase 2, but active throughout every feedback loop.

2. **Communication** – Making ideas visible, shared, and emotionally resonant.
   → Critical in stakeholder engagement, branding, and feedback structures.
3. **Community** – Not just inclusion, but belonging.
   → Surfaces in mapping exercises, decision-making, and co-creation spaces.
4. **Branding** – The narrative coherence of your purpose, identity, and voice.
   → Emerges through purpose discovery, strategic alignment, and visual storytelling.
5. **Empathy and Shared Language** – The emotional intelligence and conceptual clarity to bridge gaps.
   → Core to every IDT tool—without it, even great design falls flat.
6. **Holistic Design Thinking Methodology (HDTM)** – The integration of it all.
   → Your connective tissue. The "how" behind the "what."

These imperatives aren't steps. They are lenses. And when you apply them consistently, your transformation work becomes more than effective—it becomes **ethical**, **equitable**, and **enduring**.

Why This Matters (More Than Ever)

We live in systems that are:
- Too complex for linear thinking
- Too fragmented for siloed strategies
- Too urgent for top-down control

What they need are change agents who can **sense complexity**, **design for emergence**, and **lead with compassion**. IDT gives you the tools—but it also gives you the mindset.

This chapter, in particular, has focused on **creative-thinking tools** not as fluff, but as **critical infrastructure for systems change**. Tools that:
- Make the invisible visible
- Create structure without rigidity
- Help organizations navigate uncertainty without defaulting to control
- Build relationships that can hold tension and transformation at once

---

Pro Tips for Practice
- **Lead like a researcher** – Ask more than you answer. Observe without needing to control. Analyze holistically.
- **Facilitate, don't prescribe** – Let people find their voice. Guide with humility, not authority.
- **Always co-define value** – If you don't invite others into the "why," your "how" won't hold.
- **Use reflection as strategy** – Pause more. Listen more. Your best insights often hide behind your assumptions.
- **Test, learn, adapt, repeat** – Implementation isn't the end—it's the next iteration.

Time for Reflection

Use the following prompts to help your team, organization, or self integrate what this chapter has offered. Journal, dialogue, or even build a short workshop around them:

1. **Which of the six imperatives is strongest in our organization right now? Which needs development?**
2. **Where did our team feel the most energy or breakthrough in using these tools? What might that tell us?**
3. **What assumptions are we still carrying—and how might they be limiting our imagination?**
4. **Where are we mistaking action for progress?**
5. **How well are we capturing and communicating value—not just to funders, but to our people and partners?**
6. **Are our systems designed to evolve? Or just to deliver?**
7. **What does 'success' feel like—not just look like—for our community?**
8. **What would it mean to scale not just outcomes, but also empathy, trust, and purpose?**

Final Note: The Practice of Practicing

This isn't about mastering every tool perfectly. It's about showing up **again and again** to the work of listening, sensing, designing, reflecting, and refining.

You are not just using a toolkit.

You are building a *culture* of inquiry, care, and courageous imagination.

So, stay with it. Use these tools not as answers, but as **invitations** to deeper seeing, stronger collaboration, and more regenerative strategy.

Because when change is led with integrity, and when systems are designed with empathy, the transformation isn't just effective—it's beautiful.

10 Leading Organizations Toward a Sustainable Future

This final chapter is not a conclusion.

It's a **beginning**.

What you've explored through Integral Design Thinking (IDT) is more than a set of tools or frameworks. It's a **discipline of practice**, a **lens for leadership**, and a **living methodology** for transforming complexity into coherence—and purpose into action.

Now, the real work begins.

Because change doesn't happen because we read something inspiring. It happens because we do something consistently. It happens when we create the conditions—**within ourselves and our organizations**.

I offer practical guidance on how to bring IDT to life through training, coaching, and cultural embedding. Let's celebrate progress. We look ahead to what's still unknown. And I leave you with a challenge: to keep going.

Let's begin with where all learning becomes lasting—through **practice, reflection, and community**.

10.1 Training, Coaching, and Celebrating Success

Sustainability doesn't become real through strategy slides. It becomes real through behavior.

Sustainability leadership isn't only about designing the future; it's about building the capabilities needed to carry it forward. The practice of Integral Design Thinking (IDT) doesn't stop at the development of strategies or artifacts—it thrives through the continuous learning and support of those involved in the work. This is where training and coaching come in, forming the bedrock of sustainable transformation.

Training in IDT should be immersive and reflective. It's not enough to transfer knowledge; participants need to experience and embody the principles of empathy, systems thinking, and co-creation. Whether through workshops, simulations, or facilitated sessions, training programs should provide opportunities to work with the IDT tools—like the Interactions Matrix or Building Purpose model—in real organizational contexts. This grounds theory in practice and builds a culture of creative agency.

Coaching is the personal dimension of capacity-building. As change unfolds, individuals need support to reflect, recalibrate, and grow. Coaching helps leaders move through uncertainty, deepen self-awareness, and hold space for complexity. Whether peer-to-peer, team-based, or led by an external facilitator, coaching cultivates the kind of inner resilience required for sustainable leadership.

https://doi.org/10.1515/9783111705286-011

And let's not forget celebration. Transformation is hard work. Celebrating small wins and shared learning moments builds momentum and embeds a sense of progress into the culture. Celebration reinforces that the journey itself matters—not just the outcome. It also signals to the organization that values like gratitude, connection, and joy are part of what sustainability looks like in practice.

That's why one of your most powerful levers for lasting impact is training and coaching—not as one-off events, but as embedded practices of support and shared learning.

Growing the Capacity to Carry Change

One of the most powerful moments in any transformation comes when the original team steps back—and others step forward. That's when you know the change is not dependent on a single leader or initiative. It's becoming **shared, owned, and lived** across the system.

This section focuses on how to **build that capacity**:
- How to train others in Integral Design Thinking (IDT)
- How to coach and mentor leaders across roles and levels
- How to mark progress through celebration—without losing momentum

Because transformation is not just what you design.

It's what you **grow in others**.

Training

Training in IDT goes beyond skill development—it's about shifting mindsets, building trust, and cultivating relational intelligence. Your goal isn't to turn everyone into designers. It's to give them the **language, tools, and confidence** to see complexity and respond with care.

Recommended Approaches:
- **Experiential workshops** focused on real organizational challenges
- **Peer learning cohorts** that foster reflection and shared sensemaking
- **Design labs** with safe-to-fail prototypes and iterative feedback
- **Micro-trainings** embedded in existing leadership programs (e.g., empathy mapping, systems loops, co-design basics)

Tip: Always include a reflective element—design and insight grow together.

Train not just for knowledge transfer, but for mindset shift. When designing your training programs:
- Center empathy, systems thinking, and real-world scenarios.
- Use IDT tools like *Building Purpose*, *Value Creation Mapping*, or *Intervention Design* to ground learning in action.
- Make space for **reflection** as much as for frameworks. Questions are more powerful than checklists.

Coaching

Coaching leaders in the IDT framework requires presence and patience. This is not just about strategic advice—it's about helping leaders:
- Sit with ambiguity
- Lead through listening
- Reframe failure as feedback
- Stay connected to purpose under pressure

Coaching Touchpoints:
- One-on-one inquiry: "What's emerging in your leadership now?"
- Leadership reflection cycles (monthly or quarterly)
- Shadowing and real-time feedback on facilitation, framing, or group dynamics
- Development plans aligned with the IDT capacities: empathy, complexity navigation, creative prototyping, systems thinking, and cultural alignment

Outcome: Leaders who don't just implement change—but **embody it.**

Coaching is where change becomes personal. It's the bridge between concept and behavior. Use coaching:
- To help leaders navigate uncertainty with confidence.
- To embed reflective practice as a leadership skill.
- To create safe spaces for vulnerability, learning, and feedback.

Remember: In complex systems, there is no finish line. Leaders must learn to coach themselves—and each other—through ongoing emergence.

Celebrate Success

Celebration is not a luxury—it's a **design decision**. It sends a signal: *This matters. This is who we are.* But in high-pressure organizations, celebration is often skipped or seen as "soft." In IDT, we reclaim it as **strategic energy renewal.**

How to Celebrate Meaningfully:
- Storytelling events where teams share impact, surprises, and learnings
- Visual journeys (timelines, storyboards) reflecting the transformation arc
- Recognition rituals that honor not just outcomes, but values lived
- "Wisdom harvests" where participants reflect on what they now know

Important: Celebration is also a pause—a moment to notice, name, and nourish what's next.

One of the most underused strategies in sustainability work is **celebration**. We often rush past small wins, waiting for big milestones. But sustainable transformation is long work. We need joy. We need pause. We need shared moments of recognition.

- Celebrate **learning**, not just outcomes.
- Highlight **stories**, not just metrics.
- Recognize not just individuals—but **communities of practice** that made change possible.

Because celebration builds momentum. It tells your culture: "This matters. Let's keep going."

> ***Pause and Reflect: Integrating All Three,*** *Together, training, coaching, and celebration form a **feedback and growth loop**:*
> 1. *Training equips others to act.*
> 2. *Coaching deepens their insight.*
> 3. *Celebration renews their energy.*

This loop is a living practice—not just a phase. Use it to sustain the spirit of transformation across time, teams, and generations of leaders.

10.2 Embed into Company Culture

You can have the best strategy in the world—but if your culture doesn't live it, it won't last.

Embedding IDT into the DNA of an organization means shifting from 'project-based change' to a way of being. Culture is the container that either supports or resists transformation—and it must be intentionally shaped to align with the values and principles of sustainability.

Modeling is the first and most powerful tool. When leaders visibly engage in reflective practice, use IDT tools in meetings, and speak in a language of possibility and care, they give permission for others to do the same. This creates a ripple effect of cultural change that goes beyond formal policies or training.

Rituals are another powerful mechanism. These are the repeated behaviors that encode values into the rhythm of daily work. Simple practices—like starting meetings with purpose-alignment check-ins or ending quarters with storytelling circles—build coherence and deepen commitment. When sustained, these rituals become the heartbeat of a regenerative culture.

True cultural embedding also means integrating IDT into systems and operations. Hiring criteria, performance evaluations, decision-making frameworks, and communication strategies should all reflect the core imperatives of the IDT strategy framework. This ensures that sustainability isn't just a department—it's a way of leading and learning across the organization.

Embedding IDT into your organization is not about adding something new—it's about **revealing what's already possible** when people feel seen, heard, and connected to purpose.

Here's how to start:

Model the Mindset

Culture shifts when leaders walk the talk. Let leadership teams:

- Practice reflection and presence.
- Invite feedback and dissent.
- Use IDT tools in real decisions—not just workshops.

Create Rituals

Rituals are powerful carriers of culture. Use them to keep sustainability and design front of mind:

- Begin meetings with a reflection from the *IDT Purpose Tool*.
- Close projects with a retrospective using the *Value Capture* model.
- Invite team storytelling sessions focused on shared learning.

Integrate into Operations

Don't silo sustainability into one department. Embed it into:

- Hiring practices
- Onboarding experiences
- Budgeting and procurement decisions
- Annual planning and performance reviews

Let IDT become the **language your organization speaks**—visually, emotionally, and strategically.

10.3 Future Research Agenda

IDT is not a static framework. It's a living, breathing system of inquiry.

As Integral Design Thinking evolves, so too must the research that supports it. This framework opens up a vast terrain for inquiry (visualized in Figure 34)—into sustainability practice, creative leadership, systems change, and participatory research. The following areas offer a roadmap for future scholarship and applied experimentation.

In sustainability management, key questions remain: How do we measure transformation beyond compliance? What new metrics reflect regenerative impact, cultural alignment, or stakeholder well-being? Future research must expand what 'success' looks like—and how it's evaluated in diverse global and local contexts.

The field of IDT artifacts is still emerging. As organizations continue to design tools, narratives, and processes through IDT, researchers can explore how these artifacts evolve over time. How are they adapted in different sectors? What design features support sustained engagement? How do they influence decision-making and sensemaking?

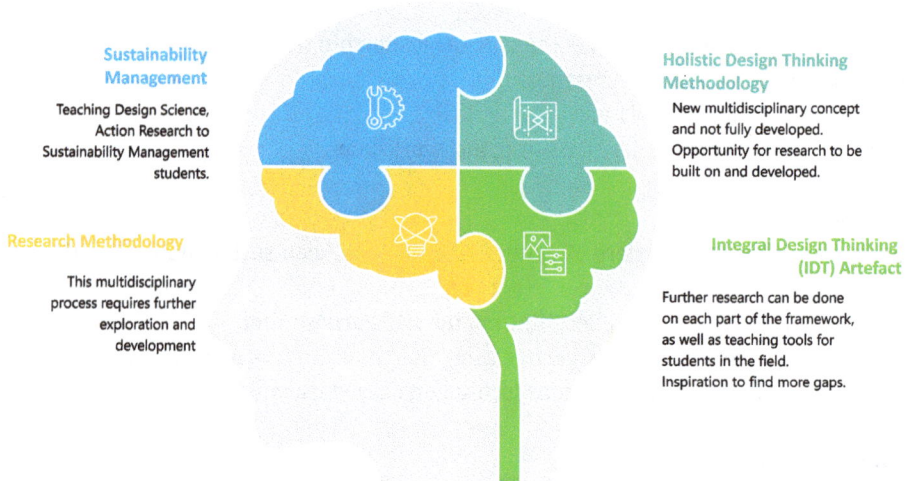

Sustainability Management

Teaching Design Science, Action Research to Sustainability Management students.

Research Methodology

This multidisciplinary process requires further exploration and development

Holistic Design Thinking Methodology

New multidisciplinary concept and not fully developed. Opportunity for research to be built on and developed.

Integral Design Thinking (IDT) Artefact

Further research can be done on each part of the framework, as well as teaching tools for students in the field. Inspiration to find more gaps.

Figure 34: Future Research Opportunities for Sustainability and Change Management Fields (Source Author).

Holistic Design Thinking Methodology (HDTM) also offers a rich ground for inquiry. It challenges the separation of thinking and feeling, of design and research. Exploring HDTM's impacts on leadership development, team dynamics, and organizational learning could yield powerful insights. Cross-disciplinary partnerships—with educators, artists, ecologists, and community leaders—can enrich the methodology even further.

Finally, research methodology itself must continue to shift. Design Science and Action Research offer a starting point, but there's room to explore hybrid models that include storytelling, embodied inquiry, and indigenous epistemologies. The goal is to expand not just what we know, but how we know—and to ensure our ways of knowing reflect the complexity and humanity of the systems we seek to change.

As I close this book, I open a door—a door to possibility, iteration, and continued learning. The Integral Design Thinking (IDT) framework is not a fixed set of rules but a living practice. It evolves as the world evolves. And just like sustainability itself, IDT thrives through inquiry, experimentation, and adaptation. In this section, I invite readers not just to implement but to *build on* what's here. The following areas are not just research topics—they are invitations. They ask you to join a growing community of thinkers, doers, and changemakers committed to designing systems that heal, uplift, and regenerate.

10.3.1 Sustainability Management

The conversation around sustainability must expand beyond compliance and risk re-duction into a dialogue about *regenerative futures*. One critical question is how IDT can be adapted for the **Global South**, where power dynamics, colonial histories, eco-logical degradation, and resource inequities intersect in profound ways. How do we honor and elevate local knowledge while applying global design tools? What does sus-tainability look like when led by those most impacted?

Further, the growing influence of **ESG (Environmental, Social, and Gover-nance)** standards presents an opportunity: Can IDT reshape how organizations re-port, communicate, and act on ESG goals—not as a performance, but as an authentic cultural transformation? Long-term research could explore how embedding IDT into ESG strategies impacts outcomes, accountability, and stakeholder trust.

And perhaps most importantly, how do we move beyond "less harm" into the realm of *regeneration*? Instead of measuring what we've reduced, can we measure what we've restored? What new indicators are needed—ones that reflect soil health, social cohesion, intergenerational equity, and psychological well-being? These are the kinds of metrics our future depends on.

> *Pause and Reflect: How can IDT be applied in global South contexts, where power, equity, and environment intersect differently? What are the long-term impacts of integrating IDT into ESG reporting and strategy? How can sustainability leaders measure **regenerative outcomes**, not just reduced harm?*

10.3.2 Integral Design Thinking Artefacts

Artefacts are not just tools. In the IDT framework, they are **embodied knowledge—**expressions of shared values, strategies, and stories. As workplaces become increas-ingly **digital and hybrid**, we must ask: What new artefacts are needed in this con-text? How do we design tools that bridge physical and virtual spaces while still hold-ing emotional resonance and narrative power?

Co-design becomes even more vital when artefacts are created with—and for—communities most affected by climate change, displacement, or systemic injustice. These artefacts are not passive. They must become **platforms for collective story-telling and sensemaking**, able to hold conflict, complexity, and emerging hope.

Imagine artefacts that don't just sit in a strategy binder but live as rituals, plat-forms, apps, or public installations. Imagine a sustainability pledge turned into a liv-ing art piece. A policy framework transformed into a participatory board game. These are the kinds of innovations waiting to emerge.

Pause and Reflect: What new types of artefacts are needed in the digital/hybrid workplace? How do arte-facts evolve when co-designed with communities most affected by sustainability issues? Can artefacts become platforms for collective storytelling and sensemaking?

10.3.3 Holistic Design Thinking Methodology (HDTM)

HDTM, the backbone of the IDT process, deserves deeper exploration—especially in terms of its **cognitive and emotional impacts** on leaders and teams over time. What changes when leaders are trained not just to think critically, but to feel collectively? What happens to team culture when systems thinking is paired with inner reflection?

Scaling HDTM across **diverse sectors** is also a frontier. From public health systems grappling with equity to educational systems needing radical redesign, HDTM offers a scaffold for innovation. But scaling requires customization, cultural sensitivity, and political awareness. How can we translate this methodology without diluting its soul?

Finally, how might HDTM evolve by engaging with **indigenous knowledge systems**, **circular economy models**, or **non-Western design traditions**? This is where some of the most powerful innovation lies. The future of sustainability is not just about technology—it's about wisdom. And HDTM must continue learning from the world's oldest systems of balance, stewardship, and community.

Pause and Reflect: What are the cognitive and emotional impacts of using HDTM over time in organizational leadership? How can this methodology be scaled across sectors—from education to public health to government? How might HDTM intersect with indigenous knowledge systems and circular economy models?

10.3.4 Research Methodology

Research in IDT is not just a means to validate—it is itself a form of **transformation**. And yet, traditional research methods often fall short when it comes to the dynamic, participatory nature of change work. This is why the integration of **Design Science** and **Action Research** is so essential. But there is more to be done. How can these two paradigms be further combined to support *real-time transformation* that is rigorous *and* relational?

We also need to investigate **embodied forms of inquiry**—the kind that involve art, movement, metaphor, and the wisdom of the body. These modes may seem unconventional, but they tap into emotional and intuitive intelligence that analytical tools often miss. What role could embodied learning play in shaping a deeper, more holistic form of organizational intelligence?

And finally, what if research itself was reimagined—not just as analysis, but as a tool for **cultural healing**? What if the process of inquiry helped repair trauma, rebuild trust, and restore dignity? This is the promise of participatory design. Of story circles. Of healing-centered research. It invites us not just to study systems, but to transform them—with humility, courage, and care.

> *Pause and Reflect: How can Action Research and Design Science be further integrated to support **real-time transformation**? What role does embodied learning (e.g., art, movement, metaphor) play in design research? How might research itself become a **tool for cultural healing**, not just problem-solving?*

This Is Where You Come In

Whether you are a scholar, practitioner, policymaker, or student—you are now part of this evolving field. The questions you ask, the stories you gather, the artefacts you create—they all shape what comes next. You don't have to have all the answers. What matters is that you *keep asking*. Stay curious. Stay courageous. Stay committed to imagining a world that works—for all.

The work ahead is not easy. But it is meaningful. And you are not alone in it.

10.4 Sub-section Research Possibilities and Ideas

A Call to Collaborative Inquiry —This section doesn't claim to have all the answers. Instead, it invites researchers into shared authorship of a field still becoming.

As you read the sub-sections, consider:
- What's already been studied—and what's been overlooked?
- What are you seeing in your practice or organization that academia hasn't named yet?
- Where could your lived experience contribute to scholarly insight?

The next breakthroughs in sustainable transformation will come **not just from research**, but from researchers willing to design *with* the world, not just study it.

10.4.1 Sustainability Management

Designing for Regenerative Impact—Sustainability management has come a long way—from compliance and reporting, to ESG frameworks, circular economy models, and regenerative leadership. Yet even as tools advance, the field still struggles with fragmentation, short-termism, and a focus on metrics over meaning.

Integral Design Thinking (IDT) offers a way to shift sustainability management from *doing less harm* to **designing for collective thriving**.

The next evolution in sustainability won't come from more dashboards.

It will come from more integrative, relational, and creative ways of thinking and leading.

Key Research Questions

- How can IDT support the transition from sustainability as risk management to sustainability as systems transformation?
- What leadership capacities are required to implement sustainability through an IDT lens?
- How does IDT influence decision-making across different industries (e.g., manufacturing, tech, education, urban planning)?
- What are the barriers to embedding IDT in corporate sustainability strategy—and how can they be addressed?
- How can IDT frameworks better align with planetary boundaries and social thresholds?

Emerging Areas of Inquiry

1. **Sustainability as Design Capacity**
   Moving from compliance checklists to design literacy. Research can explore how building IDT capabilities across organizations supports innovation, resilience, and employee engagement in sustainability.
2. **IDT and the Circular Economy**
   Investigating how IDT principles (empathy, systems awareness, prototyping, feedback loops) enhance the design of circular products, supply chains, and services.
3. **Governance Through Design**
   Studying how participatory and co-design methods can shape governance models for sustainability—especially in complex stakeholder systems like cities, cooperatives, or climate coalitions.
4. **Cultural Shifts as Strategy**
   Understanding how IDT can support cultural change initiatives aimed at embedding sustainability values—not just sustainability policies.

Suggested Research Methods

- Participatory action research (PAR) in sustainability teams
- Case studies of organizations applying IDT in environmental or social innovation
- Longitudinal studies tracking cultural shifts post-IDT integration
- Mixed-methods research combining organizational outcomes with qualitative reflection from participants

Contribution to the Field

By integrating IDT into sustainability management, future research can help shift:
- From output to **impact**
- From best practices to **emergent, adaptive practice**
- From separate "green teams" to **organization-wide design culture**

This is sustainability as a **relational design endeavor**—where people, planet, and process align through purpose.

10.4.2 Integral Design Thinking Artifact

Making the Invisible Visible — Every framework is an artifact. It holds within it a worldview—a way of seeing, structuring, and engaging with reality. Integral Design Thinking (IDT) is no exception.

As a methodological artifact, IDT integrates systems thinking, creative practice, sustainability theory, and holistic design. It is not just a tool—it is a **container for transformation**. Studying it as an artifact allows us to examine its form, function, evolution, and application across contexts.

The IDT artifact is more than a model—it is a **mirror of mindset** and **map for meaningful change**.

Key Research Questions
- What makes IDT distinct from other design thinking and systems-based frameworks?
- How does the IDT artifact evolve in different cultural, organizational, or disciplinary settings?
- What role does the visual, conceptual, and experiential design of the IDT artifact play in shaping its adoption?
- Can the artifact itself be co-designed by practitioners and scholars—and how does that affect legitimacy or utility?
- How does the IDT artifact perform in digital learning environments or hybrid teams?

The IDT Artifact: Dimensions of Study
1. **Conceptual Form**

   The philosophical structure of IDT—its integration of parts, wholes, relationships, feedback loops, and regenerative intent. Research might explore how these concepts are experienced differently in management, education, or governance.

2. **Visual and Spatial Representation**
   Studying how diagrams, maps, and toolkits influence how people understand and apply IDT. What makes a framework legible, inviting, or transformative?
3. **Language and Narrative**
   Exploring how the language of IDT—terms like wholeness, empathy, prototyping, emergence—shapes user engagement and meaning-making.
4. **Embodied Practice**
   Investigating how the IDT artifact is not only conceptual but **experiential**—how people move through it, reflect within it, and adapt it to fit real-world challenges.

Methodologies for Exploration

- Ethnographic observation of teams using IDT in real time
- Comparative analysis of IDT vs. traditional design thinking tools
- Participatory design workshops to co-evolve the artifact with users
- Semiotic and discourse analysis of how IDT is communicated and received

Contribution to the Field

Studying the IDT artifact creates an opportunity to:

- Treat frameworks as **living systems**, not static models
- Engage users as **co-authors** of design knowledge
- Reflect critically on the tools we use to shape organizations and change

This is research as dialogue—with the framework, with each other, and with the future of design itself.

10.4.3 Holistic Design Thinking Methodology

Designing From Wholeness—Most design thinking methods emerged from engineering, innovation labs, or product development environments. While useful, these origins often carry assumptions of speed, linearity, and efficiency.

Holistic Design Thinking, as practiced in IDT, challenges those assumptions.

It asks not just "How do we solve this problem?"

But "What kind of thinking—and being—does this system require from us?"

This section invites research into the **deep structure** of IDT as a holistic, integrative methodology—one that blends reflection, systems thinking, co-creation, and regenerative logic.

What Makes IDT Holistic?
–   It centers **humanity and interdependence**—not just utility or function
–   It honors **emergence** over linear planning
–   It incorporates **emotional, relational, and spiritual dimensions**
–   It views problems as *living systems*, not as isolated technical issues
–   It invites **multiple ways of knowing**: intuitive, rational, embodied, ecological

This positions IDT as a **post-disciplinary methodology**—one that crosses boundaries and embraces complexity as creative material.

Key Research Questions
–   How does holistic design thinking differ in methodology from traditional human-centered or double diamond models?
–   What philosophical or epistemological roots inform IDT? (e.g., phenomenology, systems theory, ecology, Eastern philosophy)
–   How can holistic methods be studied without fragmenting them into parts?
–   What practices support practitioners in developing the presence and perception needed for holistic design?
–   How do organizations respond differently to holistic versus linear methods of transformation?

Research Pathways
1.   **Methodological Reflexivity**
     Exploring how researchers and practitioners engage *with* the method, not just through it. This invites autoethnography, narrative inquiry, and reflective practice.
2.   **Comparative Method Analysis**
     Studying the outcomes and experiences of teams using IDT vs. conventional design methods—especially in complex systems (e.g., healthcare, education, sustainability governance).
3.   **Philosophical Foundations**
     Mapping the roots of IDT in holistic paradigms: Integral Theory, deep ecology, indigenous knowledge systems, second-order cybernetics, etc.
4.   **Embodied and Experiential Learning**
     Investigating how holistic design methodologies can be taught and scaled—especially through immersive experiences, arts-based methods, or contemplative pedagogy.

Contribution to the Field

This line of research brings design out of its industrial origins and into a new lineage: one that is relational, regenerative, and rooted in **being, not just doing**.

It helps future scholars and practitioners:

- Reframe design as **a way of knowing**
- Honor complexity without reducing it
- Make space for mystery, intuition, and emergence
- Design with life—not just for users

In a time of ecological and social unraveling, holistic design offers not just methods—but **medicine**.

10.4.4 Research Methodology

Research as a Living Practice—Integral Design Thinking (IDT) is not just a framework for organizations—it is also a **methodological invitation** for researchers. To study it well, researchers must **embody its values**: empathy, reflection, co-creation, and systemic awareness.

IDT doesn't just ask *what* you research—it asks *how* you research.

And who you become in the process.

This section proposes approaches to research methodology that are aligned with IDT's purpose: transformation. It encourages methods that are iterative, reflexive, dialogical, and ethically grounded in context.

Key Research Questions

- What methodologies can capture the relational and dynamic nature of IDT in practice?
- How can researchers study change without objectifying it?
- What forms of data (stories, metaphors, visuals, embodiment) are legitimate in IDT research?
- How do researcher and participant co-evolve through the research process?
- Can research itself be designed as an **act of regeneration**?

Recommended Research Approaches

1. **Participatory Action Research (PAR)**

   Rooted in collaboration and reflection, PAR allows participants to be co-researchers. It aligns perfectly with IDT's ethos of shared inquiry and real-world experimentation.

   PAR asks: "How can we learn from change *as we make it*?"

2. **Autoethnography and Reflective Practice**
   IDT researchers often play multiple roles—designer, facilitator, leader, learner. Autoethnography allows them to reflect on their own experience and positionality, turning personal narrative into collective insight.
   Why it matters: In living systems, **your perspective is part of the data.**
3. **Systems Mapping and Narrative Inquiry**
   To study IDT's impact, researchers may combine systems analysis (e.g., feedback loops, leverage points) with narrative tools that capture emotional, symbolic, and social meaning.
   – What changed?
   – What stories are being told?
   – What new relationships emerged?
4. **Design-Based Research (DBR)**
   A strong fit for educational or organizational settings, DBR involves iterative design, testing, reflection, and adaptation. It blends theory and practice—just like IDT.
5. **Mixed Methods with Qualitative Depth**
   Quantitative data (e.g., engagement scores, system performance metrics) can be used alongside interviews, visual tools, and observational field notes. But qualitative depth is essential for capturing **what it *feels* like** to be in a transformation.

Ethical and Epistemological Considerations
– Use **consent as conversation**—not just as a form.
– Treat participants as **knowledge holders**, not just subjects.
– Make space for discomfort, contradiction, and emergence.
– See research not just as extraction, but as **exchange**.

The research process itself should reflect the world we are trying to build.

Contribution to the Field
This research agenda invites scholars to move from detached observers to engaged stewards of transformation. It encourages work that is:
– Situated and systemic
– Humble and hopeful
– Creative, relational, and rigorous

In short, it is research that does not just study change—but **participates in it**.

10.5 Final Thoughts: A Call to Keep Designing

We live in a time of great complexity. But we also live in a time of great capacity.

As you reach the final pages of this book, know this: the work is just beginning. You now hold not just a framework, but a mindset—a way of seeing and shaping that centers empathy, systems, and possibility. This is Integral Design Thinking not as theory, but as life practice.

In a world of rapid change and rising complexity, your presence matters. Your ability to listen deeply, act wisely, and hold space for emergence is what will shape the futures we co-create. This isn't about having the perfect plan. It's about asking better questions—and inviting others into the inquiry. We live in a world where problems are layered, intersecting, and urgent. Where quick fixes don't stick. Where old models can't hold what's emerging.

That's why this book has insisted on:
– Reflection, not reaction
– Systems awareness, not silos
– Purpose, not just process
– Healing, not just innovating
– Wholeness, not perfection

Because the future doesn't need more experts.

It needs more **whole humans**—willing to show up, stay with the complexity, and co-create what comes next.

You are the most important tool in the IDT toolbox. Your story, your reflection, your courage to lead differently. Sustainability is not just about reducing harm—it's about designing with intention, aligning with values, and building systems that support life. That begins with you. Whether you are a strategist, coach, educator, designer, changemaker, or CEO—your role is not just to implement a model.

Your role is to:
– Invite people into deeper questions
– Design spaces where transformation can happen
– Notice what's alive, and nurture it
– Make decisions that align with values and vision
– Tell stories that restore hope and agency

You are not just a reader of this work. You are its **continuation**.

So keep designing. Keep questioning. Keep gathering around the table with others who care. Whether you're leading a global team or a local classroom, your work matters. Let this book be your companion—not as a map, but as a compass. You're not alone. And the journey is worth it. Let this book be a spiral, not a line. Return to it. Reframe it. Revise it with others. Adapt it for your context. Add your insight. Your culture. Your contradictions. Your brilliance.

Integral Design Thinking (IDT) is not a product to be delivered.

It is a *practice to be lived*—again and again.

Notes

Leadership mindset

1 Burns, James MacGregor, 1978. Leadership. 1st ed. New York: Harper & Row.
2 Scott, Susanne G. and Reginald A. Bruce, 1994. "Determinants of innovative behavior: a path model of individual innovation in the workplace", Academy of Management Journal(3), 37:580–607. https://doi.org/10.5465/256701
3 Greenleaf, Robert K., 1970. The Servant as Leader. Indianapolis: Robert K. Greenleaf Center.
4 Nauman, Shazia, Sabeen Hussain Bhatti, Hassan Imam, and Mohammad Saud Khan, 2021. "How servant leadership drives project team performance through collaborative culture and knowledge sharing", Project Management Journal(1), 53:17–32. https://doi.org/10.1177/87569728211037777

Chapter 1 – A New World Economy & Leadership For the 21st Century

5 Burns, T. (2012). The sustainability revolution: A societal paradigm shift. *Sustainability*, *4*, 1118–1134; doi:10.3390/su4061118, www.mdpi.com/journal/sustainability.
6 Ferdig, M. A., and Ludema, J. D. (2005). Transformative interactions: Qualities of conversation that heighten the vitality of self-organising change. In Pasmore, W. and Woodman, R. (Eds.). Research in Organisational Change and Development, (p. 15). Emerald Publishing Limited ISBN 978-1-78052-807-6, DOI 10.1108/S0897-3016(2012)20
7 Gitsham, M. (2019). The changing role of business leaders, and implications for talent management and executive education. In G. G. Lenssen and N. C. Smith (Eds.), *Managing sustainable business* (pp. 671–682). Springer Netherlands. https://doi.org/10.1007/978-94-024-1144-7_31
8 Ferdig, M. (2007). Sustainability leadership: Co-creating a sustainable future. *Journal of Change Management*, *7*(1), 25–35, DOI: 10.1080/14697010701233809 (p. 33)
9 Trompenaars, F., and Hampden-Turner, C. (2002). *21 leaders for the 21st century*. McGraw-Hill.
10 Elsbach, K. and Stigliani, S. (2018). Design thinking and organisational culture: A review and framework for future research. *Journal of Management*, 1–33.
11 Johansson-Sköldberg, U., Woodilla, J., and Çetinkaya, M. (2013). Design Thinking: Past, present, and possible futures. *Creativity and Innovation Management*, *22*, 121–146.
12 Dunne, D., and Martin, R. (2006). Design thinking and how it will change management education. *Academy of Management Learning and Education*, *5*, 512–23.
13 Liedtka, J., and Kaplan, S. (2019). How Design Thinking opens new frontiers for strategy development. *Strategy and Leadership*, *47*(2), 3–10.
14 Martin, R. (2009). *The design of business: why design thinking is the next competitive advantage.* Harvard Business School Press.
15 Greenwood, R., and Hinings, C.R. (1996). Understanding radical organizational change: Bringing together the old and the new institutionalism. *The Academy of Management Review*, 21(4), 1022–1054.
16 Romanelli, E. and Tushman, M.L. (1994). Organisational transformation as punctuated equilibrium: an empirical test. *The Academy of Management Journal*, 37(5), 1141–1166.

https://doi.org/10.1515/9783111705286-012

Chapter 2 – Designs for Life: Sustainability Business, Sustainable Organizations

17 Camou, M., and Green, L. (2016). Modeling sustainability futures: Cultural shift strategies for sustainability leaders case study New York City's Department of Education's Office of Sustainability. *The International Academic Forum (IAFOR) ECSS/ECSEE/ECSEE/ECPEL/EBMC Conference*, 53–69.

18 Goodall, C (2012). *Sustainability: All that matters.* McGraw-Hill Education.

19 Singh, S. K. (2019). Sustainable business and environment management. *Management of Environmental Quality: An International Journal, 30*(1), 2–4.

20 Martinez, F., Peattie, K., and Vazquez-Brust, D. (2019). Beyond win–win: A syncretic theory on corporate stakeholder engagement in sustainable development. *Business Strategy and the Environment, 28*(5), 896–908. https://doi.org/10.1002/bse.2292

21 IBM, 2021. Comsumers want it all: Hybrid shopping, sustainability, and purpose-driven brands, downloaded from IBM.COM, 2025. https://www.ibm.com/downloads/documents/us-en/10c31775c8540243

22 World Economic forum, 2025. The Future of Jobs Report 2025, downloaded 2025. https://reports.weforum.org/docs/WEF_Future_of_Jobs_Report_2025.pdf

23 Braineet.com, Customer Co-Creation Examples: 12 Companies Doing It Right, Open Innovation, referenced 2025. https://www.braineet.com/blog/co-creation-examples

24 United Nations, 2020. Urban Climate Action Is Crucial to Bend the Emissions Curve 5 October 2020, Article referenced 2025. https://unfccc.int/news/urban-climate-action-is-crucial-to-bend-the-emissions-curve

25 C40 Cities 2025. Website referenced 2025, https://www.c40.org/

26 NYC Gov, 2025. Website accessed 2025, https://www.nyc.gov/site/buildings/codes/ll97-greenhouse-gas-emissions-reductions.page

27 Hallin, J., Fredriksson, E., Altman, R., and Zhou, S. (2016). Developing a Human Centred Business Index – Leading with Purpose, Empathy, Systems-Approach and Resilience in 'Business Beyond Sustainability.' *European Public and Social Innovation Review, 1*(1). https://doi.org/10.31637/epsir.16-1.3.

Chapter 3 – Evolution of Perception and Theoretical Frameworks

28 United Nations, 1987. Report of the World Commission on Environment and Development, p. 54, retrieved 2025. https://digitallibrary.un.org/record/139811?v=pdf

29 Brown, L. (2006). *Plan B 2.0: Rescuing a planet under stress and a civilization in trouble.* Norton and Company, Inc.

30 United Nations, 2015. SDG History, retrieved from website 2025. https://sdgs.un.org/goals

31 Dryzek, J., Norgaard, B., and Schlosberg, D. (2012). *The Oxford handbook of climate change and society.* doi: 10.1093/oxfordhb/9780199566600.003.0001

32 Capra, F. (2002). *The hidden connections: A science for sustainable living.* Anchor Books.

33 Senge, P., Smith, B., Kruschwitz, N., Laur, J., and Schley, S. (2008). *The necessary revolution: how individuals and organisations are working together to create a sustainable world.* Doubleday.

34 Brown, L. (2006). *Plan B 2.0: Rescuing a planet under stress and a civilization in trouble.* Norton and Company, Inc.

35 Sachs, J. (2005). *The end of poverty: Economic possibilities for our time.* Penguin Books.

36 Seelos, C., and Mair, J. (2005b). Sustainable Development: How social entrepreneurs make it happen. [Working Paper]. IESE Business School, University of Navarra.

37 McKnight, J. (1993). *Building communities from the inside out: A path toward finding and mobilizing a community's asset.* ACTA Publications.

38 Blue Podcast Network. 2024. How to Protect the Ocean. 4Ocean: 40 Million Pounds and Counting – The Impact of 4ocean on Ocean Cleanup Efforts. Retrieved 2025, https://www.speakupforblue.com/show/speak-up-for-the-ocean-blue/4ocean-40-million-pounds-and-counting-the-impact-of-4ocean-on-ocean-cleanup-efforts/

39 Laszlo, C. (2003). *The sustainable company: How to create lasting value through social and environmental performance.* Island Press.

40 Capra, F. (2002). *The hidden connections: A science for sustainable living.* Anchor Books.

41 Senge, P., Smith, B., Kruschwitz, N., Laur, J., and Schley, S. (2008). *The necessary revolution: how individuals and organisations are working together to create a sustainable world.* Doubleday.

42 Wilber, K. (2001). *A theory of everything: an integral vision for business, politics, science and spirituality.* Shambhala Publication, Inc.

43 Wilber, K. (2007). *The integral vision.* Shambhala Publications, Inc.

44 Image retrieved from Jaber, M., 2021. Integral Design Thinking: A Novel Cross-national Framework for Sustainability Management, PhD Thesis, pg. 24.

45 Young, J. E. (2002). A spectrum of consciousness for CEOs: A business application of Ken Wilber's spectrum of consciousness. *International Journal of Organisational Analysis, 10*(1), 30–54.

46 Pavez, I., Kendall, L., and Lazlo, C. (2020). Positive-impact companies: Toward a new paradigm of value creation. *Organ Dyn,* https://doi.org/10.1016/j.orgdyn.2020.100806

47 Hallin, J., Fredriksson, E., Altman, R., and Zhou, S. (2016). Developing a Human Centred Business Index – Leading with Purpose, Empathy, Systems-Approach and Resilience in 'Business Beyond Sustainability.' *European Public and Social Innovation Review, 1*(1). https://doi.org/10.31637/epsir.16-1.3.

48 Schultz, P.W., (2000). Empathizing with nature: The effects of perspective taking on concern for environmental issues. *J. Soc. Issues, 56*, 391–406.

49 Czap, N.V., Czap, H.J., Khachaturyan, M., Lynne, G.D., and Burbach, M.E., (2012). Walking in the shoes of others: Experimental testing of dual-interest and empathy in environmental choice. *J. Socio. 41*, 642–653.

50 Elsbach, K. and Stigliani, S. (2018). Design thinking and organisational culture: A review and framework for future research. *Journal of Management*, 1–33.

51 Image retrieved from Jaber, M., 2021. Integral Design Thinking: A Novel Cross-national Framework for Sustainability Management, PhD Thesis, pg. 26.

52 Scharmer, O. (2007). *Theory U: Leading from the future as it emerges.* The Society for Organisational Learning, Inc.

53 Schein, E. (1992). *Organisational culture and leadership.* Jossey Bass.

54 UN Global Compact, 2023. The 12th United Nations Global Compact–Accenture CEO Study. Accessed 2025. https://www.globalcompactusa.org/news/the-12th-united-nations-global-compact-accenture-ceo-study

55 Doppelt, B. (2003). Overcoming the seven blunders of sustainability. *The systems thinker, 14*(5), 2–7.

56 Doppelt, B. (2014). Leading change toward Sustainability: A change-management guide for business, government and civil society. *International Journal of Sustainability in Higher Education.* Volume 5 Issue 2 https://doi.org/10.1108/ijshe.2004.24905bae.005.

57 Doppelt, B. (2003). Overcoming the seven blunders of sustainability. *The systems thinker, 14*(5), 2–7.

58 Image retrieved from Jaber, M., 2021. Integral Design Thinking: A Novel Cross-national Framework for Sustainability Management, PhD Thesis, pg. 28.

59 Image retrieved from Jaber, M., 2021. Integral Design Thinking: A Novel Cross-national Framework for Sustainability Management, PhD Thesis, pg. 29.

60 Peter Drucker, 1950's to 2000's, a renowned management consultant, educator, and author who wrote extensively about management and organizational culture, this phrase came from his writing.

61 Laszlo, C. (2005). *The sustainable company: How to create lasting value through social and environmental performance.* Island Press.

62 Image retrieved from Jaber, M., 2021. Integral Design Thinking: A Novel Cross-national Framework for Sustainability Management, PhD Thesis, pg. 32.

63 Robertson, Roland (1995). "Glocalization: Time-Space and Homogeneity-Heterogeneity," in *Global Modernities*, edited by Mike Featherstone, Scott Lash, and Roland Robertson. Sage Publications.

Chapter 4 – Strategy and Strategic Thinking

64 Freedman, L. (2013). *Strategy.* Oxford University Press.

65 Porter, M. (1986). *Competitive strategy.* Harvard Business School Press.

66 Andrews, K. (1980). *The concept of corporate strategy,* (2nd ed.). Dow-Jones Irwin.

67 Mintzberg, H. (1994). *The rise and fall of strategic planning.* Prentice-Hall

68 Mintzberg, H., and Quinn, J.B. (1996). *The strategy process: concepts, contexts, cases.* Prentice Hall

69 Engert S., Rauter R., and Baumgartner R.J. (2016). Exploring the integration of corporate sustainability into strategic management: A literature review. *J. Clean. Prod.,* 2833–2850.

70 Steiner, G. (1979). Strategic Planning. Free Press.

71 Porter, T. (2009). Three views of systems theories and their implications for sustainability education. *Journal of Management Education,* 33(3), 323–347

72 Liedtka, J., and Kaplan, S. (2019). How Design Thinking opens new frontiers for strategy development. *Strategy and Leadership,* 47(2), 3–10.

73 Johnson, G., Whittington, R., Scholes, K., Angwin, D., and Regner, P. (2017). *Exploring strategy: Text and cases,* (11th ed.). Pearson.

74 Bouhali R., Mekdadb Y., Lebsirc H., and Ferkha L (2015). Leader roles for innovation: Strategic thinking and planning. *Procedia – Social and Behavioural Sciences, 181,* 72–78.

75 Liedtka J.M. (1998). Lining strategic thinking with strategic planning. *Strategy and leadership,* 30–35.

76 Boon, I. (2001). Developing strategic thinking as a core competency. *Management Decision, 39*(1).

77 Graetz, F. (2002). Strategic thinking versus strategic planning: Towards understanding the complementarities. *Management Decision, 40*(5).

78 Reed, G. (2006). Leadership and systems thinking. *Defence ATandL,* 10–13

79 Checkland, P., and Haynes, M. (1994). Varieties of systems thinking: The case of soft systems methodology. *System Dynamics Review, 10*(2–3), 189–197.

80 Porter, T. (2009). Three views of systems theories and their implications for sustainability education. *Journal of Management Education,* 33(3), 323–347

Chapter 5 – Design Thinking

81 Simon, H.A (1969). *The sciences of the artificial.* MIT Press.

82 Retrieved from Jaber, M. (2021). *Integral Design Thinking: A Novel Cross-national Framework for Sustainability Management.* PhD Thesis, Birmingham City University, retrieved pg. 43.

83 Schon, D. (1983). *The reflective practitioner: How professionals think in action,* (pp. 102–104). Basic Books.

84 Krippendorff, K. (2006). *The semantic turn: A new foundation for design.* Taylor and Francis.

85 Cross, N. (2011) Design Thinking: Understanding how Designers Think and Work. Berg Publishers Ltd., Oxford.

86 Lawson, B. (2006). *How designers think: The design process demystified*, (4th ed.). Architectural Press.

87 Buchanan, R. (1992). Wicked problems in design thinking. *Design Issues, 8*, 5–21.

88 Brown, T. (2009). *Change by design*. Harper Collins.

89 Liedtka, J., and Kaplan, S. (2019). How Design Thinking opens new frontiers for strategy development. *Strategy and Leadership, 47*(2), 3–10.

90 Martin, R. (2009). *The design of business: why design thinking is the next competitive advantage.*

91 Forbs,Timmes, M. 2022. *Millennials And Gen Z: Now Is The Time To Reshape Businesses To Harness Their Power*, Article publisher June 27,2022. Retrieved 2025, https://www.forbes.com/councils/forbescoa chescouncil/2022/06/27/millennials-and-gen-z-now-is-the-time-to-reshape-businesses-to-harness-their-power/?

92 Elsbach, K. and Stigliani, S. (2018). Design thinking and organisational culture: A review and framework for future research. *Journal of Management*, 1–33.

93 Senge, P. (1990). The fifth discipline: The Art & Practice of the Learning Organization. Doubleday.

Chapter 6 – Organizational Change Management

94 Moran, J. W., and Brightman, B. K. (2001). Leading organisational change. *Career Development International, 6*(2), 111–118.

95 Cooperrider, D. L., and Srivastva, S. (1987). Appreciative inquiry in organisational life. In R. W. Woodman and W.A. Pasmore (Eds.), *Research in organisational change and development*, (pp. 129–169). JAI Press.

96 Graetz, F. (2000). Strategic change leadership. *Management Decision, 38*(8), 550–562.

97 Senior, B. (2002). Organisational change (2nd ed.). Prentice Hall.

98 Kotter, J. P. (1996). *Leading change*. Harvard Business Press.

99 Burnes, B. (2004). *Managing change: A strategic approach to organisational dynamics*, (4th ed.). Prentice Hall.

100 Lewin, K. (1947). Frontiers in group dynamics. Human Relations, 1, 5–41.

101 Judson, A. (1991). *Changing behaviour in organisations: Minimizing resistance to change*. Basil Blackwell.

102 Kotter, J. P. (1995). Leading change: Why transformation efforts fail', *Harvard Business Review*, 59–67.

103 Rieley, J. B. and Clarkson, I. (2001). The impact of change on performance. *Journal of Change Management, 2*(2), 160–172.

104 Burnes, B. (2004). *Managing change: A strategic approach to organisational dynamics*, (4th ed.). Prentice Hall.

105 Dawson, P. (1994). *Organisational change: A processual approach*. Paul Chapman.

106 Beer, M., Eisenstat, R.A., and Spector, B. (1990). *Why change programs don't produce change*. Harvard Business School Press/.

107 Hiatt, J.M. (2006). ADKAR: *A model for change in business, government, and our community: How to implement successful change in our personal lives and professional careers*. Prosci Research.

108 Kanter, R.M., Stein, B., and Jick, T.D. (1992). *The challenge of organisational change: How companies experience it and leaders guide it*. Free Press.

109 Galpin, T. (1996). *The human side of change: A practical guide to organisation redesign*. Jossey-Bass.

110 Stouten, J., Rousseau, D., and Cremer, D. (2018). Successful organisational change: Integrating the management practice an scholarly literatures. *Academy of Management Annals, 12*(2), 752–788.

111 Cameron, E., and Green, M. (2015). *Making sense of change management* (4th ed.). Great Britain, Kogan Page Limited.

112 Bicheno, J., and Holweg, M. (2009). *The lean toolbox, the essential guide to lean transformation*, (4th ed.). Production and Inventory Control, Systems and Industrial Engineering (PICSIE). Books.

113 Nonaka, I. (1994). A dynamic theory of organisational knowledge creation. *Organisation Science*, 5(1), 14–37.

114 Porter, T. (2009). Three views of systems theories and their implications for sustainability education. *Journal of Management Education*, 33(3), 323–347

115 Mann, D. (2010). *Creating a lean culture* (2nd ed.). CRC Press, Taylor and Francis Group, Ltd.

116 Liff, S., and Posey, P. (2004). *Seeing is Believing*. American Management Association, AMACOM.

117 Edmondson, A. C. (2002). The local and variegated nature of learning in organisations: A group-level perspective. *Organisation Science*, 13, 128–146.

118 Clark, S. M., Gioia, D. A., Ketchen, D. J. Jr., and Thomas, J. B. (2010). Transitional identity as a facilitator of organisational identity change during a merger. *Administrative Science Quarterly*, 55, 397–438.

119 Rodell, J. B. and Colquitt, J. A. (2009). Looking ahead in times of uncertainty: The role of anticipatory justice in an organisational change context. *Journal of Applied Psychology*, 94, 989–1002.

Chapter 7 – Discussion and Framework Introduction

120 European Union, Eu Taxonomy for sustainability activities. Retrieved 2025, https://build-up.ec.europa.eu/en/resources-and-tools/links/eu-taxonomy-sustainable-activities

121 European Union, Corporate Sustainability Reporting. Retrieved 2025, https://finance.ec.europa.eu/capital-markets-union-and-financial-markets/company-reporting-and-auditing/company-reporting/corporate-sustainability-reporting_en

122 European Commission, Fit for 55: Delivering on the proposal. Retrieved 2025, https://commission.europa.eu/strategy-and-policy/priorities-2019-2024/european-green-deal/delivering-european-green-deal/fit-55-delivering-proposals_en

123 European Commission, Circular Economy Action Plan. Retrieved 2025, https://environment.ec.europa.eu/strategy/circular-economy-action-plan_en

124 Urban Food Alliance came into existence to meet NYC's Zero Waste Initiative and targets. This non-profit organization was created as a collaborative by school food service professionals in 2012 to address the unique needs of the nation's largest school districts.

Chapter 9 – IDT Strategy Framework Creative-Thinking Tools

125 Jaber, M., 2021. Integral Design Thinking: A Novel Cross-national Framework for Sustainability Management, PhD Thesis, BCU, UK.

126 Jaber, M., 2021. Integral Design Thinking: A Novel Cross-national Framework for Sustainability Management, PhD Thesis, Section 5.3.3, pg 13.

Glossary

Archetypal & Symbolic Analysis A method for uncovering the deeper meanings behind human behavior and culture, by examining patterns, recurring characters, metaphors, and symbols. Think of it as decoding the myths and stories that live beneath the surface of organizational life.

Artefacts The tangible expressions of your design work. These are tools, documents, or activities developed to address organizational challenges—each one a building block of change.

Autoethnography and Reflective Practice A personal, introspective approach to research that combines storytelling with critical analysis, allowing you to learn through your own lived experience and reflect on your role in the process.

B Corporation Certification A gold-standard verification that a company meets rigorous standards for social and environmental impact, transparency, and accountability. It reflects a business model where profit and purpose coexist.

Branding More than a logo—this is about crafting the visual and emotional identity of an organization. It defines how a company presents itself and what it stands for.

Change Agent Someone inside or outside the organization championing a shift toward sustainability. They see the bigger picture, ask tough questions, and push for courageous change.

Co-Creation Model A participatory process where stakeholders—employees, customers, partners—actively collaborate to design meaningful solutions together.

Communication The connective tissue of any organization. This refers to the intentional systems, strategies, and messages used to engage stakeholders internally and externally.

Community A network of people bound by shared purpose, values, or location. In organizations, community includes employees, customers, partners, and local groups—all brought together by mutual goals.

Complex Adaptive Systems (CAS) Approach A way of seeing organizations not as machines, but as living systems—dynamic, evolving, and interconnected. This approach emphasizes patterns and relationships over linear cause and effect.

Contradictions The tensions or inconsistencies that arise in organizations. For example: promoting ethical sourcing while depending on exploitative labor elsewhere. Recognizing these tensions is the first step to resolving them.

Corporate Sustainability Reporting Directive (CSRD) A European Union regulation that requires companies to publicly report on their environmental and social impact, ensuring greater transparency and accountability.

Creative Analysis A research approach that uses creative methods—like storytelling, visual mapping, or design prompts—to uncover insights that traditional data analysis might miss.

Design-Based Research (DBR) A research method rooted in real-world experimentation, where solutions are prototyped and refined through cycles of design, implementation, and feedback.

Design Thinking A human-centered problem-solving approach that uses empathy, creativity, and iteration to reimagine systems and design impactful solutions. It's about designing with—not just for—people.

https://doi.org/10.1515/9783111705286-013

Design Science Research A research methodology that focuses on the creation and evaluation of artifacts (tools, models, systems) to solve real-world problems, blending theory and practice.

Dynamic Equilibrium A state where balance is maintained through constant change and adaptation. It's not static, but stable in motion—like riding a bike.

Emergent Approach A flexible, adaptive strategy that evolves in response to what's happening on the ground, rather than following a rigid plan.

Emergent Behavior Unexpected patterns or behaviors that arise from the interactions within a system—often greater than the sum of the parts.

Empathy The ability to deeply understand the needs, emotions, and perspectives of others. It's the foundation for meaningful, inclusive leadership and design.

Empathy-Based Synthesis The art of drawing insights from what people say and feel—tuning into tone, emotion, and lived experience to find deeper meaning in their stories.

Empathetic Leadership A leadership style grounded in compassion, curiosity, and a genuine desire to understand others. These leaders listen first and act with integrity.

Feedback Loops Circular systems of input and response that help organizations learn and adapt. They show us what's working—and what's not—in real time.

Fragmentation The disjointed, siloed ways of working that can prevent organizations from seeing the whole picture. Healing fragmentation starts with integration and shared purpose.

Framework A structure or model that helps us make sense of complexity and guides thoughtful action. A good framework provides clarity without oversimplifying.

Holistic Seeing the whole system, not just its parts. This approach integrates mindsets, methods, people, and processes.

Holistic Design Thinking Methodology A blended approach that merges traditional design thinking with systems thinking and complexity science to navigate change across entire organizations.

Human-Centered Orientation A mindset that places people—their needs, hopes, and experiences—at the heart of every decision and design process.

Humility A vital leadership quality that embraces not knowing, listens to others, and recognizes that the best ideas often emerge from collaboration.

Inner Alignment The harmony between your values, beliefs, and actions. When leaders and organizations are inwardly aligned, their outward impact is more authentic and effective.

Integral Whole, complete, and connected. This approach considers multiple perspectives and dimensions—mind, body, culture, and systems—in every decision.

Integral Design Thinking (IDT) A holistic strategy framework that bridges human and organizational needs. It guides the breakdown of outdated systems and the building of new, purpose-driven ones.

Integrated Leadership Mindset A way of leading that balances logic and empathy, vision and pragmatism. It's about showing up fully—head and heart—in service of meaningful change.

Interdependencies The invisible threads that connect people, processes, and systems. Recognizing these helps us design solutions that consider the ripple effects.

Intergenerational Equity The ethical responsibility to ensure that future generations inherit a planet and society no worse—and ideally better—than what we've received.

Learning Ecosystems Environments where continuous growth and shared knowledge are the norm. These systems support innovation through collaboration, reflection, and experimentation.

Learning Mindset An attitude of curiosity, openness, and willingness to grow—even (and especially) through failure.

Learning Organizations Organizations that prioritize learning as a core value. They reflect, adapt, and evolve based on experience and new insights.

Mental Models The internal maps we use to make sense of the world. Surfacing and challenging mental models is key to shifting organizational behavior.

Narrative Inquiry A qualitative research method that explores the stories people tell—and the meaning behind those stories—to understand experience and culture.

Organizational Culture The invisible force that shapes how things get done. It includes values, rituals, communication styles, and the unspoken rules of belonging.

Participatory Action Research (PAR) A collaborative research approach where participants are co-researchers—actively involved in studying and shaping their own realities.

Participatory Leadership A leadership style that emphasizes collaboration, shared power, and inclusion. Everyone has a voice; everyone helps shape the vision.

Purpose-Driven Alignment Ensuring that all strategies, actions, and behaviors are guided by a clear and meaningful purpose.

Purpose-Driven Work Work that connects to something bigger than profit or productivity. It's about impact, legacy, and meaning.

Reflection-in-Action The practice of thinking on your feet—pausing in the moment to assess, adjust, and improve your approach.

Relational Alignment Building trust and coherence between people, teams, and departments. It's about being on the same wavelength, even in moments of challenge.

Servant Leadership A leadership approach focused on serving others. Coined by Robert K. Greenleaf, it emphasizes empathy, listening, and support over command and control.

Silence and Absence Analysis The thoughtful exploration of what's *not* present—voices unheard, data omitted, perspectives missing—and why it matters.

Silos Isolated departments or teams that operate independently, often to the detriment of collaboration and shared goals.

Social Construct An idea or concept created and sustained by collective agreement. These influence our behavior, assumptions, and organizational norms.

Social Sustainability Creating systems and practices that support human wellbeing, equity, and social cohesion—inside and outside the organization.

Soft Systems Methodology (SSM) A systems-thinking approach focused on human activity and messy problems. SSM helps groups clarify goals, explore perspectives, and find workable solutions.

Stakeholder Anyone who affects or is affected by the organization's work—from employees and customers to communities and ecosystems.

Strategic Culture The shared values and beliefs that influence how strategy is developed and executed in an organization.

Strategic Energy Renewal Intentionally cultivating energy, focus, and purpose—especially during periods of transition or stress.

Strategic Fatigue The exhaustion that results from too many competing initiatives, unclear priorities, or lack of visible progress.

Strategic Flow When people, purpose, and processes are aligned and momentum builds naturally. It's a state of energized clarity.

Strategic Lever A high-impact area where small, targeted changes can unlock major transformation.

Strategic Positioning Defining your unique place in the ecosystem and aligning your actions, values, and messaging to support that identity.

Structural Alignment The coherence between strategy, culture, systems, and structures. When aligned, everything works in harmony.

Sustainability/Environmental, Social and Governance (ESG)/Corporate Social Responsibility (CSR) Different terms that live under the same umbrella: creating organizations that are environmentally conscious, socially just, and ethically governed.

Sustainability Leaders or Leadership (Change Agents) Individuals leading the charge for change. These are the change agents building bridges between vision and implementation.

Systems Mapping A visual method for exploring relationships and dynamics within complex systems. It helps identify leverage points and opportunities for change.

Systems Thinking A mindset that considers the whole system and how its parts interact. It helps leaders see patterns, not just events.

Thematic Clustering A tool for organizing qualitative data by grouping similar ideas into meaningful themes. It helps make sense of complex insights.

Tactical Action Concrete steps taken to bring a strategy to life. Where vision meets execution.

Transdisciplinary Collaboration Bringing together experts from different fields to co-create solutions that no one discipline could achieve alone.

Transformational Leadership A style of leadership that inspires bold change. It's about vision, authenticity, and helping others grow into their potential.

Transitional Identity The space between what was and what's next. A liminal state where growth and reinvention happen.

United Nations Sustainable Development Goals (SDGs) A global roadmap of 17 interconnected goals designed to end poverty, protect the planet, and ensure prosperity for all by 2030.

List of Figures

https://doi.org/10.1515/9783111705286-014

List of Tables

https://doi.org/10.1515/9783111705286-015